Organizing the South Bronx

✳

SUNY Series, The New Inequalities
A. Gary Dworkin, Editor

Organizing the South Bronx

Jim Rooney

Foreword by Nathan Glazer

State University of New York Press

Published by
State University of New York Press, Albany

For information, address State University of New York Press,
State University Plaza, Albany, N.Y. 12246

Production by M. R. Mulholland
Marketing by Fran Keneston

Library of Congress Cataloging-in-Publication Data

Rooney, Jim, 1948-
    Organizing the South Bronx / Jim Rooney ; foreword by Nathan
Glazer.
        p.   cm. — (Suny seies, the new inequalities)
    Includes bibliographical references and index.
    ISBN 0-7914-2209-7 (CH : acid-free). — ISBN 0-7914-2210-0 PB :
acid-free)
        1. Industrial Areas Foundation.   2. South Bronx Churches.
    3. Community organization — New York (N.Y.) — Case studies.
    4. Housing policy — New York (N.Y.) — Citizen participation — Case
    studies.   5. Church and social problems — New York (N.Y.) — Case
    studies.   6. Bronx (New York, N.Y.) — Social conditions — Case
    studies.   I. Title.   II. Series.
    HN80.N5R66   1995
    307.1'416'097471 — dc20   93-49671
                                                                    CIP

10 9 8 7 6 5 4 3 2

*To my children Kevin and Flynn
my mother Margaret
and in memory of my father*

✳

Contents

Foreword

The South Bronx is the national emblem of urban decay. "Decay" is, indeed, too modest a term for what happened in the South Bronx. It was urban destruction on a scale that rivaled the worst that the planes of World War II could do to British and German cities. What made phenomenon even more astonishing was that the Bronx had been built up largely of solid apartment houses, not modest one-family or two-family houses, in dense neighborhoods embellished with grand public buildings. Hundreds of thousands of units of housing were destroyed long before the time of their natural lives. "The Borough of Universities," it was once called, somewhat grandly but not unreasonably (there were three substantial ones). The city seemed incapable of stopping the destruction that went on through phases of abandonment by landlords, stripping of buildings by vandals and drug addicts, and their final destruction through arson. Nor could greater powers do anything to rebuild the South Bronx: presidential candidates stood amid the ruins and promised that something would be done. And, on occasion, things were attempted. But as one elected official said of one plan, "Why should we build more housing for people who are burning down what they have?" This was a simple and forceful summary, even though it could not encompass the complexity of the process of destruction.

One classic urban study already has been written on the destruction of the South Bronx, Jill Jonne's *We're Still Here: The Rise, Fall, and Resurrection of the South Bronx* (Atlantic Monthly Press, 1986). Jim Rooney's account of a key episode of its rebuilding will be another. It is the story of a group of organizers, rather strange from the point of view of the South Bronx, for they were neither Puerto Rican nor Black nor the heirs of the poverty program. They were, rather, the heirs of Saul Alinsky, founder of the Industrial Areas Foundation, with a distinctive philosophy of how to bring ordinary people to the point where they can improve their lives. Both in Jill Jonnes' book and in *Organizing the South Bronx*, local churches play an important role: not the storefronts that dot the neighborhoods of the South Bronx and similar urban areas inhabited primarily by Hispanics and Blacks, but mainline churches which have remained in the devastated areas and which, together with the organizers from the Industrial Areas Foundation, have had remarkable success in building single-family houses in the moonscapes left behind by the destruction.

Rooney had full access to the organization and its work. He describes its leaders and how they work, and the leaders of the churches who became their partners and connected them to the people of these areas, who were at the very bottom in poverty and social disorganization and ineffective institutions. The organizers' style incorporates a remarkable distrust of government, even though they need government if they are to achieve any improvement for the people they organize. We see them here confronting Mayor Ed Koch and his officials and the New York City business establishment in order to rebuild their way. Theirs is a way that creates more than housing. It creates a community ready to defend itself. Rooney is not completely enamored of the IAF style. He does more than tell the story, fascinating as that is to the urbanist and those concerned with the fate of our greatest city. He also evaluates the work of the IAF and the South Bronx Churches and considers whether the path they chose was the best for the rebuilding of this traumatized urban fabric.

The organization described in *Organizing the South Bronx* is by no means the only one that has had some success in the South Bronx. I am particularly aware of Banana Kelly, named after a curved stretch of a street on which my family lived in the 1930s. Oddly enough, the modest three-story buildings of Banana Kelly in which we lived have survived; the apartment houses, so much grander in architectural detail, so much soldier, that we moved to in the West Bronx fell victim to the forces that consumed so much of the Borough. (Now all of the area of destruction is called "South Bronx"—we would have been surprised to hear we lived in the South Bronx.) There is a lesson here that Rooney's work fully illuminates and explores. One could say—for areas like the South Bronx, struggling with the trauma of decay of neighborhoods, families, and institutions—"small is beautiful." One can only rebuild by creating communities painfully, encounter by encounter, meeting by meeting, demonstration by demonstration, house by house. Government cannot do it, though it can provide resources and then get out of the way. As Jane Jacobs convinced us a long time ago, government works on too grand a scale, and its flood of money can demolish more easily than it can rebuild.

But that is only one lesson from *Organizing the South Bronx*. Readers will find many others in this meticulous and fascinating account of the rebuilding of the South Bronx.

Nathan Glazer

Acknowledgments

I wish to express thanks for the help many people gave me during the course of this project.

I am deeply grateful to the leaders and activists of South Bronx Churches who have been so generous with their time and trust. My regard for John Heinemeier is inexpressible; one of the most lasting benefits from this work is my friendship with him. Inspiring leaders like Jim Drake and Ed Chambers helped me learn by their honest and challenging bluntness. Tony Aguilar, Maria Verona, and Manny Colon at SBC were also kind to spend so much time helping me understand their work.

I owe a huge debt to my advisors. Nathan Glazer's interest in my work, his steady encouragement, and his mastery of New York City politics contributed to my sorting out many problems. Professor Glazer arranged two Fellowships from the Bradley Foundation which allowed me to continue my work at a crucial juncture. Author Roland Barth challenged me to think harder, probe more deeply, and, by the example of his luminous prose style, forced me to write more clearly. I have been very lucky in teachers and mentors, but no one has influenced me more than Harvard's Donald Oliver. His originality of thought is tremendously stimulating. I have tried to learn from his integrity, boldness, and wit.

I would like to thank other people who generously gave of their time to talk with me and help clarify my understanding. Especially helpful were Kathy Wylde, Kathleen Dunn, Sam Kramer, I. D. Robbins, Mike Gecan, Erie Cortez, Larry McNeil, Arnie Graf, Father John Flynn, and Blanca Ramirez.

Scholars who offered advice and encouraged me in this line of research were Courtney Cazden, Joel Perlmann, Joe Maxwell, Terry Tivian, Bobby Starnes, Ellen Faith, Rich Maxson, Bob Verado. I am grateful also for generous encouragement from Columbia's Teacher's College Press editor Brien Ellerbeck, scholar Mary Anne Raywid, and the University of Illinois' William Ayers.

I would also like to thank Dr. Leo Rosenberg whose steady, methodical, almost superhuman devotion to research set a standard I have not attained. Dr. Terry Tolefson and Geoff Tegnell both spent many hours in conversation helping me to sharpen my thinking and writing. Jim Sleeper's brilliant and dazzlingly-written book, *The Closest of Strangers* vividly demonstrates how vital chronicling political activity in New York City's inner-city neighborhoods can be.

My debt to my friend the hyper-literate Marilyn Grumet is beyond repaying.

Asking friends to spend hours reading one's work can put a strain on friendship, and only the most generous will comply. I have been extremely fortunate in getting valuable feedback and shrewd comments from Agnes Prostick, Etta McDonnel, Tom Edwards, Bill Shine, Carol Clarke, Corinne Mond, Gayle Monaster, Maggie Gallagher, Peg Anderson, Peter Freiberg, Chris Coleman, Martha Sweeney, Geo Armand, Pat Addeo, and Nancy Stowell.

Introduction: The Design and Purpose of the Study

This book is an inside story about heroic and articulate individuals who were able to defy overwhelming odds and build affordable housing in the South Bronx. It is about the process of teaching citizens in a low-income neighborhood how to participate in public life.

Very little is written about the catastrophic and precipitous collapse of the South Bronx, although its fate is universally cited as emblematic of urban hopelessness. This inquiry focuses on community organizers who are sifting through the wreckage and making progress in battling an inept municipal government and the centrifugal forces of decay. The locus is a coalition of forty minority congregations who battled the city of New York for vacant land in order to build owner-occupied row houses. At bottom, this is a study of how to educate adults in a democracy to find their voice and wield the power that is inherent in large numbers of organized citizens.

The study is divided into four parts with fourteen chapters. Part One includes an introduction which discusses the design and purpose of the study and looks at methodological questions like access and confidentiality. Also there is an outline of the history of the South Bronx and its abrupt collapse. A third chapter reviews the sociological literature and speculates on the reasons for the devastation that engulfed the borough.

Part Two analyzes the fifty-year tradition of the Industrial Areas Foundation (IAF), the organizing network which sponsors South Bronx Churches (SBC), the group that built the homes. A chapter examines Saul Alinsky and Ed Chambers, the two key IAF figures, and locates their work in the larger tradition of citizen movements. There are two other IAF groups in New York City, and their history is also explored. The innovative housing that SBC erected was first constructed in Brooklyn, and its builder, I. D. Robbins, discusses this work. Another chapter details how South Bronx Churches was created. The last chapter of this section examines an unsuccessful attempt by SBC to bring its relational organizing style to a failing South Bronx high school.

Part Three contains a fine-grained examination of the effort to construct Nehemiah rowhouses. Information about this struggle comes from attendance at SBC rallies, planning and evaluation meetings, and extensive interviews with participants both from SBC and the city.

Part Four offers an analysis of both the suitability of the low-density housing that SBC built and extracts general guidelines for organizing citizens in low-income communities.

My work in the South Bronx is driven by the belief that the greatest challenge presently facing America is the virtual abandonment by our society of minority citizens living in the inner city.

I have an abiding interest in the South Bronx. I grew up on its fringes in the 1950s and 1960s, just across the *Maginot Line* of the Cross Bronx Expressway. In the early part of my teaching career, my wife and I worked as group home parents in the Bronx. We lived with nine "emotionally disturbed" adolescent girls who had previously lived in nearby Spanish Harlem and on some of the roughest streets in the South Bronx. The girls attended local Bronx high schools, where they were systematically miseducated.

There is scandalously little written about the appalling conditions of this part of New York City.[1] Though the South Bronx more resembles Beirut of the 1980s than it does any other municipality and serves as a synonym for urban collapse, there is a paucity of specific information that deals with the precise texture of these wrecked neighborhoods. I also realized that even modestly adding to the abiding despair of policy makers and other interested observers by specifying in excruciating detail all the things that are wrong with the South Bronx would be an exercise in willful futility. Instead, I reasoned that it would be more interesting to put a little spin on the ball and try to uncover things that were actually succeeding there. My first inclination was to look at schools and locate educators who were doing exemplary work under difficult conditions.

Narrowing the Problem

I began by plowing through the short shelf of works on the South Bronx. An important resource for me in this investigation was The Bronx Historical Society's research library, which has the best collection of holdings in this field.[2] After a while I got to know the Historical Society's director, Gary Hermalyn, who has edited, published, and written a number of commercial, as well as scholarly, books on the history of the Bronx. We discussed various contemporary South Bronx topics, focusing primarily on those concerned with the borough's schools.

I was drawn particularly to Morris High School, the first and, arguably, the most famous secondary school in the Bronx. Its fortunes have mirrored the rise and decline of its South Bronx neighborhood, and so it provides a humanizing lens for chronicling the fate of the South Bronx.[3]

Hermalyn, instead, suggested a look at PS 61, an ancient South Bronx elementary school at the foot of Charlotte Street. This school's neighborhood has equally compelling symbolic importance: it is where President Carter, President Reagan, and even Pope John Paul swooped down to make lightning visits and grand pronouncements. Both U.S. presidents vowed to marshal the resources of the federal government to rebuild on the rubble of the wrecked blocks of the South Bronx. Charlotte Street, therefore, offered another powerful narrative device for telling the story because its history vividly embodies what has happened across the entire South Bronx.

Charlotte Street's heyday was in the first half of the twentieth century, when it bustled with a vibrancy reminiscent of the turn-of-the-century Lower East Side; but, in the late sixties and early seventies, it abruptly spiraled out of control, gripped by a drug-induced social pathology. By the time of the presidential visits in 1976 and 1980, it had been burned, vandalized, and subsequently bulldozed flat. In the early eighties, a handful of grotesquely inappropriate suburban-style ranch houses, less than a dozen to an acre, complete with (one assumes) ironic white picket fences were inserted on these cleared blocks, giving the neighborhood a macabre, almost surreal air. The local school, PS 61, had been slated for demolition twenty-five years earlier because of the precipitous population decline in the wake of the "fires of the seventies," but it managed to survive and now serves the remaining population as well as the new homeowners.

Researching this school seemed like a suggestion bristling with possibilities, so I wrote the principal telling her I was interested in understanding more about schooling in the South Bronx. I worded the letter carefully, asking only for permission to speak with her, at her convenience, for less than an hour. This is a wholly unremarkable request, one routinely granted to fellow principals as a professional courtesy. I ended by saying I would call her to follow up a few days later. Thus began a frustrating odyssey through the ramifying corridors of New York City schools' notorious bureaucratic labyrinth. Rather than my recounting the dispiriting details of this vain attempt to gain access, suffice it to say that I made no fewer than thirty phone calls and sent a number of letters to various officials, only to discover at the end of six weeks that the matter was finally resolved and permission for me to talk with the principal summarily denied, with no explanation, by the district superintendent.

Friends and colleagues told me that this startling outcome should ignite suspicions, even in the most trusting, that perhaps this district had something to hide from outsiders. Though I thought that explanation a little harsh and too conspiratorial, subsequent events lent it plausibility.

After having been spurned by the district superintendent, I intended to take the matter up with the local board of education which held monthly public meetings, but I was unable to attend the last one of that year, in June of 1988. Shortly thereafter, the *Village Voice* ran a brief item hinting at outrageous improprieties in the district. A few months later in the fall of 1988, the *New York Times* weighed in with a major piece of investigative journalism, billboarding the face of the district's superintendent across its pages and recounting the colorful story of how he had gotten his job.[4]

This district's schools, which are demonstrably in collapse and which have the lowest reading and mathematics scores in the entire city, are politically cleaved into two hostile and competing camps, one Black and the other Hispanic. The superintendent, Wilfredo Abreu, got his job, according to the *Times*, by the tie-breaking vote of a board member who was, at the time of the balloting, a homeless crack addict who was occasionally dusted off and hustled to a board meeting in order to cast a key vote.[5] The *Times* went on to detail a wide range of petty larceny and pilfering by Abreu's other colleagues on the school board, as well as illegal "job trading" among politically connected administrators in the schools.[6] A month or two after that, another local principal in a neighboring South Bronx district, allegedly a no-show crack head, was arrested for narcotics sales.[7]

I have to confess, all this incompetence and seemingly petty, but, in its cumulative impact, hair-raising corruption piqued my interest. On another level, it was clear that researching this project would present various thorny and perhaps insurmountable problems of access; nonetheless, it offered an almost Dickensian opportunity for vivid writing about extreme conditions. In the end, I decided not to pursue this line of research because even successfully delimiting the degree of tragic school mismanagement would just confirm the conventional wisdom of what most people think they already know: inner-city children get a rotten education.

From the beginning of this investigation I was absorbed by the problem of getting my bearings in an alien neighborhood and cultivating contacts and informants. Another initial concern, candidly, was that of safety. I was spending a lot of time in neighborhoods where extreme violence was common. From the seething weed garden of alarming statistics about the South Bronx, it is possible to choose from the predictable ones, like the percentage of teenagers who drop out of school, or men who are out of the labor force, or households receiving welfare to extremely troubling ones like the weekly death toll resulting from the virulent crack trade.[8] I never encountered any problems in all my days and nights on the street, although I confess to having felt a bit uneasy at times. I attribute this lack of menace to the fact that I am six foot two, over two hundred pounds, and ethnically so Irish looking, with a face the color of a side of beef, that people on the street automatically assume I am a cop.

During an early visit to the South Bronx I called up Father John Flynn, a Catholic pastor, who had been a charismatic teacher and decisive influence in my Bronx parish when I was growing up and who, for the past twenty years, ministered to some of the harshest neighborhoods of the South Bronx. I have for the past two decades diligently followed news accounts of the South Bronx, and, from time to time, I noted mention of his name in connection with various housing protests and other grass-roots political activity.

We met in October of 1988 and taped a number of wide-ranging interviews.[9] He is extraordinarily articulate and candid, a man of luminous intelligence and compassion whom I admire for his dedication to this difficult and discouraging work. I began to think that profiling him would give me an interesting entry point for discussing exemplary educational work under difficult circumstances. For instance, when I asked him about a typical day, he rattled off an astonishing itinerary:

> Part of the day yesterday was for the instruction of adults who are looking toward confirmation. Then a trip over to the hospital for a man who is going to have a heart transplant. Also a visit to a psychiatric hospital to a man who was taken in in a catatonic state. Two phone calls to the housing organization on how we are going to build ourselves into a management orga-

nization that takes care of some of the houses they are going to build for the homeless so that we can involve ourselves in the management of those houses. The day may also be just giving a sandwich to someone who is out front or who has come to the rectory door. A lot of stuff is like working on a sermon, trying to get an education piece going. It's really a variety of working in the parish school, teaching in school, taking care of the organizational arm of People for Change. Being on the Board of Directors for the Department of Health Ambulatory Health Care and a youth organization that majors in karate and English as a second language. It's everything. And it's really dealing with people with their individual needs: a lot of counseling, a lot of being with people in their suffering.

We buried a kid who was shot in the subway last week because of a fight between his school and another school. Somebody beat somebody up too hard. So we buried him and consoled the family. We are burying too many people who are 26, 31, 18. AIDS, drugs; and you stay with the families: you have to be with them. See if you can keep them in hope. I think that is probably the key: the hope. You know that life is worth living. Kids are talking about suicide, not wanting to live anymore.

I was heartened to hear that a decade earlier he had helped found a still-functioning social action group called South Bronx People for Change, which is a Catholic parish-based advocacy organization linking twelve churches. Its work focuses primarily on stemming the abandonment and subsequent leveling of vandalized buildings, as well as dealing with various local issue initiatives like driving junkies out of a particular school yard. Father Flynn described the group:

an empowerment organization that works off the premise that God has given a responsibility to the people not to stay smothered by oppression and injustice. People sort of just let that happen to them. They have a responsibility over their own lives and in order to use that power they have to learn to organize. If they see something that is not just they just don't stand by and do nothing.

In the Church we have one of the best organizations in the world, but it's organized for church things. We take the Virgin to houses, we sing, and we do well in catechetical instruction.

But when it comes to street stuff like garbage collection, drug addicts, or the lack of safety in buildings we are at a total loss. That's politics, and we don't get involved in politics.

The People for Change theory is that God came to bring his people into a kingdom. The kingdom means you do not live in oppression, you don't live in sin, and you don't live with the effects of sin which are injustice and oppression. So we work with these people to organize them so they can live in a dignified neighborhood. So they can bring up their children without a great deal of fear. They can take on the Powers That Be in terms of anyone causing their kids to be in jeopardy. If, indeed, the police department is not doing its job then they go down in force and insist on their rights to be protected. If the schools are not teaching what they are supposed to be teaching, if their kids are three grades lower than they are supposed to be, we got to get involved in parent associations. Or, indeed, they have to go the principal or the school board. They need to find out why they are not getting quality teachers or quality education.

I next spent some time with the director of South Bronx People for Change, Blanca Ramirez,[10] and she introduced me to other housing activists, including one former homeless woman who urged me to spend some time at Bronx Housing Court. This nightmarish seat of justice barely functions in decrepit quarters in the basement of the county judicial central office, but because it brings together the poor, landlords, and city officials in one place it is an extremely alluring locus for research. I spent time in these makeshift courtrooms interviewing a number of judges, people connected with various tenant advocacy groups, dispossessed tenants, landlord attorneys, and others.[11]

Meanwhile another muscular local activist group, also a church-based, grass-roots organization, was dramatically making its presence felt in the South Bronx. Various accounts detailed the efforts of a group called South Bronx Churches to bring some order to a notorious local hospital, which was run by an alleged "poverty pimp," a man who had made significant contributions to the neighborhood in the late sixties during the height of the devastation, when federal money flowed in a vain attempt to stem the destruction, but who now settles merely for dispensing patronage and enriching himself.[12]

I was surprised to discover that both South Bronx Churches and South Bronx People for Change considered themselves, not nat-

ural allies, but rivals, fiercely vying for the overlapping loyalty of
Catholic pastors. It is, in the words of Father John Flynn "an awful
case in the South Bronx of the good fighting with the good." This enmity is especially unfortunate because a strong case can be made that
the only viable institutions with deep roots in the South Bronx are
the churches and, regrettably, the booming drug trade. A comparison
of the two advocacy groups gradually suggested itself as a fruitful
topic for investigation.

Access

Gaining access to groups struggling to improve conditions in
the South Bronx did not turn out to be a monumental problem. In
January of 1989, after reading some newspaper accounts of South
Bronx Churches (SBC) actions, and after repeatedly encountering
their name in conversations with other South Bronx activists, I
phoned them blind and got a recorded message saying "South Bronx
Churches: Sign Up and Take Charge! No one is in the office now, but
if you . . ." I called a few more times and became annoyed that no
one ever seemed to be in the office. Later I learned that this is a tip-
off that the group probably has its priorities straight: you can't organize a community from inside an office. After a few more calls I
reached a staff organizer and interviewed him in a relatively well-
equipped office above the chapel of St. Jerome's Church in the southern depths of the South Bronx. He told me about his boss, Lead
Organizer Jim Drake, who he said had been "the main man behind
the famous {California Farm Workers} grape boycott."[13] Drake
sounded intriguing, but when I called him he was decidedly reluctant to talk, explaining that his time was expensive and paid for by
funds raised from local impoverished South Bronx churches. However, he did agree to meet with me briefly to check me out, and luckily we had a stimulating opening conversation.[14] He subsequently
took me out to lunch ("No, that's okay, you don't have to pay; this
is on the Cardinal."—a reference to the fact that the New York City
Archdiocese is a contributor to SBC).[15]
    This sort of hospitality is standard operating procedure with
SBC organizers. They believe that their ultimate aim, the empowerment of citizens in low-income communities, can be best accomplished by laboriously building a firm foundation anchored on solid
relationships with many people. As Jim Drake put it a few months
later in September of 1989 to a group of community activists who
were being trained to revitalize Morris High School, "There are two
kinds of power. One, which I call linear power, is the ability to lord

it over others. The second kind of power is *the ability to act,* what I call, relational power."[16] In his view this relational power ultimately is derived from people who first begin by talking to one another in "one-on-one meetings." In retrospect, it is likely that Drake's initial motivation for talking with me was in part an attempt to assess whether I could be of use to SBC. At the end of our lunch he made a proposal, asking, "How would you like to do what I do—agitate and organize?"

Early in 1989 I began attending various public meetings and rallies arranged by SBC. At one meeting in a church basement organizing people living in a huge bleak, and highly dangerous housing project called Claremont Village, the home (to chose one from a long list of alarming statistics) of all the shooting victims of subway vigilante Bernard Goetz, I met one of the most admirable men I have ever encountered, Rev. John Heinemeier, a white fifty-year-old Lutheran preacher. Pastor Heinemeier was the chairman of the Sponsoring Committee which invited the Saul Alinsky-inspired organizing network, the Industrial Areas Foundation, to the South Bronx and which, in turn, sparked the creation of South Bronx Churches in 1985.[17] Subsequently I have had many meetings with him in the incongruous white rural-looking parsonage of St. John's Lutheran Church in the Morrisania section of the South Bronx and elsewhere, and he has turned out to be one of my most candid key informants. Our discussions have been numerous and ongoing.[18]

Coincidentally I made contact just as SBC was gearing up for its penultimate organizing challenge, an attempt to wrestle from the city large parcels of land that had been lying fallow for twenty years in order to build affordable housing for South Bronx residents. Making the stakes even higher and the confrontation more vivid, 1989 was a mayoralty election year in New York City, and SBC had inserted itself into the middle of a bruising election campaign.

Battling SBC for possession of some of the vacant land of the South Bronx are various New York City agencies, departments, and other arms of government. Access to the municipal point of view has been difficult. Not all public servants are scrupulous about returning phone calls. My strategy has been to go from the lower level officials and work my way up the ladder. I found I needed to be "credentialed," to be able to say that so and so said I should call. I began this process with Kathy Wylde, the housing director for the NYC Partnership, the group designated by the city as the coordinator for development of key parcels in the South Bronx. I first phoned her leaving a message with her secretary. She didn't return the call. I next wrote her a letter[19] saying that, at a recent downtown rally, SBC officials had attacked her mercilessly and that I was working on a book and hoped to spin off some articles, so I wanted to get her response to the charges leveled against her. As soon as she received the letter, I got a call and an appointment.

Confidentiality

My access to SBC is substantial: I am permitted to attend all their strategy sessions and the assessment meetings afterwards where the activists evaluate their own effectiveness. The issue of confidentiality has not directly come up. I have made no promises to anyone, and, although I have refrained from taping sensitive inside strategy sessions (at the suggestion of Jim Drake who usually dominates), even in these meetings I have openly taken copious notes.

By and large the SBC people I am working with are candid, many to the point of bluntness, and familiar with dealing with the press in confrontational situations. They are by no means unsophisticated about issues of confidentiality. I attribute my easy access to the fact that they appreciate that I am genuinely fascinated by their work, eager to understand how they construe it, and do not attempt to conceal my interest behind a neutral stance. I find that they are often pleased to talk with someone who appreciates the audacity of what they are attempting, and I think many of them derive satisfaction from reflecting on their work with a sympathetic listener.

To those who are curious, I have described in detail the outline of how I am structuring the research I have gathered. I have told them that my purpose is to try to extract from the work of SBC ideas, tactics, and strategies that may have wide application to others working with disenfranchised people. To Jim Drake, John Heinemeier and IAF Director Ed Chambers, I have shown drafts of the manuscript, and they have made suggestions.[20] Others, like Kathy Wylde of the NYC Partnership, another principal player in this chronicle, have been more circumspect in talking with me. At numerous points in our conversation[21] she asked me to turn off the recorder when she wanted to convey sensitive background material; at the end of the interview she asked me to promise to tell her in advance ". . . if you are going to use me in a way that will get me in trouble." Other public officials like Kathleen Dunn, Assistant Commissioner for Planning and Development at the Department of Housing, Planning and Development (HPD) and Samuel Kramer, the Director of Bronx Planning at HPD, have generously given me the red-carpet treatment and made themselves available for follow-up clarifications.[22]

This is not to say that all problems of access and confidentiality have been smoothly negotiated. When I first sat down with Ed Chambers, the abrasive national director of the Industrial Areas Foundation, the spawning group of South Bronx Churches and twenty-five similar groups nationwide, I inadvertently got off on the wrong foot. Chambers presides over this remarkable organizing network from a dreadfully nondescript office above a store in an anonymous Long Island suburb. After some introductory pleasantries, I asked if he would mind if I taped his remarks in order to get his quotes exact, and he suddenly lashed out, "You have only one tape recorder? Or have you got two?" When I looked puzzled, he responded incredulously, "You mean you don't know the rules of tape recording?" Back-pedaling, I guessed: "You mean you want a copy of it?" Chambers replied as if he were talking with a dim-witted child: "Well yes. Shit, you might be CIA, FBI! They are always infiltrating us." "Is that right?" I responded lamely. "Sure," he said. "The proof of it is all these news clips. How does an IRS guy collect all this information, file it back, and shove it up your ass?"[23]

He was referring to an angry phone conversation he had had minutes before with Jim Drake, the Lead Organizer of South Bronx Churches. I gathered that Drake had told him that he had just received a fat envelope from the IRS filled with news clips of SBC political activity. The IRS was citing these newspaper accounts to challenge SBC's tax-exempt status, based on partisan political involvement. Though I had heard only one side of the phone conversation, I was perversely heartened to note that Chambers talked in the same irritated, impatient way with Drake as he did with me. He advised Drake to get on the phone with New York Senator Daniel Moynihan and "get that son of a bitch to do something for us for a change."

In general, my line of attack has been to attend SBC meetings, rallies, and strategy sessions to interview their organizers, their activist ministers, and neighborhood volunteers and then to seek different perspectives from their opponents and rivals. Often these people have suggested others to talk with, and the circle has rippled outward.

I have tried to read everything available on their organization. The meager written material consisted mostly of newspaper accounts, press releases, pamphlets (Chambers, 1978) and three seminal books by Industrial Areas Foundation founder Saul Alinsky (1947, 1949, 1971), as well as a recent meticulously researched biography of Alinsky (Horwitt, 1989). As I proceeded, I realized that I needed to cast my net wider, and so I began interviewing many others not directly associated with SBC. To understand the present initiative in the South Bronx, I found it necessary to delve into the history of the IAF sister organization, East Brooklyn Churches, which pioneered the building of affordable Nehemiah homes, and, along a chain of causality, to the story of Queens Citizens Organization, the first IAF group to colonize New York City. I then went out to view the Nehemiah homes built in Brooklyn's East New York neighborhood and spent time with builder, newspaper columnist, and civic gadfly I. D. Robbins[24] who devised the affordable construction methods that make the Nehemiah homes perhaps the most economical new buildings in New York.

Road Map

In this book I have zeroed in on the problem of how SBC was engaging adult participation in community affairs in low-income areas where there is an abiding sense of powerlessness and a breakdown in spirit. How can significant numbers of citizens be mobilized and organized in inner-city neighborhoods? At bottom, this is an enterprise that seeks to educate adults in a democracy about finding their collective voice and so wielding the power inherent in large numbers of organized citizens. My inquiry is structured around the following research questions:

- In both theory and practice what is SBC's relationship to the wider world of community activism?
- How did SBC manage in just two years to create a shared sense of purpose with many community residents?
- What is the group's philosophy and *modus operandi?* How did it evolve?
- What is unique about the South Bronx and how did SBC cope with the specific conditions of this distressed community?
- Why did this highly political group center its community building work in the traditionally apolitical local Catholic and Protestant parishes?
- How is the group perceived by city officials, rival activists, and other interested observers?
- Does SBC's work in the South Bronx offer any lessons to others who are interested in teaching adults in a democracy how to engage in the effort of improving schools and creating new community institutions?

Among the sites where information for this study was gathered were:

- Mahogany-lined, lavishly appointed rectory anterooms surviving in serene isolation in otherwise wrecked neighborhoods;
- Third World delis where English is seldom spoken.
- The anguished chaos of Housing Court in the shabby basement of the still-elegant county headquarters;
- dingy walk-ups festooned with ripped posters peeling from the walls and clanging telephones that serve as headquarters for various shoestring tenants' rights groups;
- the catacomb-like depths of St. Jerome's with its endless corridors and tunnel-like passages snaking to a room above the chapel where SBC has its offices;
- the crowded periodical room of the Forty-second Street Library where hours were wasted blindly scrolling through the index*less* *New York Daily News* microfilm files;
- pews in turn-of-the-century Bronx churches where the life-affirming emotionality of church services enlivens otherwise grim precincts;
- Jewish delis in the north Bronx near the Bronx Historical Society;
- the reading room of the main branch of the Fordham Library where armed guards accompany neighborhood patrons to the rest-rooms, but on at least one occasion were unable to keep a menacing pit bull dog from aimlessly wandering through the main reading room;
- a faded but still elegant restaurant, perhaps the only conventional eating spot remaining in all of the lower part of the South Bronx;
- the modest headquarters of the Industrial Areas Foundation, up a rickety flight of stairs above a plumbing supply store in Long Island;
- the book-lined, hopelessly cluttered office of a South Bronx parsonage;
- the threadbare headquarters of another church-based activist group in a grimy basement apartment of a public housing project;
- the smog-soaked but bucolic mountains of northern Los Angeles where IAF activists are trained;
- the steps of the gleaming American Express world headquarters in the financial district of Manhattan during a demonstration by angry South Bronx activists;
- the edge of the Atlantic Ocean during a brisk, splashing walk with a South Bronx preacher, trying vainly to keep my tape recorder dry;

- the midtown corporate offices of the NYC Partnership on Madison Ave., across from the opulent former mansion of J.P. Morgan;
- the public rooms of patrician old-line Protestant churches like St. Bart's on Park Avenue; and
- up and down the shattered streets of the Bronx, map in hand, trying to get oriented in a place that seems more like Dresden than the imperial city of New York.

Startling to me was that the more time I spent wandering in these unfamiliar settings, the more normal these ruined streetscapes seemed. When I first tentatively ventured onto these streets, I was dumbfounded by the horribly bleak vistas. There were acres of weed-choked, garbage-strewn open fields where bustling tenements once stood, or lone buildings forlornly surviving on otherwise empty blocks like the remaining teeth in a diseased mouth.

I tried to fight the sense of accepting these now-familiar scenes as unremarkable. Sticking in my mind was a stray comment in David Byrne's offbeat film, *True Stories.* Byrne, a lower Manhattan artist and musician, chose an alien, flat, and empty area of Texas as the setting for his movie. As the on-screen narrator, he says at the end of the movie,

> When I see a place for the first time, I notice everything, the color of the paper, the sky, the way people walk, doorknobs, every detail. Then, after I've been there for a while, I don't notice them anymore. Only by forgetting can I remember what a place is really like . . . so maybe for me forgetting and remembering are the same thing.[25]

I entered into this research a few years ago with few preconceptions about exactly what I wanted to study, beyond that of trying to understand how good educational work is done under difficult circumstances. I have tried to stay open to "the story" and to be prudent about drawing any sweeping conclusions.

I

✳

Context

The Bronx: "The City Without a Slum"

Dominating the top of a hill in the South Bronx, presiding over the once-luxurious Grand Concourse, an expansive tree-line boulevard ambitiously patterned on Paris's Champs Elysees in the early part of this century, sits the Bronx County Building. The majestically imposing building, a ten-story limestone, Neoclassical-Art Deco fortress, is festooned with elaborate friezes depicting highlights from the history of civilization; at the top of the monumental entrance stairs are huge bronze doors decorated with fierce, carved eagles. To the extent that the Bronx is governed at all, it is from these offices and courtrooms.

On nearby side streets, many with a clear view of the looming seat of government, scores of abandoned buildings squat with their windows punched out, resembling inert, blinded, hulking giants. Parts of the South Bronx look like newsreel pictures from Beirut, or, for those with long memories, Dresden after the bombing, or, as almost everybody says, stretching to encompass the devastation, like a moonscape.

A vivid description of the Bronx County Building, also known as the Fortress, appears in Tom Wolfe's hilarious, exuberant, and appallingly reactionary, blame-the-victim novel about the South Bronx:

> The building was a prodigious limestone Parthenon done in the early thirties in the Civic Moderne style. It was nine stories high and covered three city blocks, from 161st Street to 158th Street. Such open-faced optimism they had, whoever dreamed up that building back then!
>
> Despite everything, the courthouse stirred the soul. Its four great facades were absolute jubilations of sculpture and bas-relief. There were groups of classical figures at every corner. Agriculture, Commerce, Industry, Religion, and the Arts, Jus-

tice, Government, the Law and Order, and the Rights of Man—
noble Romans wearing togas in the Bronx! Such a golden dream
of an Apollonian future!

Today, if one of those lovely classical lads ever came down from
up there, he wouldn't survive long enough to make it to 162nd
Street to get a Choc-A-Pop or a blue Shark. They'd whack him
out just to get his toga.[1]

Housing Court, located in the Bronx County Building, is where
landlords, city housing officials, lawyers, judges, and the poor con-
verge and where housing justice is dispensed. It is a fitting place to
begin consideration of the problems of the South Bronx.

A visitor walking through the imperial front doors looking for
Housing Court is directed to circle to the back of the building to
what was once a service entrance and then descend to the basement.
Before plunging into the catacombs, a visitor may note high above
this back door, chiseled into the limestone, the optimistic aphorism:
"LET IT BE REMEMBERED FINALLY THAT IT'S LONG EVER
BEEN THE PRIDE AND BOAST OF AMERICA THAT THE
RIGHTS FOR WHICH SHE CONTENDED WERE THE RIGHTS OF
HUMAN NATURE." This evocation of human nature in all its myr-
iad forms turns out to be stunningly apt.

In the bleak basement, the shabby corridor is lined with benches
and clogged with people. Thick cigarette smoke swirls against the
low ceiling; bored children race around stumbling over baby car-
riages. The noise level rising from the collective murmurings in several languages is a grating rumble. Landlord lawyers confer with each
other; housing advocates talk with poor people clutching puzzling
unfolded documents like *Dispossess Petitions, Stipulations,* and
Show Cause Orders; clerks, to be heard above the din, raucously call
out cases; and confusion reigns.

Strikingly, unexpectedly, everyone seems to be in costume. The
landlord lawyers are the easiest to spot. Straight from Central Casting, wearing dark, well-tailored suits, they are Caucasian, typically
under forty-five years of age, and usually male. Once in a while, a
rumpled lawyer can be spotted, but one suspects the dress code is un-
forgivingly strict. Attorneys for the city, to the untutored eye, are
equally well dressed but tend to have longer hair. Dapper clerks in
bright white starched shirts, black pants, dark ties, gleaming badges,
have .38 caliber guns strapped to bullet-encrusted belts, with hand-
cuffs and keys dangling. A few of these gun-totting officials in this

squalid basement affect the menacingly dark or mirrored sunglasses favored by archetypical Southern sheriffs. The housing advocates, who are usually not lawyers and who are usually not male Caucasians, are modestly but stylishly dressed, often with a bright scarf or some other distinctive touch. The poor people, and all the people who are not paid to be there are poor, are Black and Hispanic.

It is tempting to think of the South Bronx as a Third World country nested within the richest city in the world, the nerve center for world capitalism. Like all metaphors, this does not hold across the board; nonetheless, this costumed drama[2] is played out daily in Bronx. Housing Court seems right out of unsophisticated movies from the 1930s about the dispensation of justice in "Banana Republics."

Most of the official business between landlord lawyers and the poor is conducted in these dingy hallways, and renters without the benefit of attorneys' advice can be seen signing complicated legal agreements proffered by time-pressed and smilingly confident lawyers representing the apartment owners. This expediency turns Lenny Bruce's wisecrack—"In the halls of justice, the only justice is in the halls."—on its head.

Marinella Pacheo,[3] a tenant advocate with Neighborhood Economic and Educational Development group (NEED), told a visitor that, of the more than 100,000 cases that Housing Court deals with each year, most are for dispossess motions brought by landlords for nonpayment of rent. She cited a 1986 report[4] which disclosed that one-third of all cases were disposed of within five minutes.

In a warren of seven cramped, makeshift courtrooms, judges, mediators, legal assistants, landlord attorneys, and others bustle about to serve justice.[5]

The process usually begins with the landlord delivering to the tenant a "Notice of Petition and Eviction" which everyone calls a dispossess. The trigger, predictably, is nonpayment of rent. Many of the tenants in these battered buildings are on welfare, and the 1989 monthly allowance for rent did not exceed $295 a month. Even in rent-stabilized apartments where rent adjustments are supposed to be modest, the landlord is permitted to periodically raise the rent, and there are a number of legal tools that allow him to raise the rent substantially.[6] When the tenant slips behind in the payments, the landlord quickly swings into action and seeks a *judgment* against his tenant in Housing Court.

The tenant is then dispatched to the basement of the County Courthouse to answer in writing why the rent was not paid. As Carmen Olemeda[7] of the East-West Eviction Prevention Center, one of the few tenant advocates who is also a lawyer, told a visitor, most of the poor who receive these papers are not able to understand them: "First the papers are written in English which many Hispanic people can't read. And, they are written in technical language. The landlords never appear in court; they send their lawyers. The tenant almost never is represented by a lawyer." The lawyers try to short-circuit the process by collaring the renters in the hall and persuading them to sign stipulations (legally binding promises to make good on the rent) before the case is heard and before any legally embarrassing indiscretions by the landlord are raised before the judge. According to Ms. Olemeda, "They often agree to things that if they had the opportunity to get advice from lawyers, they might do something completely different." Most, therefore, never make it to the courtrooms in the drab basement. There, miniaturized justice is dispensed from an almost comically dwarfish courtroom that measures a claustrophobic thirteen feet six inches by fifteen feet. This, as the *New York Times* has noted, "makes it only slightly larger than some elevators. . . .They are tiny rooms with special tiny furniture. And, from their shrunken 'In God We Trust' signs to their shortened flagpoles bearing the red, white and blue, they contain most of the essentials of a courtroom. Only smaller."[8] Since the proceedings are technical and swift, as state Supreme Court Judge David B. Saxe candidly admits:

> An unrepresented tenant may not know that a challenge can be mounted against the validity of the rent claimed, the condition of the premises and the content and manner of the services of the required notices. Legal doctrines such as the warranty of habitability, constructive eviction and retaliatory eviction are known to housing lawyers but not to unrepresented tenants.[9]

It is tempting to see this whole process as a cruel maze concocted by predatory landlords and compliant city officials to victimize the poor, but, in truth, this is a complicated problem. Landlords need a reliable source of revenue to maintain their buildings, and they have a right to realize a profit. The fact is that, for whatever reason, many tenants do not pay their rent. Some students of the housing crisis plausibly contend that private investment has to be the cornerstone to revitalizing affordable housing in the South Bronx. And yet, the disparities are so stark, it is hard not to sympathize with the renters. If the landlord loses the case, the worst that happens is that he returns disappointed to his comfortable house, often far removed from his investment properties in the South Bronx. In the event it is his misconduct that is at issue, he may be fined, but it is still not a major setback. According to *New York Newsday*, "less than 10 percent of the fines levied against [landlords] for building violations have been collected."[10] If the tenant doesn't prevail, a Marshal may show up at her apartment the next day and dump her furniture on the sidewalk, consigning her and her children to a public shelter in a refitted armory where even hardened career criminals sleep uneasily. The issuance of dispossess notices is not rare:

> A 1986 study of the displacement pressures in the West Bronx, prepared by a number of housing groups in the borough, concluded that more than half the tenants in the area receive dispossess notices each year, the vast majority of them for nonpayment of rent. About 4,000 West Bronx tenants end up being evicted each year, the study said. Last year 91,400 dispossess notices were filed in the entire borough, Bronx Housing Court records show.[11]

Consider that; it is a startling statistic: one out of two households in this neighborhood receives a dispossess order each year. This, in an area where much of the ever-diminishing housing stock was relentlessly and systematically destroyed over the last twenty years. This, in a city where few alternatives are available, and thousands of homeless already clog the shelters or aimlessly roam the streets.

And even more discouragingly, the housing crisis is only the most visible problem in the South Bronx, an area that is racked by countless severe disorders. It was not always so. Even during the hard times of the Great Depression, the Bronx was proudly known as "the city without a slum."

Indeed, Lewis Morris, patriot and signer of the Declaration of Independence wrote in 1783 to the newly elected Congress proposing that the South Bronx be declared the new capital of the United States because, apart from its beauty and key location, "Morrisania is perfectly secure from any dangers either from foreign invasion or internal insurrection."[12] Indeed, to this day, the Morrisania section of the South Bronx remains secure from foreign invasion, but everything else has changed dramatically, perhaps even its immunity from internal insurrection.

Early History of the South Bronx

Setting a tone that would reverberate throughout the next 350 years, the first recorded real estate transaction in the Bronx was a bit one-sided. Swedish developer Jonas Bronck, an operative of the expansionistic Dutch West Indian syndicate bought a five-hundred acre tract from the Mohegan Indians in 1639 for "two guns, two kettles, two coats, two adzes, two shirts, one barrel of cider and six bits of money."[13]

On the wooded site Bronck built a stone house and three barns just across the Harlem River from Manhattan at what is now the lower tip of the South Bronx. From the land he purchased from the Indians, the ambitious white intruder carved out a grain and tobacco farm to the present 150th Street. After he died on his farm in 1643, his contemporaries named the nearby stream the Bronck River, and today the entire borough is named after its first European settler. After his death, in another instance which has contemporary parallels, the farm was abandoned.

Bronck's servants and farm hands were originally from Sweden, Germany, the Netherlands, and Denmark, and in a recent reappraisal Bronx historian Lloyd Ultan claims Bronck's legacy was "a multiethnic settlement of people from different cultures [which] presaged the following 350 years when throngs of English, Irish, African-American, Italian, Hispanic, and Asian people would come to The Bronx, live side by side, and work together . . . "[14]

Development continued, and in 1664 another large tract of land came under cultivation when a group of Englishmen established West Farms, an area to the northeast of Bronck's abandoned fields. Part of this area was later sold to Thomas Hunt and became known as Hunt's Point. Hunt raised flax and bees; the flax was shipped to Ireland to make linen, and the honey from the bees was used as a sweetener in the time before sugar became widely available.

Meanwhile the celebrated Morris family was making its way from England to Barbados and finally to New York, which had been known as New Amsterdam until it was captured by England in 1664. They purchased Bronck's abandoned farm, enlarged it, and also arranged to import slaves from the West Indies to work their huge farm. At the same time a Dutchman named John Archer, who was accumulating vast holdings, called his land the Manor of Fordham. Like present-day rival real estate barons, the Morrises countered by somewhat pompously renaming their holdings the Manor of Morrisania.

One is tempted, perhaps unjustly, to look to history for continuities, for the seeds that will later blossom into full-scale triumphs or pathologies. It is hard to resist seeing the disenfranchisement of tenants as the mortar that binds this story together. From the very beginning, these seventeenth century lords of the manor were jealous of their prerogatives: their tenants were not permitted to fish the streams or grind their grain in mills other than those owned by the landlord. This control by the landlords was substantial because gristmills and sawmills were an essential element of the local economy for two hundred years, until the dawn of modern industrialization.

The first school in the area was erected in 1683 by Connecticut settlers in Eastchester, which is now part of the northeast Bronx. Records[15] also indicate that in 1709 the Venerable Propagation Society established a local church-school. The non-unionized schoolmaster, one Edward Fitzgerald, was paid a modest eighteen pounds a year and had a seven-day work week, since he had to perform many religious functions on weekends. Mark Price cites a passage from an early history of the schools by Robert Bolton, who noted, "Whenever possible, 'moderate compensation' was exacted from pupils able to pay for their instruction, although no schooling was denied to those unable to pay."[16]

It is difficult to pinpoint exactly where the first school was located. In 1930 the Bronx Boro-Wide Association of Teachers tried to find the site without much luck. They complained that the old records were inadequate because "boundaries of estates were fixed by large trees, stone walls, and natural landmarks and small streams." By 1930, of course, the fully urbanized Bronx had obliterated any surviving natural landmarks.

The South Bronx in the American Revolution

By the time of the American Revolution there were still no towns or even villages in the South Bronx. Schooling was mostly a private family affair, and it is likely that, for the most part, only the children of the land owners could be assured of any formal instruction.

The Bronx was a battlefield during the war, with the two major land-owning families squaring off against each other. James De-Lancey, who had extensive holdings in Westchester County just north of the Bronx, was the local Tory leader. Royalist refugees from the surrounding areas coalesced around DeLancey, who helped drive

General George Washington out of the Bronx in 1776. At that point, the American forces were fleeing a British advance in Manhattan after narrowly escaping decimation in the Battle of Brooklyn. This retreat resulted in the British and their Hessian allies securely holding the Bronx for the duration of the war.

Arrayed against the Tories were the Patriots, who were led by Lewis Morris, the third and last Lord of the Manor of Morrisania. They camped in lower Westchester and skirmished with the Loyalists for the duration of the war. Lewis Morris was an authentic hero who before the War had attended the Second Continental Congress and signed the Declaration of Independence.

After the routing of the British, the Tory lands were confiscated and Lewis Morris returned to the South Bronx and prospered. He built a bridge over the Harlem River linking his estate to Manhattan. Roads were rerouted, and this bridge became an important element in his commercial success. Meanwhile, his half brother Gouverneur Morris became an influential politician and diplomat, serving as a delegate to the Constitutional Convention and American Minister to France in George Washington's administration. Theodore Roosevelt in his biography of Gouverneur Morris proclaims, "There has never been an American statesman of keener intellect or more brilliant genius."[17] Gouverneur Morris is considered the "penman of the U.S. Constitution" because he drafted its final form.[18] Before retiring to the bucolic splendor of Port Morris, the eastern part of the manor of Morrisania, he served as a United States Senator.

In 1795, the state began paying for some schooling of its young citizens. And, ten years later in 1805 the somewhat coercive "fee system" was completely abolished, and schools were made absolutely free. The population was still small; in 1795 there were only three schools within the present limits of the Bronx.

The First Half of the Nineteenth Century

The story of the South Bronx in the first half of the nineteenth century was one of modest population growth based on the early immigrant waves, impressive industrialization, and the firm establishment of free public schools.

The key South Bronx figure in the early part of the nineteenth century was Jordan L. Mott, who arrived on the scene in 1828. Mott purchased a parcel from Gouverneur Morris II, which he, not surprisingly, named Mott Haven. On it he built the first iron foundry in the Bronx. There he manufactured coal-burning stoves which revolutionized kitchens which had previously been designed around open fireplaces. This factory spurred other industrial growth and attracted workers to the South Bronx.

Also at this time the monumental public works, Croton Aqueduct, which carries water from upstate to New York City, was constructed through the Bronx and finally completed in 1849. Another major infrastructure project of this era was the building of the New York and Harlem Railroad which stimulated even more growth. Wherever a station happened to be built, houses and stories immediately sprang up, and modest villages began to flourish. The first South Bronx suburbs were thus clustered around the early train stations constructed in Morrisania, West Farms, and Tremont, a new village built on three hills.

Irish laborers built these railroads,

an exhausting, dangerous work [that] led to the saying that American railroads had "an Irishman buried under every tie." Many of these Irish workmen, finding the Bronx a refreshingly quiet change from frenetic Manhattan, stayed on and settled down with their families in Highbridge, near the aqueduct spanning the Hudson, and in Melrose where the railroad entered the Bronx from Manhattan."[19]

It is worth recalling that, like the Black migrants and the Hispanic immigrants who saturated the Bronx after World War II, these Irish newcomers were viewed with hostility and dread. This time-honored pattern of bias was not totally without foundation as Jonnes reminds us:

The impoverished Irish inundated almshouses, courts, and jails. Although by the 1850s the Irish were one-third of the populace, they accounted for 55 percent of the arrests (about half for drunkenness) and two-thirds of the paupers. Police vans were dubbed "paddy wagons" after their most frequent occupants. Illegitimacy was commonplace. Native-born Americans reviled the Irish as lazy, filthy, drunken brawlers who bonded into young gangs and terrorized the streets.[20]

Post Civil War

The second half of the nineteenth century was a time of consolidation, increased industrialization, and the absorption in the 1880s of massive waves of German, Italian, and Jewish immigrants.

A century ago the now-desolate streets of the South Bronx were the summer playground of the rich. Blue bloods raised prize cattle in Hunts Point, and in Morrisania, the wealthy dabbled in thoroughbred horses. Any list of the worst streets in America in the late 1960s would have to include Simpson, Tiffany, and Fox, all named after luxurious estates where the rich had frolicked a few generations earlier.

Simpson Street is the site of the notorious Fort Apache,[21] the police station of the forty-first precinct. According to a report in 1977:

> Fort Apache's station house is one of only three buildings in that particular block of Simpson Street that are still intact. Of all the precincts in the city, Fort Apache has been the most violent. But because of the widespread burning and the rapid exodus of the neighborhood's population, the level of crime has fallen in the last two years. Fox Street, once thought to be the street with the densest population in the country, is burned out and practically deserted now; ninety-five percent of its population is gone. The forty-first precinct still has a population of some 170,000, predominantly Puerto Rican and Black; 40,000 are on welfare.[22]

By 1993 the neo-Renaissance building that houses the forty-first precinct was abandoned when the police moved to a sleek postmodern structure seven blocks away. The worn station house was "known from here to Hollywood as Fort Apache, a solitary outpost in a neighborhood of death and decay and gangs with grandiosely macabre names, according to a *New York Times* article."[23] Indeed, twenty-five years ago it was a common sight on these streets to see young men wearing the colors of the Savage Skulls, Savage Nomads, Ghetto Brothers, Black Spades, Spanish Mafia, Seven Immortals, and Seven Crowns. With a 1992 per capita income of only $5,379 (as compared to a city average of $16,281), it is still one of the most impoverished areas of the city where drug dealing and prostitution still flourish openly on the streets but where murders, which use to run between 120 and 130 a year, are now down dramatically to around fifty. Partly that is the result of a drastic population decline from 93,900 in 1970 to 39,443 in 1990, but it also stems from other more positive changes which are beginning to stir.

In 1874 there were approximately twenty-eight thousand people living in the South Bronx when it was grafted politically to Manhattan. Even more tangible bonds were forged: horsecar transit lines had connected Manhattan with the South Bronx since the time of the

Civil War, but in 1888 a rail link was built that decisively ended the isolation of the Bronx. Manhattan's Third Avenue El, an elevated track, pierced the Bronx, stopping at the southern tip of Morrisania. In subsequent years this track stretched the length of the Bronx, and unlike the earlier more expensive commuter line it was affordable to the working class.[24]

In 1874, as these first steps of what some observers called the "colonization" of the Bronx took place, there were fourteen schools in the Bronx, with five of them clustered in Morrisania. All together there were 155 teachers and principals, and the operating costs, including all salaries and janitorial supplies, were $135,000 a year."[25]

Elementary school lasted until the eighth grade, and most found this amount of instruction adequate to cope with the demands of the world. High schools were not intended for everyone and were, in fact, called "the people's colleges." It was not until 1897, when the Mixed High School set up temporary quarters, that the Bronx even had a secondary school. When the school moved to its permanent location in 1904, its name was changed to Morris High School.

Before the Bronx opened its first high school, it did have a number of private colleges operating in the rural stretches of the borough. St. John's College, run by the Jesuits and later renamed Fordham University, has been a Bronx landmark since 1841. In the northwest tip of Riverdale at the edge of the Bronx, the Sisters of Charity ran the Academy of Mount St. Vincent which, by the turn of the century, was an accredited college. Also, New York University built a campus on a bluff above the Harlem River in the 1890s.

The Bronx also proved to be a congenial place for research. At this time, in the late nineteenth century, the South Bronx became home to the Bronx Zoo, which, in addition to being the most celebrated institution to exhibit exotic animals in the country, was also a major center for scholarship. It coordinated efforts to save the American buffalo when it was on the brink of extinction. In fact, all the herds of buffalo in the American West today spring from the original Bronx herd, and "the model for the old Buffalo nickel was raised at the Bronx Zoo."[26]

This was also the time of mass immigration from Italy and eastern Europe. The Italians, who initially settled in Little Italy or East Harlem, began to ride the El up to Melrose, a neighborhood north of Mott Haven, and to an area near Fordham called Belmont that remains a South Bronx Italian stronghold to this day. The Jews initially settled in Manhattan's Lower East Side, but the more prosperous and adventurous soon rode up the Third Avenue tracks and clustered in Mott Haven. The earlier immigrant groups, the Irish and the Germans, were already well established by this time. Prosperous Irish lived along Alexander Avenue, and Cortlandt Avenue drew so many Germans that it was known as "Dutch Broadway." Bronx historian Gary Hermalyn describes Bronx neighborhoods at the turn of the century.

> Despite the fact that the Bronx was part of the great metropolis, most Bronxites thought of themselves as living in a small village. For example, if asked where he lived, a Bronxite would usually reply Mott Haven, Kingsbridge, or Morrisania. In the 1890s the small villages were usually only a few blocks long and surrounded by farmlands, orchards, and meadows. The streets were mostly dirt roads, and each village supported only a few stores. The larger towns contained factories, mills and breweries.

> The ethnic population of The Bronx at the turn of the century was not very diverse, and most often one ethnic group dominated the village. For example, in Melrose and Morrisania, where the new Morris High School building was opened in 1904, the dominant population was German, consisting of immigrants who came to the country in the 1860s. The Irish dominated in Mott Haven, where many worked in the Mott Iron Works or the Stephens' coal yard. The wealthy Irish doctors settled along Alexander Avenue, which was known as "Irish Fifth Avenue." The Irish were also well represented in Kingsbridge and Riverdale, where they served as gardeners and servants to the rich and Anglo-Saxon families.

> Early in the twentieth century, Black families came to the Morrisania section and into Williamsbridge. At the same time, Jews settled in Mott Haven on land purchased by the Baron de Hirsch Fund. Other Jewish families could be found in the Hunts Point and Morrisania sections as well.[27]

In 1898 New York City, which had previously consisted of only Manhattan and half of the Bronx, was consolidated into the present five boroughs of Brooklyn, Queens, Staten Island, all of the Bronx, and Manhattan.

This political change, coupled with the massive deluge of immigrants, refashioned the Bronx fundamentally. The local schools, which were the primary route for advancement and assimilation, also had to change profoundly. Mirroring a change that was sweeping the country, Price observes:

Until the end of the last century, education in the Bronx had been largely a process of teaching academic subjects to boys and girls who were capable mentally and physically of absorbing instruction. Following the transition from the town system to the borough system, there began a gradual enlargement of the concept of public education and a corresponding enlargement of the educational services—both of which continue on an ever-expanding basis to this day.[28]

Price wrote at the end of World War II, but his generalization about the expansion of educational services remains true today, although he perhaps would be surprised to see the direction this movement has taken. In our time this instructional extension has embraced all manner of special educational services, including drug-abuse prevention programs, unwed mother instruction, alternative schools for the disruptive, etc. It has to be remembered that Price was writing at a more innocent time when he exulted: "The classroom . . . is now regarded as a workshop, a laboratory, a studio, a library, a place to practice gracious living."

The Early Twentieth Century

In the early twentieth century, the South Bronx boomed. The population mushroomed from 200,000 in 1900 to over one million by 1925. Subways sliced along the north-south axis of the borough, bulging with new immigrants. Apartment buildings sprang up near the subways; real estate developers were having a field day. The Simpsons, Tiffanys, and Foxes sold their estates and beat a hasty retreat to more exclusive precincts. The South Bronx suburbs were overwhelmed and quickly metamorphosed into densely populated, genuinely urban neighborhoods.

The Mott Haven iron foundries gave way to piano factories and coal companies. Photos from this era depict many manufacturing plants jumbled together wtih building supply firms and lumber yards along a canal (now covered) and suggest that a laborer looking for work may not have had to travel far. In 1897 the Bronx Board of Trade listed an impressive range of factories that issued

a great variety of commodities, such as iron work of every description including stoves, ranges and furnaces, ice making machinery, church organs, pianos, refrigerators, artistic goods, electrical supplies, surgical instruments, beaten gold, china, small and enameled ware, naphtha launches, railway lamps, paper boxes of every design, both as to utility and beauty, window shades, toys, segars [sic], brushes, carpets, dyeing and printing work, mineral waters, tape, soap, silks, shirts, drums, varnish and other products of necessity and practical usefulness.[29]

And the proliferation of subways insured that there was a generous supply of workers and consumers.

In 1909 the Grand Concourse, beginning in Mott Haven and stretching north, opened for strollers and traffic. Nearby Yankee Stadium opened in 1923. Meanwhile on the Concourse, luxury apartment houses, many in the suave, streamlined Art Deco style, sprouted along both sides of the thoroughfare. To move into one of these magnificent buildings was an immigrant's fantasy:

Living in the high class apartment houses built in the 1920s, and added to during the depths of the Great Depression, were professional people and proprietors of establishments in Manhattan. Occupying the side streets and some of the posh residencies along the boulevard were many workers in the fur and clothing trade, who found it easy to get to work by using the subway beneath the Concourse. Most of these people were Jewish, and in those days the Concourse was a dream that any working-class Jew in Hunts Point or elsewhere could aspire to attain. It was the symbol of "making it" and was a combination of Manhattan's Fifth and Park Avenues.[30]

The lamentable fate of the Concourse and especially of its side streets is a staple of contemporary tabloid journalism. An article in the *New York Post* is typical of the genre.[31] Two *Post* reporters focus on Walton Street, one block west and parallel to the Concourse. Near a formerly elegant building named "The Cortile" where Babe Ruth once lived in a sixth-floor apartment, "today," the newsmen sneer, "the sidewalks are littered with garbage, shady characters are everywhere and the building is marred by graffiti, broken windows, and stomach-turning smells." Next to a photo of the ruined building is a gigantic shot of Ruth, The Sultan of Swat, looking solemn and somewhat bewildered. The headline reads, "Buy Me Some Peanuts and Crack."

The bustling growth of the 1920s came to a squealing halt when the Great Depression struck in 1929. The South Bronx managed to weather the storm partly because ambitious, local public works projects helped to pick up the employment slack. By 1935 some apartment building construction resumed along the Concourse. In fact, as Ultan observes, "No urban area in the country experienced more private residential development during that troubled decade, and the boast was often made that the Bronx was 'the city without a slum.'"[32] By the end of the decade the South Bronx was a secure, hardworking area built at a density unsurpassed by almost any other area of the country. It was home to laborers and the emerging middle class, and ordinary life was firmly rooted in distinct, stable neighborhoods.

Post World War II

If the 1930s was a time for the South Bronx to pause and catch its breath, then the 1940s, with the coming of World War II, ushered in profound changes that fundamentally realigned social patterns.

Directly after Pearl Harbor, thousands of South Bronx men were plucked from the neighborhoods and sent to the Pacific and Europe. The factories of Port Morris were retooled to crank out munitions around the clock. Factory workers were needed, and into this vacuum came new immigrants:

Shortages in the labor force operated simultaneously with the ongoing mechanization of American agriculture to accelerate one of the country's largest internal migrations. During the war years, millions of Blacks left the poverty of the rural South to work in northern and Pacific coast cities. Similar economic conditions in Puerto Rico . . . sparked a major influx of Puerto Ricans to New York City.[33]

The story of this Black diaspora is movingly told in Nicholas Lemann's classic 1991 history, *The Promised Land: The Great Black Migration and How It Changed America.*[34] This work focuses on Chicago, but New York City and the South Bronx, in particular, was the promised land for both southern rural Blacks and waves of economic refugees from Puerto Rico seeking employment.[35]

By the second half of the twentieth century, the South Bronx was saturated; there was little room for new immigrants to be shoehorned in, and so a new pattern emerged. It was as if, for every new family that came to settle in a old apartment or in one of the new high-rise public housing projects, another family moved out. In the 1950s, 100,000 people moved in to the Bronx, and perhaps 100,000 others, mostly White, left, settling in the suburbs or the more wide-open residential neighborhoods in Queens. The Southeast Bronx in

and near Hunts Point turned into a lively Puerto Rican neighborhood, and Morrisania and beyond, in the heart of the South Bronx,
grew increasingly Black.

At first in the postwar period, most of these newcomers settled
in Harlem where housing was more available and less expensive. But
a series of interrelated policy decisions fashioned in Washington had
a strikingly unanticipated impact on the South Bronx and spurred
changes that took on an overpowering momentum of their own.

Locally in 1944, rents were frozen as part of a wartime price sta-
bilization strategy, but this artificial removal of rent rates from market forces unexpectedly persisted for decades in the South Bronx. At
first, this had the effect of further stabilizing neighborhoods because
a reasonable rent was locked in for the tenant and in the tight rental
market people were reluctant to leave their apartments.

But, as we'll see, two Washington D.C. policies promulgated by
the Veterans Administration and the Federal Housing Administration interacted synergistically with the lingering rent-control regulations, resulting in systemic changes that profoundly distorted the
historical direction of the South Bronx.

These municipal and federal government policies, coupled with
the massive loss of entry-level industrial jobs triggered by a changing economy, bred dramatic changes all through New York City. In
its wake, whole neighborhoods were destroyed not only in the Bronx,
but also in Manhattan and Brooklyn. The fallout from these disloca-
tions had its most virulent impact on the South Bronx. This havoc
is especially visible in the borough's housing and schools.

The Ravaged Bronx of the 1970s and 1980s

Charlotte Street in the center of the Bronx serves as a potent
symbol for all the hopelessness of the South Bronx of the 1970s, and
now as a result of its well-intentioned but fundamentally bungled rehabilitation in the 1980s, it stands as an unlikely monument to government's deep confusion about how to restore viability to these
ruined neighborhoods.

Charlotte Street has, of course, a particular resonance because
it has been visited by the last two presidents of the United States and
its residents have witnessed the pledges made to mobilize the resources of the United States to end the disgraceful destruction of this
neighborhood.

When President Jimmy Carter strode down Charlotte Street
in 1977, there was not much left. In the early 1960s, fifty-one

apartment buildings stood on Charlotte Street and its two adjacent blocks, Wilkins Avenue and East 172nd Street, and they contained more than one thousand apartments and three thousand residents. By 1977, there were only nine buildings left. And, according to a contemporary account in the *New York Times,* "Six of them have their windows and entrances blocked off with cinder blocks and concrete, and two of them are fire-blackened hulks."[36] At the time Carter swept through, to make a brief speech, there remained only one occupied building, with thirty-seven apartments.

Robert Esnard, who was chairman of the Bronx office of the City Planning Commission during that time, said, "By the late 1960s half the buildings were gone. Abandonment had begun. The middle class had begun to leave replaced by minorities and the poor. Those on welfare and those unemployed moved into Charlotte Street."[37]

What caused this precipitous decline replicated throughout the South Bronx? According to Esnard,

Buildings were left to rot. Landlords left. Bankers wouldn't loan a dime. There was no such thing as insurance, fire or otherwise. The population turned over. Add to this the fact that Charlotte Street was selected as a site for two new schools, a public school and a junior high, and site-clearing went on and you have the final irony: two school sites cleared for a population that doesn't exist anymore."[38]

Time-worn PS 61, across Boston Road from Charlotte Street, once slated to be replaced, still serves the remaining population.

Today, more than a decade after two Presidents vowed to make changes, the surrounding neighborhood remains mostly untouched, but Charlotte Street itself has been transformed. After a grim walk along Boston Road through an urban nightmare of block after block of devastated buildings, a stroller is confronted with a sunny scene reminiscent of the suburbs in the 1950s. The one inhabited six-story building President Carter saw along Charlotte Street remains,[39] but the rest of the block has twenty modest, pastel, prefabricated, free-standing ranch homes sitting on meticulously tended green lawns. One conjures memories of photographs of War World II veterans beaming proudly in front of their identical homes in Levittown. There are some differences, however. All these homes have their tiny windows sealed by bars, except for the big picture window that does not lend itself to such protection, although a close look reveals that many houses have even this window secured by internal bars.

The first strip of these prefab suburban houses, which were assembled in the early 1980s, had white wooden picket fences, and the later models now have steel picket fences, many with sharp points. Some plots are softened by shrubs, and one even has the archetypical suburban status symbol of a satellite dish to capture cable television signals. Even today, it is hard to know whether this preposterous block is a harbinger of hopeful transformation for the South Bronx or a grotesque footnote in the seemingly relentless debasement of the borough.

This modest beginning of reconstruction is the result of Jimmy Carter's 1977 visit. That brief presidential sojourn, which featured "startled winos [who] waved their bagged bottles happily at him [as] Black youths, cheered, calling. 'Give me a job, Jimmy,' "[40] stimulated a short-lived media scrutiny of the neighborhood. From press accounts it is possible to construct a picture of life in this neighborhood during what may have been the depths of its misery. More graphically, the heart-breaking story of Charlotte Street is told in eight detailed, well-researched chapters in Jonnes 1986 book. The residents of this classic Bronx working-class neighborhood, almost all Eastern European Jews, had "everything a family could want in the early twentieth century—a park, good public schools, convenient subways, synagogues, movie theaters, and excellent shopping."[41] Ten years after an abrupt shift in population in the early 1960s all that was left was rubble, "large stretches of eerie necropolis—charred ruins; fields lumpy with detritus; disemboweled, abandoned buildings."[42]

The schools at this time were facing unprecedented problems. Many young people were unprepared for instruction (or perhaps, it was the schools that were unprepared for these students): in some schools, few students spoke English, and schools had to contend with a potent distillation of all the ills of ghetto life, including one-parent families, pervasive drug addiction, street gangs, rapacious landlords, misguided government policies, high crime, and the lassitude bred by welfare.

There is surprisingly little written about the schools of that time. It is almost as if newspapers and magazines willfully averted their attention. What did get reported tended to focus on crime. For example, in a typical article, the *New York Times* reported on the rising violence at Samuel Gompers Vocational-Technical High School in Mott Haven. Focusing on the plight of staffers, rather than students, the article noted: "Some teachers contend that there have been at least 22 assaults recently on faculty members, including one incident in which a teacher's sweater was set afire while he was wearing it. Several women teachers said they had been molested, menaced or punched by unknown intruders from the halls."[43]

A young teacher, her idealism badly battered, admitted poignantly that she felt "more like a turnkey in a jail than a teacher" and planned to leave at the end of the term. I just don't want to get hurt," she said. The school itself was in shambles, with a charred classroom resulting from one of a reported thirteen fires set by students that year. Teenagers were loitering in the playground drinking wine. According to another teacher who wanted to leave, "The students were fine until the building started to go. That was the first sign to them that nobody cared." Added to that there were said to be forty to fifty classes a day without teachers and five hundred misprogrammed students who missed the first few weeks of school while their schedules were being straightened out. Administrators cited lack of funds caused by New York City's fiscal crisis.[44]

Of course, the city did spend some money in the South Bronx during this time. For instance, it lavished more than $100 million of public money on improvements to Yankee Stadium in Mott Haven. This money was invested in stadium amenities like ". . . its blue seats and its plazas and its VIP boxes with private bars, private bathrooms, luxurious sofas and guards, in the corridors to keep out those who do not belong. The latter category includes most of the area's residents, who can't afford to buy tickets in the more expensive parts of the stadium their money helped build."[45]

The city found funds to install high-intensity security lighting around the stadium, but "across the street . . . is a 50-year-old, unlit, ill-cared-for public athletic facility with a drinking fountain that hasn't functioned in years." Also at this time the city slashed the budget of the local Senior Citizens Center, and it could not "provide enough doctors and medicine at Lincoln Hospital—several blocks away—to stop people from dying because of inadequate treatment."[46]

Assaults on stadium fans received extensive press coverage. But relatively little was written about the marked decline in sanitation services, or the impact on health care the closing of nearby Morrisania Hospital had on the neighborhood, or the fact that "many local landlords drastically reduced maintenance on their buildings while just as drastically increasing rents."[47] Even the local YMCA and YMHA, which had provided recreation for neighborhood children for decades, closed down around this time.

The paralyzing fear of inconveniencing Yankee fans continues to galvanize government attention to the neighborhood. In 1993,

City Hall and borough officials trip over themselves to reverse the blight near the stadium when the odious team owner, George Stein-brenner, sniffs that he is worried about the safety and parking in the area. South of the stadium is a park for residents and the Bronx Ter-minal Market, a cooperative of about two dozen food merchants who supply *bodegas* and other small stores. According to the *New York Times* "during a meeting of city officials last week to discuss possi-ble parking sites, the market and a city park across the street from the stadium were mentioned among other sites."[48]

Up until recently, it was clear that the Bronx was being sys-tematically destroyed:

> In the late sixties in the Bronx the rental apartment building (a form of housing invented in ancient Rome and reliably lucra-tive in every era thereafter) suffered a dramatic demise as an economic entity, becoming in short order a worthless invest-ment. Costs had soared, rents remained controlled, while rent delinquency and vandalism were rampant. Some landlords just abandoned their buildings, others "milking" them—paying no taxes, providing no services, but collecting what rents they could. The most venal turned to arson to recoup their losses. Concurrently, "finishers" (whose vocation was invented in this time and place) and junkies mined the dying apartment houses for every item of worth. They set fires to force out tenants so they might more easily extricate pipes and other valuables. Welfare tenants, desperate to escape buildings without heat or hot water and often under siege, torched their apartments in or-der to get priority on city housing lists.[49]

Has this shattered collection of neighborhoods stabilized? What is the situation in the 1990s? Is there any way to go but up?

The Outlook for the Bronx

Obviously, it is not clear what the future holds. The signals are decidedly mixed. On one hand, building abandonment has slowed considerably. Although this is true in part because there is little left to abandon, the fact remains that the population has thinned and vast tracts of lands are now available for factories and housing. The infrastructure is already in place. The subways are functioning, an extensive network of highways offers easy truck access, and sewers and electrical lines are already buried in the empty streets.

There are a number of impressively successful, small-scale "sweat equity" reclamations of previously abandoned buildings like those launched by the innovative community development group Banana Kelly, where the new residents exchanged their labor for ownership of their apartments. There is mounting evidence that, once people have a tangible stake in their housing, they will be better able to confront the pervasive forces of neighborhood decay.

Jobs, of course, remain key to Bronx reclamation, and by the late 1980s there was some evidence that New York City's economic boom, which created numerous service sector jobs, had finally begun to trickle down to some of those living in poverty.

Yet, New York City continues to bleed manufacturing jobs, according to a study commissioned by the Bronx Borough President in 1990.[50] The report cites Bureau of Labor Statistics which estimates that there was a loss of 64,000 blue-collar jobs in New York City between 1979 and 1988. The Regional Plan Association projects that such jobs will continue to decline in the 1984–2005 time period by about sixteen percent. These are the kinds of jobs best suited to graduates of Bronx high schools.

The Bronx population is recovering from the loss of almost 300,000 residents in the 1970s. Roughly 100,000 new residents moved to the Bronx between 1980 and 1990, and the Regional Plan Association estimates that another 82,000 may be added between 1990 and 2000. Moreover, the ethnic composition of the Bronx is still in flux, with the percentage of white non-Hispanics expected to decline from 34 to 24 percent between 1990 and 2000, while the number of Hispanics and Blacks will show a healthy growth.

Where will all these new entrants live, and how will they pay the rent? The current trends projected across the last decade of the twentieth century depressingly indicate, according to the Regional Plan Association, that the poorest Bronx households will mushroom by 20 percent to 242,000. In 1987, 27 percent of people in the Bronx received some form of public assistance, and, since their numbers will grow substantially, the demand for social services in the South Bronx will expand.

This, in turn, will exacerbate the housing crisis. The Regional Plan Association found that there were in 1990 about 424,000 housing units in the Bronx, not all in occupied structures, and about 43,000 households doubled up. It is expected that by the year 2000 there will be a dire need for 570,000 housing units. These projections illuminate a serious mismatch of need and reality. This boils down to a need for 189,000 additional housing units over the next decade, which, at a low estimate of $80,000 per unit, indicates a projected investment of $15.2 billion for Bronx housing. Since the vast majority of residents cannot afford market rates, the housing situation appears bleak.

In the early 1990s evidence suggests that the economic boom of the 1980s, which in any case, largely bypassed the Bronx, was long past. The hyperthyroid real-estate market is in collapse. As always in the South Bronx, one does not have to look far to see problems.

Epidemiologists warn that the AIDS virus infects as many as one in five sexually active men in the South Bronx. Women residents are warned that, because of such rampant infection, intercourse with a neighborhood man is like "sexual Russian roulette."[51] In fact, in New York for the last few years, AIDS has been the leading cause of death for women aged 25 to 34. A recent study highlighted startling racial disparities.

> Among Whites, the AIDS death rate rose from 0.6 per 100,000 women in 1986 to 1.2 in 1988. But among Blacks, the rate was 4.4 in 1986 and jumped to 10.3 in 1988. In 1987, the AIDS death rate among Black women in New York was 29.5 per 100,000.[52]

It is said that one in every twenty babies born in Bronx hospitals is infected with the AIDS virus, and five in twenty are born with opiates in their blood.[53]

Meanwhile, another widespread scourge has descended on the South Bronx and other inner-city neighborhoods across the country. Crack cocaine. Five years after crack first hit the streets of the South Bronx in 1983, the juvenile arrest rate in New York City tripled from 386 to 1,052. Young teens are at the heart of the crack trade because they do not run the risk of the mandatory jail sentences older dealers confront.

Crack is an extremely lucrative product: according to law enforcement personnel some youngsters can make up to $3,000 a day. This money is usually spent in conspicuous consumption and ostentatious display. Like *nouveau riche* suburban adults, the young drug dealers favor gold chains, status cars, and expensive clothes.

> Gold, in fact, is a widespread obsession with inner-city youngsters. Heavy gold cables that cost up to $20,000 are all the rage, as well as chunky three-fingered rings resembling brass knuckles. Even gold dental caps are considered chic. These styles are so widely associated with drug trafficking that school princi-

ples are banning them. In New York City the principals of three high schools have forbidden the wearing of gold jewlery.[54]

The drug trade, and its resulting gang wars, have enslaved thousands of South Bronx residents and trapped others in their homes where they are still not safe from stray gunfire.

Bronx per capita income is the lowest in the Tri-State Region's thirty-one counties. Among elementary and junior high students, 78 percent are classified as poor under the school lunch formula. Bronx dropout rates are twice the state average and a quarter higher than the city average.[55]

The depressing litany can be extended almost indefinitely, but the point has been made. Anyone attempting to reverse the commanding forces of decay in the South Bronx has a monumental task. Where does one begin?

Before we turn to some hopeful stirrings, it is useful to explore the reasons for this collapse.

2

Why Did the South Bronx Collapse?

The South Bronx was, of course, not the only inner-city neighborhood that fell prey to widespread destruction in the decade between 1965 and 1975. Other parts of New York City, notably Bushwick, East New York, and Bedford Stuyvesant in Brooklyn, as well as Harlem in Manhattan, were marred by building abandonment, social dislocation, and school disaster. Also, other U.S. cities such as Chicago, Los Angeles, Detroit, St. Louis, Cleveland, Baltimore, Washington, D.C., and many midsized cities suffered extensive ruin in their ghetto areas.

Given the enormous proportions of the destruction, there surprisingly, is no clear consensus on why the South Bronx collapsed. Various specialists have compiled lists of factors.[1] But it is a complex problem, and untangling cause from effect is particularly difficult. For instance, was the genuine fear of crime, perhaps the most frequently cited reason, which drove out stable middle-class families and triggered a chain of dramatic changes in its wake, a contributing cause of the decline? or is that fear better understood as a symptom disguising a less publicized, buried cause?

In an attempt to impose order on this discussion of the causes of the collapse, I will distinguish between two primary causes and a host of proximate factors. In my reading of the evidence, the employment situation for unskilled labor, which changed drastically after World War II, and government policies, particularly postwar federal housing and highway initiatives, are the two primary culprits in the disintegration of the South Bronx. In my view, fear of crime, racism, tenant and landlord arson, the drug epidemic, the construction of the Cross Bronx Expressway, and the rise of the so-called ghetto underclass are all promixate causes that might be best thought of as symptoms. Nonetheless, it is important to remember that all of these factors have worked synergistically, and so neat division into categories inevitably is an over-simplified distortion of a complex situation.

Let's begin with the acknowledgment that the South Bronx was always a reception zone for newly arrived immigrants, a place for newcomers to get their bearings and slowly adjust to mainstream American society. This rather orderly assimilation demonstrably did not continue with newly arrived Latinos from Puerto Rico and internal migrant Blacks from the Deep South after World War II. Why was their fate radically different from the pattern of grudging but eventual accommodation to newcomers—a social response that stretched back a century to the Irish immigrants of the 1840s?

Primary Causes: 1. Jobs Disappeared

The road to success for all previous entrants to the South Bronx was integration into the local economy, but after World War II the economy fundamentally shifted gears. In a nutshell, the problem was that manufacturing jobs fled the Bronx, and the new residents were consequently excluded from employment opportunities:

Hunts Point and other industrialized areas of the South Bronx were thriving at the end of the war. Food processing, garment manufacturing, cabinet and wood-working shops employed the working class population of surrounding neighborhoods. . . . Of the 2,000 manufacturers in the South Bronx in 1959, 650 had left by 1974, along with an estimated 17,688 jobs.[2]

This loss of manufacturing jobs was not limited to the South Bronx but was happening on a massive scale in all of New York City. The drying up of low-skill jobs which were always there for earlier immigrants emerges as perhaps the key difference between the arrivals who came here after World War II and those who had been successfully assimilated into American society before the War.

This fundamental change in the economy erected higher barriers for minority youth and drastically slowed their absorption into the job market. William Julius Wilson observes:

Urban minorities have been particularly vulnerable to structural economic changes, such as the shift from goods-producing to service-producing industries, the increasing polarization of the labor market into low-wage and high-wage sectors, technological innovations, and the relocation of manufacturing industries outside of the central cities. These economic shifts point out the fact that nearly all of the large and densely populated metropolises experienced their most rapid development during an earlier industrial and transportation era. Today the urban centers are undergoing an irreversible structural transformation from "centers of production and distribution of material goods to centers of administration, information exchange, and higher order service provision." The central-city labor market, particularly in northern areas, has been profoundly altered in the process.[3]

This change means that the educational requirements of those entering the job market were now different. Since it is no longer goods but information that is being processed, job growth, according to John Kasarda,[4] has been concentrated in industries that require higher levels of education. This, at a time when the local schools have been convulsed by challenges they have not met.

The specific numbers are dramatic. In New York City, as late as 1970 there were 1,445,000 jobs that required less than a high-school education. By 1984 that number dwindled to 953,000. At the same time, there were 1,200,000 jobs in New York City that required "some higher education" in 1970, and that number has continued to expand. By 1984, 239,000 new jobs in that category were created. The result is "a serious mismatch between the current education distribution of minority residents in large northern cities and the changing education requirements of their rapidly transforming industrial bases."[5]

Other rust-belt cities were experiencing the same job loss, yet they did not implode. The scale of what happened in the South Bronx is utterly unique. As Nathan Glazer has noted:

One saw an onslaught on physical structures that has no parallel in the history of civilized urban life. There was abandonment and destruction in other American cities, but nothing on the scale of New York, even accounting for its much larger size. One sees nothing like it in England's declining midland cities, even though their populations and employment opportunities have been more radically reduced, and much of the housing stock has been demolished or is in bad repair. One sees nothing like it in the great cities of the Continent, or the developing world.[6]

One reason for the magnitude of the destruction was that, in the teeth of this job loss, New York City did little to try to save the manufacturing industries that wanted to remain. In many cases, factory owners and merchants who provided jobs to the local residents felt deserted by the city. During this period, apartment buildings were abandoned at such a rate that local government could not demolish them in a timely fashion. The result was that, by the late 1970s, throughout the city the list of buildings which were scheduled for demolition swelled to over 10,000, with more than 200 buildings added every month. The buildings reverted to the city when landlords walked away. The structures were confiscated in lieu of delinquent tax payments. Often the empty hulks were swiftly expropriated by drug dealers and squatters who used them to mount assaults on nearby occupied factories. In one such typical set of related instances in the South Bronx, "Breaking through brick walls, roofs, ventilators, loading bay doors, cellar floors and windows, the squatters since summer have burglarized two knitting-goods factories, a Christmas-trimmings plant, a construction company and a neighborhood grocer."[7] Illustrative of the brazenness of the thievery, in one case, teenagers stole a car and repeatedly rammed it into a loading bay door until they gained entry.

In addition to the threat of squatters, there was the danger of fire which "often spreads from one vacant building to adjoining occupied ones and has taken the lives of several residents and at least one fireman this year," according to a contemporary report in the *Daily News*. The article goes on to note, "Aside from the unsightliness of the buildings and their drain on property values, they harbor garbage and rats. The rats often infest the rest of the block no matter how clean and well-maintained it is, and the junkies often steal piping to sell as scarp, thereby causing flooding in the buildings."

At this time in 1977, according to the Department of City Planning, the South Bronx had lost an astonishing 100,000 residents in seven years, and "in the last few years, 7,000 fires and $20 million in insurance losses were reported; more than 1,200 [South Bronx] buildings stand vacant or abandoned."[8]

During a massive electrical blackout in 1976, extensive looting of South Bronx stores took place. The looting continued for a full night, and the next afternoon "the police were pelted with bottles and rocks from the rooftops. The entire shopping area was closed off, and teams of helmeted officers armed with baseball bats broke up groups that congregated nearby."[9] Altogether, in the South Bronx an estimated 350 stores were looted, and damage was in excess of $4.5 million.

Many merchants continued to hang on, especially in a major shopping area called the Hub in Morrisania where, in 1978, stores ". . . employed 2,000 people and generated sales of more than $100 million a year."[10] At the time, many of the businessmen agreed on one prescription for the neighborhood: as one merchant said, "The solution for the Hub and for the whole of the South Bronx has been offered over and over again. It is housing and jobs. Jobs and housing. When ways are found to provide them, the other problems will take care of themselves."[11]

Primary Causes: 2. Government Policies

The change in the nature of entry-level jobs was an economic fact. However, the federal government's complicity in the destruction of the South Bronx was not preordained. The government intervened vigorously and incompetently. It promulgated ill-conceived public housing projects; it heedlessly encouraged suburban development at the expense of the inner city; and, even more distressingly, it abjectly failed to provide adequate political leadership to galvanize forces of regeneration.

Government's first intervention was well-meaning, even idealistic. Deep in the Great Depression, the Roosevelt Administration succeeded in passing the Housing Act of 1937, which stepped up the federal government's involvement in housing from merely establishing and regulating minimum building standards, always the modest sphere of housing reformers, to that of actual construction. These ambitious efforts were founded on the disappointing experience of earlier initiatives dating to President Franklin Delano Roosevelt's First Hundred Days of 1933 when the Public Works Administration attempted to create jobs and housing simultaneously by jump-starting private development with federal loans. Even with this encouragement, precious little was built because developers continued to conclude that low-income housing was not profitable.

The new legislation of 1937 called for municipalities to organize housing authorities, bypass the private sector, and build apartments with long-term federal loans and direct Washington subsidies for construction and maintenance.

The idea was to build huge, racially integrated apartment buildings for the "deserving poor."

Massive slum clearance efforts had captured city planning, and the era of the housing project had begun. Block after block of Melrose, Mott Haven, and Claremont [a neighborhood just north of Morrisania] was leveled to make room for these "towers in gardens" in accordance with the national housing goal of a decent, safe and sanitary home for every American.[12]

But there was a fly in the ointment. As Kenneth Jackson points out in his classic study, *Crabgrass Frontier: The Suburbanization of the United States*, "Because municipalities had discretion on where and when to build public housing, the projects invariably reinforced racial segregation. A suburb that did not want to tarnish its exclusive image by having public housing within its precincts could simply refuse to create a housing agency."[13]

The result was that low-income housing was not built on the inexpensive, empty fields and potato farms of nearby Long Island, or on sites in Westchester to the north of the Bronx, but in the heart of the city, especially in the South Bronx. This had the advantage of clearing city slums, thus protecting the downtown real estate investments of the prominent citizens who typically made up the governing boards of the housing authorities, according to Jackson. This deliberate policy decision was in marked contrast to that of other industrialized countries like Great Britain and Japan, which faced similar problems but chose to build public housing on inexpensive, empty land on the outskirts of its cities.

Other policy decisions compounded the original error:

> The original concept of public housing was that it was for the "working poor," the "deserving poor," and the honest man temporarily down on his luck. Long-term welfare families, loafers, and unwed mothers were not welcomed. By the 1960's, however, this concept had been discarded, and admission policies were changed to allow welfare recipients into the structures. Thereafter, public housing came to be seen as the shelter of last resort, as a permanent home for the underclass rather than a temporary refuge for "respectable" families.[14]

So, viable but modest blocks were bulldozed flat in the name of social progress, and the promise of these high-rise projects rapidly soured. By the early 1970s their dismal failure was apparent to everyone.

> Originally conceived and carried through as major advances in ridding cities of slums, they involved the tearing down of rotting, rat-infested tenements, and the erection of modern apartment buildings. They were acclaimed as America's refusal to permit its people to live in the dirty shambles of slums. It is common knowledge that they have turned into jungles of hor-

ror and now confront us with the problem of how we can either convert or get rid of them. They have become compounds of double segregation—on the bases of both economy and race— and a danger for anyone compelled to live in these projects. A beautiful positive dream has turned into a nightmare.[15]

The most infamous example of this type of housing was the Pruit-Igoe project in St. Louis which housed some ten thousand adults and children. No scheme could make it livable, and, in a dramatic acknowledgment of complete failure, it was demolished in 1979, a mere twenty-two years after it was built.

Wilson comments:

In both housing projects and other inner-city neighborhoods, residents have difficulty identifying their neighbors. They are therefore less likely to engage in reciprocal guardian behavior. Events in one part of the block or neighborhood tend to be of little concern to those residing in other parts. These conditions of social disorganization are as acute as they are because of the unprecedented increase in the number of teenage and young adult minorities in these neighborhoods, many of whom are jobless, not enrolled in school, and a source of delinquency, crime and unrest.[16]

What is more, as Nathan Glazer has pointed out, the new subsidized public housing drew residents from the older but still viable housing stock. Without similar subsidies, the older structures could not compete economically with the low-rent projects, and this hastened their abandonment.

Today these high-rise buildings are no longer being built in New York City. In fact, during the 1980s under the Reagan Administration, hardly any public housing was constructed at all. Even worse, the meager public funds that were committed to housing initiatives under HUD were filched from the poor and, in many cases, were awarded to politically connected builders to construct middle-income suburban homes.

Meanwhile, city planners and architects are convinced that they have learned lessons from the failure of high-density housing. According to the current prevailing orthodoxy, whenever low-income housing is now built, it is invariably only two or three stories high, and customarily there are courtyards or other protected spaces so that mothers can keep their eyes on their children.

The South Bronx's detached one-family houses on Charlotte Street are the *reductio ad absurdum* of this new trend. Perhaps more tenable is other new housing stock built near Charlotte Street recently. These are two- or three-story attached "townhouse" buildings that draw their inspiration from the brownstones of the late nineteenth century. So far, there has been only a handful of developments using this new construction.

In later chapters we will examine a number of low-density, owner-occupied alternatives that may be the harbinger of a brighter future. The twelve years of City Hall administration by Mayor Ed Koch, ending in 1989, were notable for their failure to support (until its waning days) almost any of the models of nonprofit, community-based housing efforts that had sprung up fitfully across the city. In a landmark number of the journal, *Dissent,* Jim Sleeper, urban affairs specialist, editorial writer for *New York Newsday,* and now columnist for the *Daily News* wrote:

> But the mayor has failed utterly, out of what can only be described as an ideological commitment to the "free market," to hold the line against immediate causes of homelessness (itself the tip of an iceberg of "doubling up" and dislocation involving hundreds of thousands) and to support the many replicable models of nonprofit, community-based housing development that have emerged across the city. A little recouped tax incentive money would go a long way here. Instead, many successful experiments are all but dying on the vine while the city auctions its foreclosed parcels to the highest (often unqualified) bidder or sells them to upscale developers. Government doesn't so much "get out of the way" as choose between competing approaches to property relations and housing development. Demoralization and incompetence in the city's housing agency reflect the mayoral bias, compounding the crisis.[17]

Today, at this late stage, it is not clear just what can be done to reclaim those large public housing complexes. One innovative response to the problem is championed by Jack Kemp, a Republican House member from New York who was elevated in the Bush Administration to Secretary of HUD: "thousands of public housing communities across America are plagued by crime, drug abuse and vandalism. Where tenants have been empowered to take over the management of their housing communities, and even to purchase at a large discount their homes and apartments from the public housing authorities, housing projects have undergone almost miraculous transformations."[18] Whether this, or any policy, can repair the human damage done to people in some public housing projects is an open question. The atmosphere in these federally-funded buildings—"the rampart crime, the drugs, the sense of absolute apartness from the rest of the American society, the emphasis on an exaggerated and misguided version of masculinity that glorifies gang membership and sexual conquest"[19]—makes the prospects for reform daunting. However, the strategy of allowing low-income residents to own their homes as a possible solution to the housing woes of the South Bronx makes sense and will be examined in later chapters.

Another pre–World War II Washington initiative was equally well-intentioned but ultimately as disastrous to the beleaguered borough. The thought was to use federal money after the war to partially subsidize plowing over farms in Long Island and planting mass-produced, single-family detached homes for returning veterans.

In 1934 the Federal Housing Administration (FHA) was established to insure long-term mortgage loans made by the private sector to individuals. This was an unalloyed bonanza for private developers whose investments were virtually risk free. What is more, builders were permitted to charge whatever the housing-starved market would bear. The result was massive, subsidized construction of single-family dwellings outside the central city where the middle class, who could afford the ten percent down payment, found, in many cases, that it was cheaper to buy a new suburban house than to rent a comparable structure in places like the Bronx.

That this federal money was not used to build apartments in places like the South Bronx is no accident of fate. There was, as Jackson documents, a built-in anti-urban bias. Through unfavorable terms, FHA programs discouraged the construction of multifamily units. Also, the FHA was reluctant to lend money for repair of existing structures. And finally, the FHA "allowed personal and agency bias in the form of all-White subdivisions in the suburbs to affect the kind of loans it guaranteed—or equally important, refused to guarantee."[20]

Evidence for this last element of anti-city discrimination can be found in such official tools as the 1939 *Underwriting Manual* that FHA appraisers of potential loans used. The guidelines stipulated that "crowded neighborhoods lessen desirability," and "older properties in a neighborhood have a tendency to accelerate the transition to lower class occupancy,"[21] factors that increase loan risk and therefore should be avoided.

Famed Levittown is the archetypical result of FHA largess. The Irish and the Jews from the South Bronx were two groups who, in large numbers, eagerly took advantage of the opportunity of participating in the American dream of home ownership. This new escape valve siphoned from the South Bronx huge numbers of stable middle-class jobholders and taxpayers. Subsidized suburban housing undermined the economic diversity of many South Bronx neighborhoods and the vacated apartments were often filled by families who were ill-equipped to enter the remaining job market.

The destructive legacy of the federal intervention of the FHA to the South Bronx is hard to overstate. Its policies bolstered the racial exclusivity of New York City's outlying suburbs and, at the same time, discouraged the building industry from serving inner city residents. More blatantly, huge areas of the South Bronx were, in effect, designated as poor risks and therefore ineligible for loan guarantees. This redlining of major sections of the South Bronx went uninterrupted until the mid-1960s when community organizers began focusing on the issue, but by then the damage was done.

Moreover, other federal mortgage agencies hastened the transfer of funds from the heart of the South Bronx, where it was needed, to suburbs in other states. Both the Federal National Mortgage Association (Fannie Mae) and the Government National Mortgage Association (Ginnie Mae), which allow mortgage investment funds to easily flow nationally from, for instance, the Northeast to the Southwest, had a devastating impact. "A typical result was that savings banks in the Bronx invested only about 10 percent of their funds in the 1970s in the borough and only about 30 percent in New York State. The rest went for investments elsewhere in the country, a result that would not have been possible except for Fannie Mae."[22]

Encouraged by the federal example, local banks and savings and loan companies began to redline certain neighborhoods in the South Bronx and deny improvement loans to local businesses. Then insurance companies followed suit, and an ironclad self-fulfilling prophecy of destruction and rot expanded.

For instance, in 1975, "The Dollar Savings Bank, the biggest bank in the Bronx (and the fifth largest savings bank in the nation) gave only thirty-two mortgages in the entire borough, while the Bronx Borough President's office released a 1977 survey showing that even after the uproar about redlining, the bank had reinvested less than 7 percent of its assets in the area."[23]

Meanwhile, rent control was also having an enormous impact. This "temporary" war measure of a half-century ago persists on the books in one form or another to this day. It has had an undeniably profound impact on housing availability and landlord-tenant relations, although its precise effect on the rampant owner abandonment of buildings is still a matter of dispute.

After World War II, the Grand Concourse remained Jewish, and the west Bronx was also slow to change, in large part because rent control kept people committed to the better housing stock in these districts. On the other hand, rent control also ossified the area because, even as the population got older in those baby-booming years, there were few empty apartments where younger residents could start families and move into their old neighborhoods.

Also, while rent control is a hugely popular government regulation with tenants, some critics maintain that it has contributed to social changes that over the long haul have made it profitable for landlords to cut back on maintenance, milk a property dry, and then, profits in hand, walk away.

Landlords charge that rent control makes it impossible to realize a profit on rental buildings in the Bronx. It is true that the lower end of housing stock in the South Bronx had been abandoned by the late 1970s. However, William Tabb cites a Columbia University study that found that,

> "almost half of the housing units renting for under $150 in 1975 had disappeared three years later: 60,000 were abandoned, and 46,000 were upgraded. But the latter created a bulge in their new price range, and, without a population able to pay the rents, they slipped back into abandonment: it is not rent regulations that hold down rents but lack of effective demand, even when families pay a disproportionate share of their income for shelter."[24]

Owners of the most run-down apartment buildings couldn't raise rents because there was not enough demand, and they couldn't lower rents and still make mortgage payments. The result?

> "Disinvestment is clearly the most sensible policy for a landlord who gets behind in real estate taxes, utility bills, maintenance, and so on. Most cannot refinance and sell. Once a landlord abandons a building—or even before, when an apartment cannot be rented and is closed off—it is a prime target for drug addicts, thieves, and others who prey on the remaining residents."[25]

Peter Salins[26] argues that the interaction of rent control and the details of the welfare system that paid the rent for substantial numbers of South Bronx residents led to the extraordinary situation of landlords abandoning their apartment buildings. He notes that, welfare clients, owing to the huge number of social problems that plague their lives, are not usually sought out by landlords. The soft housing market in the mid-1960s, exacerbated by rent control, combined with the reliable stream of rent payments from the Welfare Department to permit landlords to reap robust short-term profits by taking in welfare tenants. However, at some juncture a point of diminishing returns was reached, and the landlord found it cost effective to cease providing costly maintenance or even heat and hot water; and, after the building had been thoroughly "milked," sometimes a convenient fire allowed landlords to cut losses and collect insurance.

Primary Causes: 3. Failure of Leadership

As if misguided urban renewal and public housing policies, tax breaks and highway construction that tilted the more prosperous residents towards the suburbs, and a one-sided politically expedient rent-control policy were not enough, the South Bronx was also plagued by an ignoble failure of political leadership.

The local government was unable or unwilling to take positive corrective action. For instance, the schools were demonstrably in collapse, yet no coordinated effort was mounted to check the decline. Medical services were cut: two South Bronx municipal hospitals were closed between 1967 and 1977. Political bosses gerrymandered the area so that constituents had no single government representative responsible for the South Bronx. Most poignantly, the schools were left to fester.

As Glazer writes, what remained was

the apparent inability or unwillingness of the city to restrain the destruction. The authorities were as if paralyzed, and while television and movie crews (particularly foreign ones, deprived of war-destroyed urban landscapes by postwar rebuilding) regularly filmed scenes of destruction fascinated by a sight unequaled in the civilized (or uncivilized) world, the city and its political leaders were remarkably mute. It is true from 1975 on they were in the throes of a financial crisis that threatened bankruptcy and seemed to have attention for nothing else. But analysts were also struck dumb, though journalists described what was happening in fascinated horror again and again.[27]

Indeed, it was more than political ineptitude; there was flat-out venality. In an enterprisingly researched book, muckrakers Jack Newfield and Wayne Barrett detail the pervasive political corruption of Bronx politicians. Democratic Party county leaders have ruled the Bronx for a generation. The last of the Irish leaders, Patrick Cunningham, was

> indicted in July 1981 for tax evasion, obstruction of justice, and making false statements to federal officials. His coverup attempts in early 1978, just before his resignation, unraveled when the feds flipped the associates he had persuaded to lie about cash payments to him. He was convicted at trial, was sentenced to three years in prison, and lost his license to practice law.[28]

Cunningham's successor, the repugnant Stanley Friedman, was anointed by Edward Koch in his book, *Mayor*, as "one of the smartest, ablest, most loyal people I know." As Newfield and Barrett point out:

> Friedman was given almost total control over his borough by the mayor. Any businessman who wanted to develop city-owned land, who wanted a franchise, a contract, a permit, a zoning variance in the Bronx had to go to him. Not holding any public office, and thus having no obligations to make financial disclosures, Friedman was free to become a millionaire through his political influence.[29]

It is worth underscoring that:

> Although the Bronx was 75 percent Black and Latino, under Friedman every significant position in its government— borough president, district attorney, surrogate, and county leader—was still occupied by a white male.[30]

Friedman was eventually sentenced to jail for conspiracy, racketeering, and mail fraud. He installed his hapless protégé, Stanley Simon, as Borough President. In the tradition of his mentor, Simon was subsequently found guilty of extortion, racketeering, lying to a grand jury, and income-tax evasion and was sentenced to five years in prison.

It was not just the local political elite who ran afoul of the law: Bronx politicians on the federal level were also preoccupied with lining their pockets while the South Bronx burned. Local Congressmen's roles in the convoluted Wedtech scandal earned them jail terms. Wedtech, a South Bronx munitions factory, was hailed by President Reagan as the epitome of the entrepreneurial spirit, and, in a way, it was. It was considered by supply-side Republicans as the crown jewel of the South Bronx.

But, in fact,

> Wedtech was a scam operated by corrupt and greedy executives whose main concern was milking the company and bribing officials. "They paid everybody," said Mario Merola, the Bronx District Attorney who investigated Wedtech. "They thought that was the way of doing business."[31]

When the dust cleared, the dean of Bronx Congressmen, ten-term Mario Biaggi, was convicted of extorting stock worth $1.8 million, filing false tax returns, racketeering, and perjury. He was sentenced to eight years and fined a quarter of a million dollars. Puerto Rican Robert Garcia, a local political hero and Congressman, was convicted of extortion and conspiracy for having received $175,000 in checks and illegal loans from Wedtech and a $1,900 necklace for his wife.

It was not just the corruption of elected politicians that diverted funds which could have gone to housing or education. The reigning unelected "Baron of the South Bronx," Ramon S. Velez, wielded enormous power and became a millionaire by dominating government-financed antipoverty programs for more than a generation. Velez "has practically written the book on how to seize power and use it in an impoverished neighborhood and on how to pull the interlocking levers of social services, politics and personal gain."[32]

With entrepreneurial zeal, Velez had parlayed his control of numerous community organizations into an empire built on efficiently delivering his employees as campaign workers to hungry politicians, who, in turn, award him contracts for more programs. He further feathers his nest by hiring himself as a consultant to these agencies at exorbitantly lucrative rates. Into the 1990s, his empire still delivers the goods: he is responsible for electing the majority of the Latino officials in the Bronx, according to Marlene Cintron, who heads Mayor David Dinkins' Office of Latino Affairs.[33]

Velez presides over a half dozen corporations from which he has amassed, according to the *New York Times*, more than $1 million in pensions and annuities on a claimed annual salary of almost $300,000. Just one of his corporate entities, the powerful Hunts Point Multi-Service Center has spent over $300 million for programs dealing with housing, health care, drug treatment, day care, and services to the elderly since its founding in the sixties. In addition to this fiefdom, he also prevails over other local institutions, including the powerful community advisory board of South Bronx's troubled Lincoln Hospital.

Despite all the public money poured into the borough and filtered through his network of agencies over the past twenty-five years, the evidence of improvement to Bronx residents is slim. The list of leaders spawned by these agencies is nonexistent.

Some scholars argue that focusing on crooked politicians or "poverty pimps" (Mayor Ed Koch's memorable phrase) misses a larger, more blameworthy target: the bankers, insurance brokers, and corporate executives who made conscious decisions to go overseas for low wage jobs (some at fifty cents an hour in Sri Lanka). Investors, corporate heads, and developers all shape urban growth through banking institutions and private corporations, and they consciously avoided investing in areas like the South Bronx after the population changed and economic conditions grew less predictable. These more global forces exacerbated the local realities of systematic institutional bias on the part of realtors, appraisers, insurers, lenders, and other private actors who redlined neighborhoods and who also bear some responsibility for the abandonment of the people of the South Bronx.

The list of villains is long; the list of effective, seasoned, principled leaders is short.

Secondary Causes: A. The Role of Racism

No responsible observer can doubt that job and housing discrimination, along with racism (both in its blatant forms and in its more subtle guises), is a large part of the story of the decline of the South Bronx. However, teasing out the precise causal impact of bigotry on the deterioration of the borough is a delicate operation.

For instance, in 1966 when landmark civil rights legislation was already on the books the unemployment rate for Blacks in the U.S. was 7.3 percent, but by 1984 the numbers of Blacks out of work almost doubled to 14.4 percent. One would think that discrimination would have been worse in 1951, before the Brown Decision, and yet Black unemployment then was only 5.3 percent.[34]

Wilson concludes:

It should also be emphasized that, contrary to prevailing opinion, the Black family showed signs of significant deterioration not before, but after, the middle of the twentieth century.[35]

Discrimination, particularly job discrimination, played a significant role in blocking the entry of Black and Hispanic residents into the middle class. Beyond that there was the institutional racism of real-estate steering and bank and insurance company redlining of minority neighborhoods. As Sleeper charges:

> Nor, when all is said and done, can the role of unemployment and discrimination in deepening the suffering be overemphasized. When the full history of the agony of the South Bronx and central Brooklyn in the 1970s is written, the pathologies of "multi-problem" speculators and other, mostly white, schemers will assume greater prominence alongside the pathologies of the large welfare families who were the ultimate victims of bank redlining, blockbusting, and mortgage insurance scams. And not only the minority poor: the true Job of the neighborhood racial change in New York is the black lower-middle class family that scrimps to buy a home in a predominantly white area only to find its own arrival used by brokers as a signal to divest, prompting general white flight.[36]

Secondary Causes: B. Landlord and Tenant Arson

"Between 1970 and 1975, there were 68,456 fires in the Bronx—more than 33 each night. Most of these were the South Bronx burning."[37] People burned their own dilapidated apartments because they would be relocated then to new public housing projects and, in the process, given up to $3,000 to cover losses. Junkies then systematically stripped buildings of copper pipes and other salvageable fixtures, making rehabilitation almost impossible. There is also abundant evidence that, in order to collect insurance payments, landlords hired professional "torches" to incinerate apartment buildings that had lost their profitability.

In 1972 fireman Dennis Smith wrote a classic book about the fires of South Bronx called *Report From Engine Co. 82:*

> There are four [fire] companies working out of the firehouse on Intervale Avenue and 169th Street. Each . . . is now averaging 700 runs a month. It is safe to say that ours is the busiest firehouse in the city—and probably the world.

Around the corner from the firehouse is the Forty-first Precinct House. It is the busiest police station in the city. There are more homicides per square mile in this precinct than anywhere in the United States, more drug traffic, more prostitution.[38]

The book vividly details the working life of a fireman in those days when an alarm could signify everything from a fatal fire to a call to a family quarrel, or a holdup or homicide, or just a malicious false alarm, one of some 2,000 fraudulent calls for assistance the fire company responded to that year. According to Jonnes, the fires reached a peak in 1976 when South Bronx fireman responded to 33,465 fires of all kinds, ranging from those in commercial dwellings, apartments, and vacant buildings to cars and garbage in empty lots.

Arson accounted for most of the burning of the South Bronx in the 1970s, although the role of inadequate wiring, stacked garbage, and ovens and space heaters used to warm apartments cannot be discounted. The burden of evidence indicates that two groups were responsible: the tenants and the landlords. It is hard to fathom the desperation that would drive an apartment resident to incinerate his own dwelling, but the opportunity to be bumped to the head of the waiting list for public housing was motivation enough for some.

A more cold-hearted impulse drove the landlords to hire professional arsonists to follow through on a business decision that endangered people's lives. Often the unprofitable building had been fully milked but had changed hands from one paper corporation to another before it went up in flames. Each deal artificially hiked up the ledger value of the building and so swelled the insurance settlement.

Where does the responsibility for this lie? William Tabb in a Marxist interpretation of the New York City urban crisis concludes there is no lack of perpetrators:

Tenant groups blame the banks, which refuse to finance improvements in their neighborhoods; insurance companies, whose agents collude in inflating property settlements in order to get larger commissions and who fail to investigate suspicious fires because it is easier to pay than to prove arson; the city governments, which do not insist that there be accurate records as to who owns what building and what previous fire insurance claims have been made, and which do not conduct arson investigations and refuse to tell tenants the amounts of insurance purchased.[39]

Secondary Causes: C. The Fear of Crime

"The number of reported assaults in the Bronx rose from 998 in 1960 to 4,256 in 1969; burglaries rose from 1,765 to 29,276. The principal increase in these boroughwide statistics came from the South Bronx."[40] This, of course, coincides with the enormous rise in heroin addiction in the 1960s.

As these statistics demonstrate, the fear of crime was a genuine worry. Residents in a position to move out generally did. Glazer, along with Jonnes, considers fear of crime to be absolutely decisive. Glazer concludes flatly: "Crime was the key element which changed what would have been a thinning out of a population into a plague of destruction, in which 40,000 units a year were abandoned."[41]

The headlines at the time tell a grim story. *Youth Held in Murder of Bronx Man Locked in Closet Three Days; Grandmother Is Raped and Robbed by a Burglar in Her Bronx Home; Elderly Bronx Couple, Recently Robbed, Take Their Own Lives, Citing Fear; Two More of the Aged Killed in the Bronx.*[42]

The population in the South Bronx was by now overwhelmingly Black and Hispanic, and they tended "to be a mixture of working people and welfare families with few elderly members, while the [remaining] whites are mostly elderly Jews living on social security payments. They have remained in the area either for sentimental reasons, or because they cannot afford to move." The elderly Jews, and other white ethnics who remained in the South Bronx when the population changed, faced a particularly harrowing fate. For many of them, it was a life of "push-ins," "crib-jobs," and "shut-ins."

According to law enforcement agents, the criminals were often youngsters in their early teens who preyed on the aged because they were vulnerable and so afraid of retaliation that they would not go to court to testify. Many of the elderly were so fearful that they left their apartments only once a week to shop for food, staying shut-in the rest of the time. Many who ventured out went only to the Senior Citizen Centers. They were terrified that, when they returned and opened their apartment doors, teenagers lurking in the dark hallways would shoulder them from behind, push-in and rob their apartments. The young criminals call these crib-jobs, because it is so safe that it is like taking candy from a baby.

Secondary Causes: D. The Cross Bronx Expressway

In the 1950s when centrifugal forces in the South Bronx were building, Washington's impact was again felt. Vast sums of money were poured into the federal interstate highway system, which helped speed the way for people to move to the suburbs and still retain their jobs in the city. This was, of course, true all across the country, but the highway builders bear a particularly large responsibility for destroying viable parts of the South Bronx.

Apart from the individual neighborhoods that were obliterated by the imposition of the Cross Bronx Expressway, the massive public works project itself gripped the popular imagination of Bronx residents in deeply symbolic ways. When asked what destroyed the southern half of the borough, it is a rare Bronxite who does not put high on the list the construction of this gargantuan expressway which dead-ended numerous streets and became the de facto northern border of the South Bronx.

As Robert Caro writes in his Pulitzer Prize-winning biography of Robert Moses, the man responsible for ramming the Cross Bronx Expressway through the heart of the borough, "These were roads like no other roads in history, for these were roads through a city. . . . Moses had to hack paths through jungles of tenements and apartments houses, to slash aqueducts in two and push sewers aside, to lift railroads in the air or shove them underground."[44]

One of the most conspicuous parts of the South Bronx, seen every day by tens of thousands of suburban commuters, is East Tremont, a neighborhood sliced apart and wrecked by the building of the Cross Bronx Expressway in the late 1950s. The tragedy of this willful destruction illuminates in microcosm how outside forces unintentionally conspired to undermine the entire South Bronx, neighborhood by neighborhood.

Up until the 1950s, this was a bustling, mostly Jewish neighborhood with vibrant schools: "The Jews of East Tremont were luckier than those who had to stay behind on the Lower East Side, but not so lucky as the Grand Concourse Jews. They were not the milliners or the cloak-and-suiters but the pressers, finishers, and cutters who worked in the bare workrooms behind the ornate showrooms of the garment district."[45]

Schools were terribly important to the people of East Tremont (a quarter of a century after their kids had graduated, some parents could still remember the precise student-teacher ratio in their classes), and East Tremont had good schools. They were old—PS 44, at 176th and Prospect, the neighborhood's junior high, had been built in 1901, and the city said there was simply no money to replace it—but there were no double sessions and standards were high. PS 67, off Southern Boulevard, was the first elementary school in New York to offer lessons—and supply instruments—for any child who wanted to learn to play the violin. And all the schools were close, close enough for kids to walk to."[46]

East Tremont was more than just a viable community; it performed an essential service for the South Bronx. It provided what sociologists call a *staging area,* "a place where newcomers who had lived previously in America only in slums, successful at last in their struggle to find a decent place to live, could regroup, and begin to devote their energies to consolidating their small gains and giving their children the education that would enable them to move onward and upward—to better, more 'fashionable' areas."[47]

As Blacks and Puerto Ricans began flooding the South Bronx, communities like East Tremont remained stable and even welcomed the newcomers. "But the influx stayed slow and no whites left because of it. By 1950, there were approximately 11,000 nonwhites in East Tremont, 18 percent of the neighborhood's 60,000 population. And the neighborhood was still holding just fine."[48] East Tremont was an ideal staging area for these new immigrants, a place that would allow them to consolidate their strength, a place with strong neighborhood schools that specialized in urbanizing newcomers and teaching them the skills they needed to cope with raising their own families in New York.

But, as we've seen over and over, the viability of the South Bronx and its schools was sabotaged from the outside by well-meaning but ignorant policy makers.

This short highway turned out to be the most expensive road in history, estimated to cost some $250 million. It triggered a chain reaction as apartments near the construction emptied out as the long years of building devastated the adjoining streets. Into that vacuum streamed poor rural Blacks and Puerto Ricans who were welcomed by the landlords because, every time an apartment changed hands, the rules of rent control allowed the landlord to boost the rent by 15 percent. The rents that were artificially frozen since the war now began to surge forward, propelled, in part, by welfare payments that helped absorb the increase. Even still, by 1960 when the East Tremont part of the Expressway was finally opened, 25,000 Jews still lived in the area, but changes were inexorably in motion: break-ins and vandalism increased; insurance premiums for shopkeepers soared; buildings close to the relentless racket and poisonous fumes of the expressway began emptying; and the pathology of drugs began taking its toll. Anyone who could afford to get out moved, and the children of the older residents never dreamed of settling in their old neighborhood. As Caro says, "Faster and faster they left, and faster and faster, wider and wider, spread the urban decay."[49]

Caro vividly described the streets of East Tremont eighteen years ago:

> The streets of East Tremont are carpeted so thickly with pieces of shattered glass that they shine in the sun. Garbage, soaked mattresses, bits of broken furniture and, everywhere, small pieces of jagged steel fill the gutters. The sidewalks are full of holes, the streets—particularly the streets overlooking the expressway, for the expressway has made them dead-end, reducing traffic to a minimum—with the hulks of stripped automobiles. Once East Tremont, while the expressway was being built, had had the look of blitzkrieged London, now it looked as London might have looked, if after the bombs, the troops had fought their way through it from house to house. It had the look of a jungle.[50]

It is tempting to say that this catalog of despair remains accurate even today, but that is not quite fair. In 1983 the City of New York swung into action and took steps to soften these eyesores and, in their words, "lift the morale of residents, discourage vandals and addicts who haunt abandoned buildings and make a better impression on the thousands of motorists who pass the area daily."[51] On scores of these crumbling tenements, city workers pasted over the smashed windows with vinyl decals which depicted brightly colored curtains and shades and cheerful flowerpots with bright yellow daises.

Anthony B. Gliedman, then New York City's Commission of Housing Preservation and Development (HPD), who, perhaps appropriately, now works for glitzy real estate developer Donald Trump, justified this effort by making the philosophically intriguing but pragmatically absurd observation that "Perception is reality."[52]

If we step back from East Tremont and view the destruction of the South Bronx as a whole, we find that the story for each neighborhood differs in details, but the overall shape of the problem is strikingly the same.

Secondary Causes: F. The Rise of the Ghetto Underclass

Ghettos were always a part of the history of American cities. There is nothing new about the grinding poverty in minority neighborhoods. But by the mid 1970s a qualitative change was making a desperate situation hopeless. A constellation of interrelated tragedies struck as the rates of inner-city joblessness, teenage pregnancy, out-of-wedlock-births, female-headed families, welfare dependency, and serious crime mushroomed:

> These increasing rates of social dislocation signified changes in the social organization of inner-city areas. Blacks in Harlem and in other ghetto neighborhoods did not hesitate to sleep in parks, on fire escapes, and on rooftops during hot summer nights in the 1940s and 1950s and whites frequently visited inner-city taverns and nightclubs. There was crime, to be sure, but it had not reached the point where people were fearful of walking the streets at night, despite the overwhelming poverty in the area. There was joblessness, but it was nowhere near the proportions of unemployment and labor-force nonparticipation that have gripped ghetto communities since 1970. There were single-parent families, but they were a small minority of all black families and tended to be incorporated within extended family networks and to be headed not by unwed teenagers and young adult women but by middle-aged women who usually were widowed, separated, or divorced. There were welfare recipients, but only a very small percentage of the families could be said to be welfare-dependent. In short, unlike the present period, inner-city communities prior to 1960 exhibited the features of social organization—including a sense of community, positive neighborhood identification, and explicit norms and sanctions against aberrant behavior.[53]

When New York State's U.S. Senator Daniel Patrick Moynihan called attention[54] to the breakdown of the Black family in 1965, he triggered a firestorm of verbal abuse for dwelling on these troubling issues. His work was interpreted as an attack on racial minorities. Nervous liberal scholars, taking cautionary note of the vitriolic criticism he received, trimmed their sails. According to University of Chicago sociologist William Julius Wilson, "The liberal perspective on the ghetto underclass has become less persuasive and convincing in public discourse principally because many of those who represent traditional liberal views on social issues have been reluctant to discuss openly or, in some instances, even to acknowledge the sharp increase in social pathologies in ghetto communities." According to Wilson, this avoidance takes a number of forms. "One approach is to avoid describing any behavior that might be construed as unflattering or stigmatizing to ghetto residents, either because of fear of being charged with 'racism' or with 'blaming the victim.' "[55] This cowardly abdication of responsibility of liberals has left the door wide open for conservative social critics to provide their own interpretation for the causes of this social pathology. Focusing on the importance of different ethnic group values and the blunting effect various government policies have had on individual initiative, they have largely ignored economic explanations. In the absence of a countervailing explanation for the exclusion of so many from the mainstream of America, many have found this simplistic hypothesis compelling.

By way of illustration, how is one to interpret devastating statistics like these:

- In 1959, 15 percent of all Black births were out of wedlock. In 1982 it was 57 percent.[56]
- Real wages for poor Black men dropped 50 percent during the 1970s. Approximately one-third of Black men from poor areas are arrested on drug charges by the age of 30. Nearly one in four Black males between the ages of 20 and 29 is in prison, on probation, or awaiting trial,[57]
- In 1989 in the Bronx there were 484 murders, 604 rapes, 16,220 robberies, 20,659 burglaries, 9,577 felonious assaults, 29,698 cases of grand larceny, and 11,438 other felonies. Of the twenty-five elementary schools with the lowest reading scores in New York City, thirteen were in the Bronx. There were 161,000 children living in families below the poverty line. There were 756 reported cases of AIDS.[58]

Large fractions of the population of the South Bronx are mired in poverty, educationally disenfranchised, and perhaps permanently excluded from participation in the labor market. What will happen to them? Are they destined to be a permanent brake on any possible recovery for the South Bronx?

Scholars risk the serenity of their ivy towers by grappling forthrightly with these issues. Yet courage, which seemed to be in short supply until recently, is now rising. Social historian Michael B. Katz proposes that we reframe the whole question of pubic policy towards the poor and, in the process, step back from the overpowering particularities of the degradation of the South Bronx and struggle to view it in a broader context:

For two centuries of American history, considerations of productivity, cost, and eligibility have channeled discourse about need, entitlement, and justice within narrow limits bounded by the market. In every era, a few people have counterpoised dignity, community, and equality as standards for policy. But they have remained outsiders, unable to divert the powerful currents constraining the possibilities for social thought and public action.[59]

Katz argues that this formulation ignores the perspective of the powerless and accepts the *status quo* as natural. What's more, he charges:

When Americans talk about poverty, some things remain unsaid. Mainstream discourse about poverty, whether liberal or conservative, largely stays silent about politics, power, and equality. But poverty, after all, is about distribution; it results because some people receive a great deal less than others. Descriptions of demography, behavior, or beliefs of subpopulations cannot explain the patterned inequalities evident in every era of American history. These result from styles of dominance, the way power is exercised, and the politics of distribution.[60]

Poverty is now less a natural occurrence than a social product, although that is not how Americans think about poverty, Katz argues. This is so, he maintains, for two reasons. First, the discourse of capitalism defines people by their ability to generate wealth and condemns anyone who, for whatever reason, does not contribute to the production of material prosperity. Also, this constricted debate about poverty accurately reflects the language of politics in the United States:

American workers failed to develop a language of class that included both economics and community. As a result, for over a century American political discourse has redefined issues of power and distribution as questions of identity, morality, and patronage. This is what happened to poverty, which slipped easily, unreflectively, into a language of family, race, and culture rather than inequality, power and exploitation.[61]

How can we sort out this problem? Is the undeniable existence of a minority underclass a result of behavior failings (that, in many cases, include such extreme behavior as the male abandonment of children they father), as conservatives hold? Or, is this social disaster a result of structural forces and misplaced faith in the benign workings of the market economy, as Tabb and Katz argue?

Cornel West, the director of Princeton's Afro-American program, contends that we must begin by acknowledging that "structures and behavior are inseparable, that institutions and values go hand in hand." Further,

> we must delve into the depths where neither liberals nor conservatives dare to tread, namely, into the murky waters of despair that now flood the streets of Black America. To talk about the distressing statistics of unemployment, infant mortality, incarceration, teenage pregnancy, and violent crime is one thing. But to face up to the monumental eclipse of hope, the unprecedented collapse of meaning, the incredible disregard for human (especially Black) life and property in much of Black America is something else.[62]

West asserts that the most fundamental issue now facing Black America is the "nihilistic threat to its very existence." It is "primarily a question of speaking to the profound sense of psychological depression, personal worthlessness, and social despair so widespread in Black America."

For West, nihilism is the lived experience of coping with a life of horrifying meaninglessness, hopelessness, and, he says, most importantly, lovelessness.

Is this bleakness unalterable? West holds out some hope. He thinks that there is value for people in hellish places like the South Bronx in investing energy in institutions that promote self-worth and self-affirmation. He cites "grassroots democratic organizations [that] put forward a collective leadership that has earned the love and respect of the community, and, most important, has proved itself *accountable*. . . . This collective leadership must exemplify moral integrity, character, and democratic statesmanship within itself and within its organization."

The rest of this book tells the story of one such democratic grassroots organization.

II

✳

The IAF in New York City

3

Alinsky, Chambers, and Citizen Movements

Like a spider in a web with tensile lines stretched to the South Bronx, Baltimore, San Antonio, Los Angeles, and various other American cities, Industrial Areas Foundation Director Ed Chambers sits in his nondescript office in a Long Island suburb and fields telephone calls from a battery of lead organizers. When one of IAF's twenty-eight church-based agitating groups[1] gets into a bruising fight with some municipal authorities, a filament of the web vibrates and Chambers stirs.

One of the IAF's community development organizations is based in the South Bronx. This group, South Bronx Churches, is trying to politicize substantial numbers of local citizens, bind them into a muscular, power-oriented collective and incite them to exercise their organized clout to challenge the complacent political leadership who have, perhaps unwittingly, collaborated in the ruin of the South Bronx.

Since its official launch in 1987, SBC has built a powerful coalition of forty-five dues-paying churches; launched a petition drive that garnered one hundred thousand signatures to demand better schools, affordable housing, and other civic reforms; compelled a local hospital to improve its formerly mismanaged emergency room; and turned out eight thousand angry residents for a housing rally—an unprecedented number for the South Bronx.

Chambers's office, the national headquarters of the Industrial Areas Foundation, sits atop an unpretentious plumbing supply store in Franklin Square, a modest Long Island bedroom community. At the top of a flight of rickety stairs, there are a few carpeted rooms where a lone secretary and Ed Chambers coordinate IAF activities. About this threadbare office, the white-haired, blunt-spoken Chambers harks back to Saul Alinsky, the founder of IAF in 1940. "Saul wasn't much for slogans. But he always had one over his black board. *Low Overhead: High Independence.* That's one I've remembered well and stuck to. Stay close to the field, stay close to what you do."[2]

Ironically, Chambers, like the other principal creators of South Bronx Churches Rev. John Heinemeier and Jim Drake, grew up in rural America. He is the son of an Irish laborer who completed only the second grade and who left "slave labor in Britain" to work on the railroad in America. His father went on strike in 1928 and remained out of work until 1941, according to Chambers's bitter memory of the ordeal. Recounting this family history to a group of activists attending a ten-day IAF Training session in Los Angeles during the summer of 1989, he drew this lesson: "You have to have anger to be able to be a good organizer."[3]

After high school he left Clarion, Ohio, and studied to be a Benedictine priest in Minnesota, but, as Chambers recalls, "I got thrown out of the seminary in 1953 for agitating."[4] He had harbored the then-subversive notions of celebrating the mass in English, turning the altar around to face the congregation, and further ruffled feathers by continually raising fretful existential questions, regarding the then-prevailing orthodoxy of rigid Thomism—ironically, all ideas subsequently endorsed by Vatican II.

After leaving the Midwest, "I came to Harlem. I was on my way to the Catholic Worker," the leftist, radical social-action collective run by secular saint Dorothy Day[5] on the Bowery in lower Manhattan. "But I only got to 135th Street," in Harlem. "There was a religious commune there called the Friendship House; Catholic, interracial."

Chambers remained for two years.

> That's where I began to learn about the real world. Our program was to give out old clothes and old shoes to Blacks. It was called interracial justice. I didn't see how that advanced interracial justice. So I started organizing tenants. No heat, no water. Began getting a taste of organizing. Somebody in [IAF founder Saul] Alinsky's organization heard about me, and I hired on, and been with it ever since.[6]

When he first began in 1957, he was dispatched to the steel-mill town of Lackawanna in western New York State where he organized the Citizens Federation of Lackawanna. Two years later he helped set up the Organization for Southwest Chicago (OSC). In 1963–64 he founded The Woodlawn Organization (TWO), a "Black self-determining" group, and, in the process, challenged the powerful

University of Chicago. Then, conforming to a typical pattern for IAF organizers at that time, he once again packed his bags and moved to Rochester, New York, to clash with Eastman Kodak from 1965–67. The organization there, Fight, ultimately forced the giant photo-supply corporation to hire and train six hundred unemployed Blacks.[7]

The IAF, a social-action agency that contracts to help build community organizations, was created by Saul D. Alinsky (1909–1972) in Chicago in 1940. Alinsky was a somewhat larger-than-life figure who took pride in describing himself as a "professional radical." He wrote a biography of his mentor, iconoclastic labor leader John L. Lewis, and two hard-nosed, politically candid, and pithy books that spell out his approach to empowering poor communities.[8] As his biographer notes:

> Throughout Alinsky's life there was confusion about where to place him on the political spectrum, more confusion than one would have expected of a man who had been a friend and supporter of the great labor leader John L. Lewis and the industrial labor movement in the 1930s, a self-professed radical in the 1940s, and an outspoken advocate of racial integration and civil rights in the 1950s and 1960s. But other symbols and ideas are associated with Alinsky, too: he had a powerful ally in the Catholic Church; he insisted that power—not reason—was fundamental to the achievement of social change; he often adopted an anti-intellectual pose and used and encouraged tactics that violated normal canons of good taste and civility. Such behavior made many conventional liberals uncomfortable, even hostile, while to others further to the left, Alinsky's disavowal of a class analysis made him and the importance of his work suspect.[9]

Alinsky spent his early years in a tenement in a working-class neighborhood of Chicago and later painted what his biographer calls a "somewhat selective account of 'growing up in the slums'—which, in intended effect, was probably supposed to be the urban-poor, Jewish-ghetto equivalent of the Abraham Lincoln log cabin legend."[10] In point of fact, when Alinsky was six, his father became a landlord, and the family moved to a more prosperous Chicago neighborhood. He had the good fortune to enter the powerful University of Chicago's celebrated sociology department and study with renowned scholars Ernest Watson Burgess and Robert Ezra Park, who pioneered the case study method of research and, in a somewhat novel departure for scholars at the time, routinely dispatched their students to the field.[11]

Alinsky then did some organizing for John L. Lewis's CIO (the Congress of Industrial Organization) and, in 1938, moved into the Back of the Yards, the notorious slum behind the stockyards of Chicago depicted in Upton Sinclair's 1906 novel, *The Jungle.*

In his 1971 book, *Rules For Radicals*, Alinsky describes this neighborhood as "utterly demoralized. The people had no confidence in themselves or their neighbors or in their cause."[12] And what caused this condition? According to Horwitt, in Alinsky's analysis it was an inadequate appreciation of the power of citizenship in a democracy:

> In its essence, citizenship meant participation to Alinsky; it meant being active rather than passive. It also meant that one questioned authority, took the initiative to address community problems and developed an understanding of how events and forces in the larger world affected one's own life and community.[13]

Alinsky construed his role as the organizer as someone who would "build confidence and hope in the idea of organization and thus in the people themselves: to win limited victories, each of which will build confidence and the feeling that 'if we can do so much with what we have now just think what we will be able to do when we get big and strong.' "[14]

The first fight he picked was one he knew he could win, staging what he called a *cinch fight*. "One of the major problems in Back of the Yards in those days was an extraordinarily high rate of infant mortality,"[15] he wrote. Some years before, he learned, religious elements in the community had driven out a medical clinic because it was suspected that birth control information was being dispensed. The group that funded the clinic was eager to return, although that was not widely known. Alinsky stormed into the health agency, and in a great show of anger and bluster he and his fired-up neighborhood leaders demanded that the clinic be restored without delay.

The deck was stacked. From the beginning there was never any doubt that he would win this victory and thus bolster the confidence of the citizens he organized. Alinsky admitted, "It is almost like taking a prize-fighter up the road to the championship—you have to very carefully and selectively pick his opponents, knowing full well that certain defeats would be demoralizing and end his career." This does not mean that every fight has to end triumphantly: "If by losing a certain action [the organizer] can get more numbers than by winning, then victory lies in [intentionally] losing and he will lose."[16]

Time magazine in 1940 evaluated the results of Alinsky's first efforts:

> Fifteen months ago, with the bishop's blessing, friendly, chesty, Jewish Sociologist Saul Alinsky set up a Back of the Yards Neighborhood Council. Aim: to reconcile the potentially conflicting interests of business, labor, politics and religion in a crowded, depressed industrial area. Typical Council results to date: C.I.O. leaders helping the Chamber of Commerce in its membership drive; 1,200 hot meals free each day for undernourished children; a new recreation center five blocks square; an infant-welfare station which has cut the infant death rate from ten in every hundred to four out of a hundred.[17]

Years later, Alinsky later told a *Chicago Daily News* reporter that he learned three lessons from his Back of the Yards experience.

> First, to hell with clarity. The only thing you get is what you are strong enough to get—so you had better organize. Second: You prove to people they can do something, show them how to have a way of life where they can make their own decisions— and then get out. They don't need a father who stands over them. Third: It comes down to the basic argument of the *Federalist Papers*. Either you believe in people as James Madison or James Monroe did, or, like Alexander Hamilton, you don't. I do.[18]

It was at this time in 1940, with the political support of the left-leaning Roman Catholic Bishop Bernard J. Sheil and the financial support of the philanthropist Marshall Field III, that Alinsky founded the Industrial Areas Foundations to carry forth his organizing work more systematically. In the 1950s scores of IAF organizing efforts were begun across the country from New York's midtown Chelsea neighborhood to a number of Mexican American barrios in California. Now past its fiftieth year of organizing, there are twenty-eight active IAF community organizations across the country.

Although there are no templates for this kind of organizing, the general process is similar. One of the strengths of the IAF is that Chambers and his veteran organizers have been able to boil the practice of reorganizing neighborhoods down to its essentials. This is not to say that all the efforts of IAF bear fruit: there is a high mortality rate among the many attempts. Chambers estimates that roughly 25 percent of the organizing attempts ultimately fail. "Each failure has to be analyzed separately. Generally it is more the failure of the lead organizer than a lack of money. Perhaps we have put in someone who has done well as number two but does not make the transition. Those people are no longer with us,"[19] Chambers asserts.

Citizen Movements

Alinsky was, of course, not working in a vacuum, and his insights were formed both in harmony with and in opposition to prevailing ideas. As such, they are part of a larger history of community organizing, which itself is a branch, principally, of social work.[20]

The larger story of activism in inner-city communities can be traced to the charity movements of the last quarter of the nineteenth century. At that time the largely upper-class activists were primarily concerned with documenting the dependency of the newly urbanized immigrants from Europe, and they often adopted the role of spokesperson for the poor. During the Progressive Era at the turn of the century, the activists were from the middle class and tended to be social workers centered in Settlement Houses.[21] They typically had little interest in mobilizing ghetto residents; they worked through legislatures to pass child-labor laws and housing-code regulations. According to sociologist Steve Burghardt:

> The clearest forms of this advocacy lasted until World War I, when the conservative and prointerventionist fervor of the nation swept aside the far more liberal and often pacifist-socialist sentiments of settlement house leaders like Jane Addams and Lillian Ward. But the tradition of advocacy was established and has lived on, including an emphasis on documented and observed facts about conditions affecting the poor. . . . and a self-defined role as spokesperson for the poor, not with them. Similarly, advocacy alliances were based not on class or social standing but on general agreement with the issues. . . . Advocacy was for the poor, done by professionals and others sympathetic to the cause.[22]

Three organizing tools were devised during these early struggles and permanently added to the arsenal of community organizers. These were good data-collection skills (to exploit the advantage of having the facts on your side); media-manipulation techniques (in order to put a particular sympathetic spin on a story or dramatic confrontation); and the need for sophisticated knowledge of how the legislative process works (in order to squeeze politicians at the most propitious times).

The consensus-generating approach of the Progressive Era was succeeded by a class-oriented analysis that was more ideological in substance and in its critique of American society. It grew out of the labor movement of the 1930s and the Industrial Areas Foundation is a product of this more militant strain in community organizing. Alinsky was a protégé of crusty John L. Lewis, the President of the Committee for Industrial Organization (CIO), which during the Depression organized the steel, auto, and rubber industries by relying on an analysis predicated on class conflict. The CIO was concerned, not just with higher wages and industrial reform, but looked toward the possibility of social revolution. Much of the class antagonism that drove this movement was snuffed out by the national unity that grew out of World War II.

An enduring legacy of the thirties, however, was the reliance on organizing large numbers of workers to press for change rather than depending on experts. To this day the IAF remains adamant on this point of educating indigenous leadership, elevating this precept to an Iron Rule. In a collective statement of the principles which inspire IAF organizers, Mike Gecan, Field Supervisor of IAF operations in New Jersey and Pennsylvania, defines this fundamental doctrine:

Never do for others what they can do for themselves. Never. This rule, difficult to practice consistently, sometimes violated, is central to our view of the nature of education, of leadership, and of effective organizing. This cuts against the grain of some social workers and program peddlers who try to reduce people and families to clients, who probe for needs and lacks and weaknesses, not strength and drive, not vision and values, not democratic and entrepreneurial initiative. The iron rule implies that the most valuable and enduring form of development—intellectual, social, political—is the development people freely choose and fully own.

We believe that most leaders are made, not born, and that the majority of men and women have the ability to understand, to judge, to listen, to relate, to speak, and to resolve. We find in our congregations and our blocks, in our public housing projects and barrios a vast pool of citizens, able-bodied and able-minded men and women. They are often untrained and untaught. They are ignored by almost everyone. They are even redefined as a new class or underclass, but time and again they have proved their ability to grow and develop if invested in. The heart of our organizing is the finding of talented potential leaders, the inviting of those leaders into training and relationship, and the enabling of people to decide whether they want to develop, and where, and when, and how fast.[23]

Historian Robert Fisher[24] boils down Alinsky's method of community organizing, invented in the 1930s and still faithfully adhered to fifty years later, into five succinct elements:

1. *The professional organizer is the catalyst for social change.* While Alinsky was seen as an apostle of democratic decision making and indigenous leadership, his method places a premium on the creative organizer "who can do it all.". . . Alinskyism stresses that a well-trained professional organizer is the most likely person to make the right choices. Democracy is important; the organizer is even more so.

2. *The task is to build a democratic community-based organization.* Democracy is defined as the process of self-determination, in which ordinary people make the decisions about things that affect them. For Alinsky, truly democratic organizations can only develop within small spatial units, like a neighborhood, where there are natural bonds of unity and identification. Unlike most other leftist approaches to neighborhood organizing, Alinsky emphasizes gathering support of traditional community leaders and institutions, people who already have local influence and a wide audience.

3. *The goal is to win power.* Only by organizing people to struggle for power can democracy be realized; only then can the "have-nots" gain control of their communities and their lives. Neighborhood organizations are seen as the interest groups of the powerless and the unorganized. . . . Alinksy emphasizes that, since people act from self-interest rather than altruism, it is self-interest rather than exalted ideals that should motivate a people's organization.

4. *Use any tactics necessary.* This element of the Alinsky method achieved widest acclaim and criticism. He argued that people built organizations and won power by winning victories. Negotiation, arbitration, protests, and demonstrations; boycotts,

strikes, and mass meetings; picketing, raising hell, being diplomatic, and being willing to use anything that might work were key elements of Alinskyism.[25] The end justifies the means, Alinsky counseled.

5. *A people's organization must be pragmatic and nonideological.* In his opinion [ideological organizations] were undemocratic because their organizers came with preconceived ideals, goals, and strategies; they did not lct neighborhood people make decisions. To let the people decide, Alinsky advocated, no matter what they decide, is the essence of democracy.

The postwar period from 1946 to roughly 1960 was a time when the pendulum shifted dramatically. If neighborhood organizing in the prewar period focused on working class disenfranchisement and powerlessness and thrived on conflict, the forties and fifties were decades when the conservative middle class organized to protect property values and preserve neighborhood homogeneity, and when civic leaders politely brought their influence to bear to grease the wheels for more efficient delivery of government services. Fisher characterizes the goals of the most prominent form of neighborhood organizing in the 1950s as twofold—enhancement and protection.

It was not until the early sixties during the civil rights struggle and the anti-Vietnam War movement that militant forms of social action were resuscitated. Alinsky's unswerving reliance on conflict made him the spiritual father of such groups as the National Welfare Rights Organization and the National Tenants' Organization[26] and, on a more political level, Students for a Democratic Society (SDS) and the Student Nonviolent Coordinating Committee (SNCC),[27] all of which emphasized the mobilization of large numbers of people.

These citizens mobilization enterprises represent two slightly overlapping strains of community organizing. One we might call *government-sanctioned,* and the other, for want of a more accurate term, *insurgent.*

The government-sanctioned efforts grew out of Lyndon Johnson's War on Poverty which enshrined equal opportunity (rather than, for instance, redistribution of wealth) and, somewhat surprisingly, community action as its two formal goals for helping the poor. As Michael Katz in his brilliant book, *The Undeserving Poor: From the War on Poverty to the War on Welfare,* points out:

Community action required the establishment of local agencies to receive and spend federal funds. As a strategy, it deliberately bypassed existing political structures, empowered new groups, and challenged existing institutions.[28]

This governmental deference to citizen participation was a decidedly unorthodox idea. As Katz quotes activist theoretician Francis Fox Piven:

[The government] gave money to ghetto organizations that then used the money to harass city agencies. Community workers were hired to badger housing inspectors and to pry loose federal welfare payments. Later the new community agencies began to organize the poor to picket the welfare department or boycott the school system. Local officials were flabbergasted; one level of government and party was financing the harassment of another level of government and party.[29]

At first this might seem to be a development that Alinsky with his zest for frustrating bureaucrats and his zeal for upsetting apple carts would find gratifying, but he horrified many community activists and heartened many conservatives by branding the War on Poverty a "prize piece of political pornography" that spread cynicism rather than opportunity.

As always for Alinsky, power calculations were at the true heart of the issue:

Poverty means not only lacking money but also lacking power. An economically stable Negro in Mississippi is poor. When . . . poverty and lack of power bar you from equal protection, equal equity in the courts, and equal participation in the economic and social life of your society, then you are poor . . . . Therefore an anti-poverty program must recognize that its program has to do something about not only economic poverty but also political poverty.[30]

Stormy relations with the social work profession and rival community organizers is a feature of Alinsky's work faithfully replicated by Chambers and most of the key organizers of the Industrial Areas Foundation to this day.[31]

The more insurgent organizing efforts, typified by the student radicals of SDS and SNCC, were more overtly political and formed the heart of the New Left. Fisher, in his history of community organizing initiatives, isolates six ingredients that he posits as defining characteristics of the New Left approach to organizing. Curiously, four of the six, *Be a catalyst, not a leader; Let the people decide; Develop indigenous leaders;* and *Create supportive personal relationships,* come straight from Alinsky. Two others, *Develop loose organizational structures;* and *Establish places in the community free of external restraints,* were unique to the New Left experiments and have not survived the test of time.

In our own era the conservative backlash of the seventies and eighties has reduced the visibility of many social action groups, yet scholars of community organizing like Fisher and theoreticians like Henry Boyte[32] remain optimistic that the future of such local organizing is limitless. A sanguine Fisher in 1984 selectively shifted the evidence and extolled the possibilities:

> In response to events in the 1960s and the economic crises that followed, a widespread interest in neighborhood organizing arose throughout the United States in the 1970s. *The Christian Science Monitor,* in a series of articles in 1977, reported a "groundswell movement of citizens calling for the return of political and economic power at the local level." More than twenty million Americans were active in hundreds of thousands of neighborhood groups throughout the nation. Several thousand block clubs sprang up in New York City alone after 1975. The National Commission on Neighborhoods listed over 8,000 larger community groups throughout the nation. . . . As people increasingly turned away from public and corporate leadership, they turned inward to spaces and interests where they could have more control, and nowhere was this more visible than at a neighborhood level.[33]

Even allowing for considerable inflation of numbers and over-optimistic faith in the potential of neighborhood organizing, this shift to local concerns offers new potential for reinvigorating grass-roots democracy. To capitalize on this latent capacity, organizers must develop new skills such as innovative fundraising and imaginative coalition-building. Also important, according to Burghardt, is "learning to work in large, collective settings with multiple agendas while still maintaining democratic procedures . . . demanding work that is the *sine qua non* of this form of social action." And further, "The social movements of the 1960s created a tremendous awareness of sexism and racism. To engage in social action now requires exploring one's own attitude towards race, sexual preference, age, and class."[34]

Despite these new challenges, IAF leaders have not deviated significantly from their time-tested tactics, but elsewhere other local social action organizations have modified Alinsky and Chambers's approach. This new strain of community organizing, called neo-Alinskyism, attempts to pay more attention to combating racism and sexism in their organizations.[35]

Ed Chambers has been at the helm of IAF for almost two decades, and, although the power-oriented tactics in the field have remained consistent in that time, he has sparked a number of institutional sea changes. "Modern IAF began about three or four years before Alinsky died, when I changed the way of operating," he boasts. Chambers, like his South Bronx Churches colleague, Lead Organizer Jim Drake, is disconcertingly blunt. Both, in what may be an occupationally related trait, are not plagued by modesty:

> We set up an institute where we train many, many organizers. Up until then we always had only two or three people on a staff doing all Alinsky's work for him, and letting him write about it. So in *Rules for Radicals*, for instance, all those stories are my work. Saul didn't have anything to do with organizing the fight in Rochester. He appeared five and a half days during two years in Rochester. That's the only time he spent there. And that was at press conferences or interviews.[36]

Chambers stretches back behind his cluttered desk and, between fielding phone calls, describes the changes he initiated in IAF:

> In those days, we had one or two efforts going on at a time. We'd do 'em for three years, and then we'd drop them and go on to another city. Trying to demonstrate that you could build self-determining, independent power bases amongst Blacks and Hispanics. I saw the futility of that and told Alinsky that we were burning out organizers. I was 36 then. This is around '65, right in the midst of the civil rights movement, '65, '66. I said "this is nonsense. We have to pull together our couple of organizers. We've got a base in Chicago. And we've got to have people come to us, and we'll teach them how to organize. And that was the beginning of what is called the IAF Institute.

That led to working with people on-going year after year, so that we didn't abandon them after three years. We provided a new organizer, we kept training our leadership, and the new leadership coming in all the time. A third comes in every year, and a third goes out. So modern IAF begins around '69 or '70. Alinsky died in '72, and I took the whole thing over.

Saul was a lecturer. Saul was on a jet all the time. Saul was an entertainer, a manipulator of media, a master of it. He had no patience. He built one organization, Back of the Yards Neighborhood Council back in 1940–41. And after that he never put his hands in the field. I started with him when I was 27 in 1957. I've been doing this stuff for 33 years. It's all I've done.[37]

Although Chambers keeps close tabs on all IAF organizing projects across the country, each is somewhat autonomous. He directly supervises only one lead organizer, but that happens to be Jim Drake, South Bronx Churches chief leader, and so he has a particular interest in seeing SBC flourish.

4

The IAF in Queens and Brooklyn

John Heinemeier, the man who founded two archetypical inner-city New York IAF organizations—East Brooklyn Congregations and South Bronx Churches, grew up in a small town in Texas in a family of preachers. He was trained for the Lutheran ministry at Concordia Seminary in St. Louis. He remembers himself as a young seminarian searching for direction:

> In my graduate year I did some work in a Black congregation in St. Louis. During that process, as well as during my youth in rural Texas, I discovered a vocation which I think has since been borne out: working in the inner city, cross-culturally, among the underclass. At seminary I asked to be placed in an inner-city congregation anywhere in the country as long as it was near salt water. So I was placed in Brooklyn in 1963—the year I was ordained—and worked there for twenty years.[1]

Heinemeier, fresh out of school and in his midtwenties, was assigned to a small congregation in Canarsie, a white working-class neighborhood in the southern flatlands of Brooklyn. A few years later, he was called to a church in the bleak community of Brownsville, a nearby minority neighborhood in eastern Brooklyn.

Meanwhile, Ed Chambers, sitting in his Chicago office, was casting a jealous eye on New York City. It was a temptingly ripe target, not just because of the infamous slums in the South Bronx, Brooklyn, and Harlem, but also because it is the media capital of the world. Any IAF triumph in New York City would be magnified, and that, in turn, would pique interest across the country.

In fact, Saul Alinsky once had a toehold in Manhattan but soon lost it. In 1957 IAF staffers began organizing in Chelsea, a diverse West Side Manhattan neighborhood with a population of sixty thousand that ranged from impoverished Puerto Ricans to prosperous brownstone owners. Without deep roots in the community, the new organizers arrived in Manhattan and, as Horwitt recounts, guile-lessly inquired:

> What are the problems? [they] would ask, and the answer gave them an agenda for a community organization: a housing short-age, pockets of juvenile delinquency, a lack of parking facilities on the waterfront.[2]

The track record of the short-lived Chelsea Community Coun-cil (CCC) was mixed. Modest victories included forcing the city to construct thirteen hundred low- and middle-income apartments in Chelsea and leading a rent strike. However, these achievements were overshadowed by the inability of the CCC to achieve a steady and in-dependent operating income and, most notably, poor success in orga-nizing the twenty thousand Puerto Ricans in the neighborhood.

Horwitt weighed the failure in Chelsea and concluded that "Chelsea was the wrong place at the wrong time. Joseph Fitzpatrick at Fordham, the expert on Puerto Ricans, had been disappointed that Alinsky had gone to Chelsea rather than into the South Bronx."[3]

Author Nicholas von Hoffman, an IAF organizer and colleague of Chambers who did not work on the Chelsea project, concluded years later in an interview with Horwitt:

> "Saul did not have the troops in Chelsea" von Hoffman thought, and challenged [Alinsky] to explain how he could possibly suc-ceed there. "I was really saying, 'What are you going to fight with? You got no army. . . . no base, absolutely no power base.' You know, New York is not Chicago."[4]

Queens Civic Organization

In most places where the IAF has built powerful local organi-zations, the opening salvo is fired when an invitation to dispatch or-ganizers comes from church leaders in a particular community who have banded together as a sponsoring committee. Ed Chambers then assesses the committee's request to see if there is a sufficiently tempting prospect to justify mobilizing IAF's resources. Even if the neighborhood looks fertile, before he will contract to supply orga-nizers, he sets specific conditions, which often include a locally gen-erated, guaranteed income flow for three years.

Since by the midseventies no invitation was forthcoming from New York, Chambers decided not to wait and short-circuited his customary process by seeding the multicultural but largely middle-class borough of Queens with a veteran organizer. This resulted in the creation of a group called the Queens Civic Organization (QCO) hatched from a nucleus of thirty Catholic and Protestant parishes the Lead Organizer had stitched together.

QCO went about its work relatively quietly, although, once in a while, its exertions would ripple beyond the neighborhood and surface in the newspapers, especially when the contentious group abrasively rubbed up against authority or brawled with city officials. Their first big scuffle was with Mayor Edward Koch, and, as *The Wall Street Journal* tartly noted, this caused the mayor to receive "considerable criticism, and QCO to receive abundant attention."[5]

As a result Larry McNeil, the original lead organizer of QCO, facetiously hails arch-enemy Mayor Edward Koch, "as our founding father." McNeil, who is now an IAF Cabinet member and a supervisor of four California organizations, says that, in 1977 when Koch was running an underdog campaign for mayor and looking for forums to address, the fledgling Queens Churches Organization invited him to one of its meetings.[6] As a *quid pro quo,* they made him sign a contract which bound him to return to their predominantly white, middle-class neighborhood after the election. According to McNeil, after his upset election, the narcissistic Koch tried to back out of the promise, but the group resolutely held him to his commitment. Upping the ante, three days before the scheduled return meeting, QCO held a noisy press conference outside City Hall and imperiously issued a "performance test" for Koch. Laying out a host of small, relatively easily accomplished municipal tasks, they gave Koch two weeks to demonstrate that he could handle the reins of power and deliver for his Queens constituents.

By the night of the meeting with Koch, the group had put almost all its eggs in one basket, hoping for a dramatic public debut, having built slowly during the previous months with many small-scale actions, including, of course, the proverbial cinch fights of Alinsky. On the appointed evening, they filled a enormous auditorium with their people and key allies. Seated at a long table on one side of the stage was the QCO negotiation team with name plates identifying their churches. Across the stage in stark isolation was a tiny table reserved for Koch. All IAF organizers take huge delight in planning the drama of confronting authorities. Perhaps it is their ecclesiastical backgrounds, with its loving attention to rituals and ceremonies, but clearly their enthusiasm for the details and rich symbolism of staged events is irrepressible.

Koch also remembers the night vividly:

When we went in I had the feeling I was in some Nuremberg stadium. There was a military band. There were more than 1,000 people, chanting. They were thumping standards on the floor. It was like mass hysteria and very militant.

I don't care, it doesn't bother me. In fact I enjoy it.

The rhetoric coming from the stage from Father [Eugene] Lynch [pastor of Saint Mary Gate of Heaven Church in Ozone Park, Queens] was to the effect that "We are going to demand that city officials come out here. We are going to put them on trial. They are going to have to answer questions. If we don't like their answers, we are going to ask them again and again until they respond to our satisfaction." It was the most hostile kind of atmosphere. So they marched me down in front and seated me very close to the stage. They then ordered me up and sat me at a small table by myself on one side of the stage. On the other side was a large table at which something like eight jurors were sitting, and then there was Father Lynch— the hanging judge—in the middle at his lectern. He said, "We are now going to place the Mayor on trial. He is going to have to answer these questions."[7]

Koch was told he would be asked questions first; immediately afterwards, they would get straight down to business, so all opening statements would be dispensed with. Koch bristled and demanded to be permitted two minutes for some prepared remarks, vowing to storm out if he couldn't speak before being pelted with questions. The pastor stood firm, and, in the stunned and confused silence of the deadlock, tension mounted. McNeil remembers that flashing before his eyes was the inglorious failure of an action that had been painstakingly planned for many months. If Koch left, all their work of building expectations and meeting quotas of assembled activists would dissolve in a puff of smoke. Two thousand people, here primed to get down to brass tacks and bargain with the new mayor, would be left hanging.

Just then, moments before Koch was about to leave in a huff, a quick-thinking political novice on the negotiating team raised her hand and broke the logjam by calling for a team caucus. In the huddle, Father Lynch reminded McNeil that one of IAF's cardinal rules for these kind of actions was always to control the agenda, and so he maintained that any yielding to Koch was unthinkable. Retelling the story, a self-deprecating McNeil said he impatiently responded, "Forget what I taught you; *let him talk.*"

The steadfast Lynch remained unconvinced, but his team overruled him and agreed to split the difference and let Koch have one minute, rather than two, for his opening remarks. Koch self-importantly balked at not getting his way and turned his back on the two thousand waiting citizens. All was almost lost until Koch, in a pattern that would become one of his distinguishing political hallmarks, blurted out what he was thinking. Overheard by a sharp-eared newsman and vividly reported in the next day's newspapers was, according to McNeil, Koch's muttered cynicism that he didn't have to stay because, after all, "it is no longer an election year."

The press gleefully pounced, keeping the story alive for days. The *New York Post* even kept a box score monitoring Koch's progress on the QCO demands. This put the group on the map and, according to McNeil, "made QCO a household word."

Koch bitterly assesses the encounter differently:

Then there was an enormous amount of flak in the press. "How could you do this?"

And I proceeded to say, escalating a little bit, "Well, you know, my feelings at the time were that this was sort of like the Jewish doctors' trial in Moscow under Stalin. I felt as if I were one of the doctors."

So everyone said, "Oh, he's accusing them of anti-Semitism." Well, maybe I was, because that is the way I felt.[8]

East Brooklyn Churches

Even before the Koch "action" Heinemeier, who had been in Brooklyn for almost fifteen years, began tracking the activities of this parish-based, ecumenical social-action group in the adjacent borough. In an interview in the cluttered, book-lined office of his South Bronx parsonage in the spring of 1989, he recalled:

I became impressed back in 1977 with some of the things that were beginning to happen in QCO. That, coupled with many years of inner-city ministry there in Brooklyn and knowing how parochial it all was, how unable any local congregation was to really effect change—I just learned that over many years

in Brooklyn. I have always had a strong ecumenical commitment in my ministry; it's been pretty gut from the beginning.
So in March of 1978 I convened a meeting after a number of
[preliminary] meetings with individual pastors. This is all before knowing anything about the IAF.[9]

A central tenet of the IAF ideology is that all change springs
from meetings where two people sit down and talk, often without a
predetermined agenda. These one-on-one relational meetings give
people an opportunity to get to know one another and create bonds
which later can be the cement that binds group action. As a result of
these meetings Heinemeier "got to know a lot of the other clergy
there in Brownsville [Brooklyn]."

It was in March of '78 at Lutheran Hospital which has now been
demolished down in East New York; I remember distinctly that
meeting. I called a meeting, and I guess fifteen or more clergy
showed up after individual cultivation [in the one-on-one en-
counters]. And there we asked, "do we want to do something
together?" And there was a readiness to say yes. And so at the
very next meeting we invited some people from QCO over.
Some of the principal leaders there, Roman Catholic, Lutheran,
just a couple, two or three. And there a kind of seed was
spawned of looking at IAF.

IAF was doing QCO. IAF had a *much* different role in QCO's
formation. And after a number of more meetings, we decided to
interview three different organizing networks, IAF being one.
One out of Chicago, one out of Washington area. I forget their
names, but they were reputable concerns. And then two Roman
priests and I called IAF and Ed Chambers; they were still out in
Chicago at that time.

We met at a motel out in LaGuardia airport. Very brass-tacks
kind of meeting with Ed Chambers. Father John Powis and
Michael Breslin and myself met with Ed Chambers in some
bedroom together there at LaGuardia Airport. There we invited
Ed to come to a kind of initial exploratory meeting of leaders.
And that happened at Our Lady of Mercy Roman Church. Must
have been around November or so in '78. And that kept pro-
gressing. On Dr. King's Birthday in '79, Jan. 15, at the Salvation
Army on Riverdale Ave. in Brownsville, a contract was signed.
I still have a picture of that.

The original contract was with seven congregations: four Roman Catholic, a Lutheran, a Pentecostal, and a nondenominational church. "A pretty humble beginning," according to Heinemeier. He continues:

> That's where it started. No staff. We set out on an eighteen-month Phase One program of raising $300,000 and getting 20–25 congregations we wanted to have in at the end of eighteen months at which time we would get our first full-time staff.

This is the classic way the IAF sinks roots in a new community. Joan Levin Ecklein and Armand Lauffer, in their 1972 book, *Community Organizers and Social Planners: A Volume of Case and Illustrative Material*, distill the Alinsky/Chambers entry strategy into four salient propositions. Although they were analyzing the IAF initiative in Rochester, decades later the pattern is still faithfully followed. In Brooklyn, as in Rochester in 1965, the ball got rolling when a coalition of church leaders invited the IAF to help them knit together a number of minority parishes in a hurting ghetto. This triggered what Ecklein and Lauffer identify as a four-step process:

Step 1. *There needs to be a nucleus of support and the availability of financial resources from outside the disadvantaged community in order to initiate an organizing process.*

Step 2. *Alinsky* [read Chambers] *set certain tests as conditions for coming, and, in responding to these conditions, the local leadership began the process of organization before Alinsky commited himself to enter the situation.*

Step 3. *Alinsky helped the local leadership meet his set of conditions.* He used a variety of devices to educate his leadership: he recounted past successes in order to convince the local leaders that it could be done; he sought to increase militancy by polarizing the situation, by identifying the enemy, and by developing a situation in terms of good guys and bad guys; he helped the leadership anticipate some of its problems, such as the role of informers and sell-outs; he provided leadership by setting goals and helping to anticipate the kind of tactics leaders would need to employ; and he schooled them over and over again in the mutual rights,responsibilities, and expectations of his role as the professional organizer and their role as the local leadership.

*Step 4. As soon as Alinsky commited himself to organizing, the de-
velopment of a militant and disciplined core of people became the overriding objective. Issues and programs were
converted into tactics to achieve that objective.*[10]

This sequence occurred in Brooklyn, with Chambers orches-
trating the demands and with the charismatic Heinemeier leading
the local pastors in complying. The result was the firm commitment of IAF to the building of one of the most innovative people's
organizations yet seen, one destined to break new ground. Heinemeier recalls:

> Mike Gecan, who is now the supervisor for New York and New
> Jersey, was our first Lead Organizer. He came, I think, in Au-
> gust or September of '80. And soon on we convinced IAF that
> we were determined to be not simply a service organization,
> but we wanted to build as well. And then, of course, their juices
> started flowing with that kind of mandate.
>
> It was [Gecan and Chambers] who found [Nehemiah builder]
> I. D. Robbins, to their credit. He found out of his work—here in
> the Bronx and elsewhere—his concept of affordable housing.
> One of our pastors, Rev. [Johnny Ray] Youngblood, named it
> Nehemiah. Somewhere around '81 or so model homes began
> building and into '82, about the time I left Brooklyn.

The culminating achievement of East Brooklyn Churches
(EBC) was the building of twenty-three hundred owner-occupied,
single-family rowhouses affordable to a range of residents in the East
New York–Brownsville neighborhood.[11] However, Nehemiah[12] came
at the end of a long road that began in 1980 when EBC started
running a series of more modest actions intended to build strength
and confidence.

For instance, they first dueled with Brooklyn Borough President
Howard Golden over the winnable issue of replacing seventeen hundred street signs that were down in their neighborhood. They packed
his office with seventy-five angry residents, and, although he had already committed himself to replacing the street signs throughout the
sprawling borough, this meeting persuaded him to start in the ghetto
communities rather than the more prosperous areas.

Constructing a democratic power organization from an inner-
city base is a slow, brick-by-brick task. Another early, membership-
building battle in East Brooklyn was a confrontation with local food

merchants over unhygienic conditions in their stores. According to Arthur Jones's account in the *National Catholic Reporter:*

> By the early 1980s, after a two-year initial organizing stage, EBC helped church people research which government agencies had jurisdiction over supermarkets; neighborhood people were organized into teams, about 100 "shopper inspectors." They asked supermarket managers for permission to send in the inspection teams; most agreed.

> Then, on Saturday mornings, the "inspectors" examined the store for non-working refrigeration units, dirty conditions, moldy food, high prices.[13]

The results of the inspections were widely aired at Sunday services at twenty local churches. EBC put ten supermarkets on probation and invited the managers to a community meeting. Father Leo Penta, a Catholic priest and one of the founders of EBC, remembers:

> You know, when you say, "All in favor, please stand," and 700 people stand up, that does something for and to people. We subsequently had a press conference to announce the new cooperation between the community and the supermarkets.[14]

Other more ambitious actions followed, including demolition of abandoned buildings that blighted the neighborhood, crackdowns on local "smoke shops" where drugs were openly retailed, and the registering of ten thousand new voters.

As Jim Gittings, writing in a religious magazine, sums up:

> In each case solid homework was done, logistical problems were solved ahead of time, initial approaches to authority were made at the highest levels, the organization's intentions or expectations were presented with clarity, and time-lines for requested actions were set. Also, when officials or bureaucrats gave good service, EBC didn't forget to say "thank you" in ways that the press was bound to report. This last practice is a habit that does much to keep the organization's relationships with public officials viable, if not always warm.[15]

The crowning glory of the organizing that East Brooklyn Churches has been doing for the last decade and a half is the construction of twenty-three hundred attached single-family dwellings, the Nehemiah homes. The erection of these houses has revitalized the neighborhood, bestowed on the organization credibility and legitimacy among the residents, and, some would say, stirred consternation among city officials who proved unable or unwilling to build affordable housing themselves.

5

Old Testament Builders
Nehemiah and Robbins

East New York in the wounded flatlands of southeastern Brooklyn is a less tightly packed, low-rise version of the South Bronx. Eerie empty streets with dilapidated detached homes and crumbling tenements stretch for blocks in bleak monotony through a neighborhood plagued by crime, drugs, high unemployment, and poor schools. Just as the corridors of decay in the South Bronx are suddenly interrupted by the riveting sight of the cleanly scrubbed suburban homes of Charlotte Street, East New York also harbors a surprise.

In the midst of the housing neglect and staggering physical rot, a visitor stumbles upon hundreds and hundreds of immaculate, orderly brick rowhouses. Brooklyn has always prided itself on its elegant late nineteenth-century brownstones, and now, in the late twentieth century in its most threadbare neighborhood, a more modest version of that quintessential urban innovation is springing up—Nehemiah homes.

Sponsored by East Brooklyn Churches and built by civic gadfly and real-estate innovator I. D. Robbins, these twenty-three hundred homes are owned by people with working-class incomes who pay roughly $300 a month in mortgage charges.

During the latter phase of construction in 1989, Robbins presided over this remarkable inner-city oasis from an office in one of the Nehemiah houses. From this unassuming headquarters with one secretary, three desks, a few file cabinets, and walls plastered with Building Department maps and blueprints, Robbins masterminded the most successful affordable housing operation in New York and perhaps the United States.

Robbins, an impeccably tailored, bluntly articulate man in his early eighties with silver hair and patrician bearing, first came to New York in 1933 from Pittsburgh to work as a newspaperman. Recounting his early career decisions, he said that after arriving in New York:

> My cousins were beginning to have some success in the construction business. They were expanding, and they asked me to join them. And I did. I don't know a trade. I took care of the financing, everything except the purchasing. It was a big company producing several thousand houses a year: tract houses, factories, apartment houses, mostly in New Jersey.
>
> After about a year and a half with them, I went into business for myself. I was thirty years old. Basically my career has been in the construction business and in finance. I know money. All business is the same: it is primarily organization and administration.[1]

He has had a distinguished career as a builder of large-scale developments and as the president of the City Club, a prominent "good government," blue-blood watchdog group he once ran for Mayor. His credentials as a builder are impressive:

> I built the Hunts Point Cooperative Market [in the South Bronx] which is the largest refrigerated plant in the world. I organized it and brought it in under the budget. And I rebuilt the Brooklyn Market, which is the second largest refrigerated plant. I built the housing for the Typographical Union, the Big Six Towers in Queens. It is a very big and successful development, probably the most successful middle-income housing ever built in New York. It is still a model, one in which for anyone who was lucky enough to get in there—they have had a glorious home. I was president of the company for a great many years after I built it. Whenever they have any problems, I usually go back there and work on them.

How was it that Robbins got interested in affordable housing? Robbins leans forward behind his desk in front of a window that looks out on a grassy backyard and a forest of Nehemiah rooftops and recalls:

> When I retired from business, I took a job as a columnist for the *New York Daily News* on public affairs generally. I'm not a Johnny-One-Note on housing. Housing is just one facet of pub-

lic issues. You've got hospitals, crime, sanitation, police, a lot of different things.

The *Daily News* was running a promotion of which housing was a part. They paid a professor at one of the universities to propose a way to get affordable housing started. He suggested a contest among architects to get the best design for affordable housing. This is nonsense, of course, because architects have nothing to do with affordable housing.

They had a luncheon for about thirty builders who were supposed to participate in this scheme. The managing editor was unaware that he had someone on this staff who had built more than all those other builders combined. I raised certain questions and sort of took over the meeting. The editor said to me, "why don't you write a piece for the Sunday magazine telling us how to do it." And so I did. They got three thousand letters. They never had an response like that.

The seminal 1978 article had the attention-grabbing title: *Blueprint for a One-Family House: For the $12,000-a-Year Income.*[2] The piece was prophetic in many ways. With imperious self-assurance, Robbins insisted that the new homes be owner-occupied because "ownership could encourage responsible community leadership. It would also be a challenge—and an invitation—to join the mainstream of American life." He also advocated reducing typical ghetto density by 80 percent or more because, he argued, this would reduce the problems of inner-city dwellers and make living arrangements more manageable.

He began the article by sketching a little history:

We have come full circle in house-building. We went from the single family house to the small multifamily tenement, to the six-story elevator building, to the 32-story apartment house and large project. Now, both the high cost of construction and the social frictions of high-density communities suggest that we go back to where we started—and take another and more respectful look at the two-story, single-family row house.

A drive through the South Bronx or a ride on the elevated [railroad] over Brownsville, Brooklyn, reveals hundreds of burned out acres. The city owns most of this land. The water supply system, the sewers, streets, electric and gas utilities, police stations, firehouses, hospitals, schools, and churches remain. And with these "off-site" improvements in place, if the city would contribute land, it would be a builder's dream, a chance to spend the money on the house.

The brisk interest generated by the article continued to mount as Robbins used his weekday column to flesh out more details. It was not only working-class readers eager to own homes who took notice of these ideas. Robbins recalls:

Finally we were getting nowhere because every time I wrote one of these things and said it could be done and how to do it, Koch would get upset and he would call Gliedman who was head of HPD [Housing, Preservation and Development, the city's central housing bureaucracy]. Gliedman was a lawyer and not a construction man, and he'd call architects and engineers and so-called specialists together. And they would say Robbins doesn't know what he's talking about. And they would write memos to Koch saying Robbins can't produce. He's a liar, a phony, and a fake. All those guys, by the way, all those guys who didn't really know the business, are gone now. I got exasperated at one point and said if they would give me a lot in the South Bronx I would build a house at my own expense to show that it could be done. They could appoint auditors or whatever they wanted to prove the costs were what I said they were.

At this point the IAF, always on the prowl for galvanizing ideas that could strengthen its grip on residents and contribute to muscle-flexing displays in its two New York organizations, contacted Robbins. He remembers:

Ed Chambers had become a steady reader of my columns, and he told Mike Gecan [the Lead Organizer of EBC], "Here's a guy who seems to know what he's talking about. Why don't you go see him?" I had a lot of people who wanted to build houses, but they didn't have any money. I didn't know how to finance them. Borrowing money from banks on a speculative venture to build affordable housing didn't seem like a very good idea. I said to Mike, "Do you got any money?" and he said, "yes." And I said, "How much?" "Oh, I think I can raise $12 million." I said, "What are we waiting for; let's go." That's how it got started. Our relationship has been an ideal one. Very nice group of people. We think alike. I support what they are trying to do. They support what I'm trying to do. You couldn't find a finer bunch of men.

Where was the IAF, with its vaunted shoe-string economics, going to get $12 million? More importantly, historically it was an IAF tenet to avoid putting energy into brick and mortar at the expense of building relationships and organizations. And, beyond that, how could they possibly forge binding ties to a millionaire retired builder without risking a fiasco of major proportions?

Mike Gecan, the low-key, cerebral EBC Lead Organizer, concedes that this was, in theory, an unlikely alliance. At a ten-day training session for IAF organizers in California in 1989, Gecan recalled that by 1980 EBC was firmly established and was slowly building its power base in the most wrecked parts of Brooklyn. A big issue was the demolition of abandoned apartment buildings which had been functioning as crack dens and as centers for all sorts of other illicit activity. EBC was successful in prodding the city to knock down some three hundred buildings that were deemed to be beyond rehabilitation. That massive removal left a wide-open vista of empty lots in its wake, and Gecan explained, "We saw the land for the first time; block upon block. Now, people asked, what are we going to do with this land?"[3] It was at this point that Ed Chambers turned over a thick file of Robbins' *Daily News* articles to Gecan.

Bubbling up from EBC's church-going membership was a perennial concern about adequate housing, now heightened by the leveling of hundreds of substandard buildings, and so according to Gecan EBC leaders "entered into a several month research and analysis phase to determine what should be done about the land." They concluded that the odds for housing transformation were slim. They were cautious about raising expectations, and when they finally made their first tentative moves it was with the knowledge that they could back out at any step along the way.

Caution was warranted. After all, as Samuel Freedman points out in his powerful 1993 biography of EBC's charismatic pastor Rev. Johnny Ray Youngblood:

For twenty years the borough's poorest neighborhoods had served as test sites for philosophy after philosophy, program after program, from Model Cities to Operation Breadbasket, from the Office of Economic Opportunity to the Comprehensive Employment and Training Act. And after the experiments in white largess and black empowerment had expired—a few, it was true, leaving pockets of renewal—the larger deprivation remained.[4]

The stakes were huge because although prudence dictated following the conventional wisdom of starting small—after all, they were novices in the building trade—their research, heavily influenced by Robbins, indicated that they needed a large-scale housing development to reach a critical mass in order to have even a stab at success. A cautious pilot project would be doomed to failure.

Robbins explains this reasoning:

> My experience over the last fifty years is that bad buildings crowd out good buildings. There is no way small amounts of good building will improve a neighborhood. There is no way to save a neighborhood when it has gone down past a certain point.
>
> It is a fundamental fact; Lewis Mumford wrote this in the twenties, he said, "[High rise apartments on] Park Ave. are great for rich people. They have all the options. They don't cause any trouble. But high density is extremely bad for poor people."
>
> If you are poor it means you've got problems. You put a lot of poor people in one place and you've got big problems. These people need to have a little air to breathe, a little room to move in.
>
> Say you got fifty-four families on a block here. Suppose you got one criminal in there. You can isolate him. People soon know who he is. They tell the police. Everything gets straightened out soon. Even if he plays the radio too loud at night. If he has reggae music with the windows open. I'm making that up, but that's probably what happens. If you are in a public housing project with 540 apartments which is common, you have ten criminals. Those ten criminals quickly form a gang. They prey on the others. And the people are poor so, therefore, they feel they have no options. They don't have any power to assert themselves, and they're not organized, and they're scared. The whole thing goes to pot.
>
> Don't be romantic about this. Poor people have problems. It is one reason they are poor.

Before construction could begin, EBC had to reach its goal of generating a fund of over $10 million. An IAF axiom: *Power is orga-*

nized people and organized money. At first, they sought money in fat-walleted allies like foundations, corporations, banks—all institutions which potentially had some incentive to improve slums. But, no dice; they were not able to shake any money loose from these repositories of excess capital, according to Gecan.

EBC then looped back to its roots and appealed to the hierarchies of the Catholic Church and main-line Protestant denominations for millions in operating capital that would be fed into an interest-free revolving fund that would capitalize the building expenses and which would be replenished, in time, when the homes were sold.

An obvious church ally in Brooklyn was the 69-year-old, progressive, antiwar Catholic Bishop Francis Mugavero. EBC leaders, including prominent Catholic pastors, approached the bishop and in a formal meeting boldly pressed him for $2.5 million to finance the untried affordable-housing concept.[5] Staggered, the bishop paused and hedged, "How about a quarter of million dollars?" A lightning-quick Catholic pastor seized the moment, proudly congratulating the diocesan leader, "Bishop, that's a great start." Puzzled, the bishop stammered, "Start?"[6]

Relentlessly, EBC advanced the gentle confrontation, requesting a half-hour meeting with Mugavero every two weeks until the rest of their request was met. According to Gecan, the bishop reluctantly agreed to the meetings, and, visibly "upset, he bolted from the room. But the key to a good action is having the next step in mind."

Three pastors met with Mugavero every two weeks for three months "to energize him. The first thing they did at those meetings was to begin conspicuously with a prayer." After a while, the bishop committed a million dollars, probably expecting to be let off the hook, and was met with an enthusiastic, "Great, bishop! We are almost half-way there!" Eventually the Catholic prelate surpassed his quota, and other conservative Protestant denominations like the Lutherans and the Episcopalians also ponied up their assessments.

At this point EBC was entering virgin territory, forging and trusting in a broader, more independent leadership team than was its custom. It included not only its own neighborhood leaders and other collaborating IAF organizers, but the "enlightened, rationalist, not-a-man-of-the-church"[7] I. D. Robbins, along with Bishop Mugavero and other ecclesiastic bigwigs.

This working group framed five governing principles that would guide this commitment to brick and mortar.

First, it would produce only single family homes, to create a clear sense of accountability. Second, the houses would be owned rather than rented, so every resident had an emotional and financial stake in the experiment's success. Third, they would be attached to one another, to hold construction costs below fifty thousand dollars per unit. Fourth, they would be built by the thousand, rather than in the small numbers of most pilot projects, to foster a renewed sense of neighborhood. And finally, they would not rely on any gifts or grants from the public sector.[9]

Early on, this unlikely team descended on IAF nemesis Edward Irving Koch. What they needed from the mayor was commitments of unencumbered, multiblock expanses of cleared, city-owned land in Brownsville; a promise of no foot-dragging by the hydra-headed municipal bureaucracy; a ten-year deferral of property tax on land that was not generating much tax revenue in any case; and a relatively humble $10,000 subsidy per house that would be repaid when the Nehemiah owner sold the home.[9]

They marshaled their forces for the confrontation with Koch. The long, relational encounters with Bishop Mugavero bore luxuriant fruit: the meeting at City Hall occurred long before the financing was firmly in place, but at the opening bargaining session the bishop flabbergasted his negotiation teammates and stunned Koch with the audacious bluff: "Ed, we got $12 million and we're ready to go."

Koch was knocked off balance. According to Gecan, Koch was left "wondering how he can say no. There is nothing he likes about the whole concept. Koch says he'll think about it. Koch stalls."

In order to crank up the temperature, EBC hired a posh hotel reception room, packed it with three hundred supporters, and confidently announced at a formal press conference that they were prepared to build Nehemiah homes.

Koch was conspicuous by his absence, and reporters clamored to know, where is the mayor? They rushed to phones, and Koch was forced to stammer, "I'm with them."

The Economics of Affordable Housing

What is Robbins' secret? How did he make good on this bold pledge to build housing, "good brick and block homes with a full basement," at a rate that was dramatically less expensive than that of any of his competitors? "It's a combination of many things,"[10] he expansively explained to a group of South Bronx activists gathered in a cramped office above the chapel of St. Jerome's in the spring of 1989.

Perhaps the key ingredient in dramatically driving down construction expenses is in skillfully eluding so-called soft costs. In an article in a weekly New York business publication, Robbins defines soft costs as those expenses "other than for labor or materials [which] are the largest single variable in house construction. In one study by the Department of Housing Preservation and Development, Nehemiah soft costs were 6 percent of the total cost compared with 35 percent for the next-lowest-cost builder. As the selling price rises, the ratio of soft costs should, in fact, fall."[11] How does one avoid soft costs? The Robbins formula includes these elements:

1. **Modest Profit.** "There are no profits; only a one-thousand-dollar fee," he told the South Bronx organizers, who in the spring of 1989 were contemplating exporting Brooklyn's Nehemiah concept to their beleaguered borough. This alone, depending on whose building you compare it to, involves a savings of anywhere from $5,000 to $8,000 per home. As Robbins advised in the business article, "Build in large volume. A builder who produces 50 houses or fewer needs to project a profit of $5,000 per house to feel reasonably comfortable. Increase the program to 1,000 houses, and $1,000 or $1,500 a house should be sufficient."

2. **No Interest Charges.** Robbins doesn't pay interest on borrowed money during construction because the sponsoring church-based organizations have generated the loan money from their hierarchies. This capital is made available for construction at no interest from a revolving fund. The money is restored to the bankroll when the houses are sold. This saves, Robbins claims, another $3,000–$5,000 per unit.

3. **No Selling Costs.** There is no expense involved in selling the homes. Instead of spending money on advertising or promotion, the member churches of EBC make housing applications available, and the expectation is that parish activists, those who struggled to win land from the city, will be the first in the long line of people eager to take their crack at the American dream of home ownership.[12]

4. **No *General Conditions*.** This is something that the wily Robbins succinctly defines as "something the builders put into their pockets" and includes security arrangements during construction and other sundries and incidentals. In most areas of

New York City, a major concern is protection of building materials before they are bolted into the house. Prudence demands that no supplies lie unguarded even for a minute. As the *New York Times* reported, the cost for security during construction on 250 Nehemiah homes in Brooklyn worked out to only $600 a house. "Fourteen security people are on the payroll, and they are on the site when construction materials can be stolen. But the speed of construction holds the cost down. From excavation to occupancy averages six months."[13]

5. **Promptness and Suppliers.** Robbins contractors buy materials for less because Robbins guarantees payment in nine days or fewer, and, of course, he buys in large quantities from original sources rather than through middlemen.

6. **Loyal Contractors.** He has better arrangements with contractors and subcontractors, "because we pay our bills in nine days, and they can feel secure in working with us," a rarity in this business. All the delays and false starts that mar most large-scale construction projects and escalate the bills are much less of a factor in his projects. According to the *New York Times*, he uses "a small cadre of five loyal subcontractors—an electrician, plumber, foundation man, excavator and carpenter—most of whom depend entirely on Nehemiah for their income. Keeping them steadily employed is a necessary ingredient of Nehemiah's success."[14]

7. **Low Administration Costs.** Robbins also has very limited administrative expenses. His company headquarters in Brooklyn employs only two full-time staffers, "my assistant and a clerk." He also retains a part-time inspector and a "full-time *expediter* at the Brooklyn Housing Department" to slice through the red tape that bogs down construction and swells the cost. Any structure more complicated is an invitation to heartache because the complexity of code compliance rises exponentially with increased building height.

8. **Fixed Architect Fee.** He saves on architect fees by paying only $200 per house instead of the going rate of roughly 5 percent to 10 percent of the selling cost. Since he builds in quantity, it is still a very lucrative arrangement for an architect, so quality plans can be easily obtained.[15]

9. **Uncomplicated Buildings.** Robbins builds what he characterizes as a carefully designed house, "one with no gingerbread, a rational house." It is not a prefab because, in his judgment, the

history of prefab construction in NYC is dismal. Robbins homes are "site built." In the business weekly article, he counseled potential developers to

> build uncomplicated buildings. The present Nehemiah house, as designed by James T. Martino, is a simple, code-compliant rowhouse, employing manufactured joists, trusses, and frames and conventional materials applied or installed on site. It is planned for a continuous cycle of construction. Sewers and water mains are located within the sites and connected once to city sewers and mains."[16]

This highlights another crucial aspect of the financial success of Nehemiah construction. Despite his prickly relations with city officials in some agencies, Robbins has achieved remarkable cooperation from the diverse array of municipal authorities who have to be appeased before a brick can be set in cement. For instance, the building code calls for each new home to make its own separate connection to the city's sewer system. As the *New York Times* pointed out, "the Sewer Department accepted Nehemiah's plan [in Brooklyn] to make a single connection to the city sewer line from all of the houses on a street, and convinced a reluctant Buildings Department to go along. Nehemiah ran its own on-site line parallel to the city's and connected in one place, saving at least $1,000 a house."[17] Robbins was also able to convince the Water Department to make a similar arrangement, and he garnered additional savings by tapping into the city's main at only two points on each block.

10. **Economies of Scale.** His modified approach to site building makes shrewd use of economies of scale. One backhoe excavates basements for as many as twenty-seven houses at once. "It takes [the operator] two days, and then he moves on to the next site," Robbins told the SBC Strategy Team. The foundation contractor then moves in and sets footings, which are 18' X 32' concrete strips that underlie the cellar. The forms which are the molds for the basement walls are "modern, advanced forms ganged up in sets of six by small cherry pickers." The joists which start above the cellar level are made in a factory and go across the full width of the house. It takes two carpenters just two days to lay the joists for the row. The house is framed in steel, "and the frames are manufactured in a New

Jersey factory owned by MLRS Inc., the general contractor, and come to the site all put together." The result, he proudly told the SBC organizers, is that "our fire rating is better than code. There are firebreaks between every home."[18]

To the SBC church leaders Robbins bragged, "Everyone is lined up and ready to go. If the land is ready to build on, we can put up ninety-three homes on four and a half acres and can move families in within five months. No, wait a second. Make that six months. We have to take into account foot dragging on the part of the housing bureaucracy."

6

Relational Organizing: Launching South Bronx Churches

As the first East Brooklyn families were moving into the newly constructed Nehemiah homes in 1982, John Heinemeier, the clergyman most responsible for firing up the engine of East Brooklyn Churches, began to grow restless. At that time he was affiliated with the conservative Missouri Lutheran Synod but increasingly unhappy with its "growingly narrow vision of its relationship with other denominations. I just simply could not with any enthusiasm espouse it any more."

> Then this opportunity came up in the South Bronx, and I'm committed to city ministry. And I was asked to come here by the bishop of this other Lutheran community, called the Lutheran Church of America. And so, after looking it over, I decided to come. It was a natural breaking point there in Brooklyn. We had just built a new parochial school there. The East Brooklyn Churches at that time was really doing well, with Nehemiah going into the ground. It was a watershed kind of time. It was a time that, if you believe in leaving when things are going well—things were going pretty well at that time. I had the sense that I had done some of the kinds of things I had wanted to do there. Kind of a mission accomplished sort of thing. It was a time to move on.[1]

The bishop wanted Heinemeier to reinvigorate St. John's Lutheran in the predominantly Black Morrisania section of the South Bronx. Morrisania is in the 18th Congressional District, the most impoverished in the nation.[2] As Heinemeier points out, it is a mere four miles from the most wealthy congressional district in the United States, Manhattan's Silk Stocking Upper East Side. Subsequently, he and his family moved into St. John's parsonage, an ancient white house tucked in an alley between the church and the parish school which presently houses a Head Start Program.

He found his new parish located in streets which were even more demolished and dangerous than the ones he had left. "I think you'd be hard pressed to find many neighborhoods like either the South Bronx or East Brooklyn," he says. "I'm always amazed when I go into other metropolitan areas of this country to see how different they are from the South Bronx, which is sort of the epicenter of urban decay. Everything is pronounced here."[3]

In spite of the efforts of a valiant handful of lay leaders, the parsonage had been vacant since the late sixties. "There was no pastor living in this house for the previous thirteen years," Heinemeier recalls. "The pastor had refused to live here. In fact, it was one of the key questions asked by leaders of this congregation when we were interviewing: would your family live in the parsonage? They were more concerned about that than any other single question."

The previous pastor had commuted to the South Bronx from a comfortable suburb in Westchester, north of the Bronx. And that absentee stewardship had consequences for the health of the congregation: "It took its toll in terms of ministry. The place was in shambles when we got here." The previous minister had been sick with a brain tumor for a number of years prior to Heinemeier's arrival. "It had been pastorally vacant for three years, and during that period it was strictly a one-morning-a-week ministry."

Heinemeier had to rebuild the congregation practically from scratch. But that "is exactly my cup of tea. I was in my element coming here. And still to this day, except for tensions sometimes in the family, I still appreciate living here. I would far rather live here than anywhere else. But," he adds ruefully, "I cannot say the same for my family."[4]

"In Brooklyn our own family situation was different. That's been a signal difference. We lived in East Flatbush where the Brownsville congregation had its own parsonage," and he daily made the short commute to his church in Brownsville. East Flatbush is an upwardly mobile Black community, with numerous residents from the Caribbean, many of whom are homeowners. It is a community that is not crushed by all the desperate pathology associated with inner-city neighborhoods where large numbers of residents are mired in the underclass.

Although all Catholic priests live in rectories adjacent to their churches, commuting to a parish in a declining neighborhood is not unusual for some other clergy. In fact, this arrangement is fairly common in the South Bronx among a number of Protestant ministers. The separate residential arrangement in Brooklyn, dictated by the location of the parsonage, afforded Heinemeier's wife and three children an opportunity to blend into a more benign community than is possible in a harsh area like the South Bronx.

"Brownsville [where the parish was located], was very much like the South Bronx, really a wasteland. Now it's somewhat different with Nehemiah."

> But as hard as the difficulty is, I am utterly committed to living in the parish. Living outside the parish is against everything I stand for, but that parish already had the house, in a nearby community. [Reflectively, he added] maybe in the long run, maybe it was even the better decision. You know, to forego those priorities for the sake of family peace and security.

In 1993 his children were 25, 23, 19 years old, so that during his Brooklyn ministry more than a decade ago they were all quite young. Many White New Yorkers, not all of whom are alarmists or racists, consider it irresponsible to merely walk along the ruined streets of the South Bronx, let alone raise children there.

His young son graduated from Fordham Prep, a solidly academic Catholic high school precariously perched on Fordham Road, the northern Maginot Line of the South Bronx. One daughter went to the celebrated Bronx High School of Science, and the remaining daughter went to a Lutheran high school. In Flatbush, his children had attended the local public schools, but, since the schools of the South Bronx were demonstrably in collapse, this was not really an option here. About the decision to forsake the public schools, he explains, "We crossed that hurdle a long time ago."[5]

Heinemeier speaks of his intention to minimize any aspect of his life which separates him from the poorest of the poor in his neighborhood but concedes:

> Now that is an impossible task, yet it is a constant invitation. With my race, my background, privilege, education—almost every aspect of who I am—I can never be in a one-for-one community with the people who live here. I can only make an attempt. But even these attempts, that desire to be part of the common life here—they are deeply felt by the local community.

For example, it would be quite hazardous for anyone in this community to touch my wife or children. They would have hell to pay—by local people. When our son was about nine years old, he was riding his bicycle in front of the church, and a bigger teenager took it away from him. Several other teenagers in the playground next door saw that happen, and, within thirty minutes, the bike was back. They had gotten it back—by knife point.

That intention to share life here is acknowledged and appreciated—with the understanding that we'll never do it profoundly.

This illuminates an unexpected and painful dimension of the commitment that is needed in order to stir up change in areas like the South Bronx. Street smarts, courage, and political savvy may not be enough. It often may be necessary for a man with a family to ask his wife and children to give up a conventional and comfortable existence to join him in the sacrifice that this work entails. "That's been a trying thing, it really has. Our kids, each one of them has tried to integrate into the community somewhat. It has been very, very difficult for them, far more so than for me."

Heinemeier arrived at St. John's on 1 January 1983 after a highly emotional farewell in his East Brooklyn church. Upon arrival he concluded:

My primary agenda was rebuilding my congregation. But right along side of that, and I had learned this from IAF, something that I had been doing informally but now did much more systematically was to initiate a series of agendaless one-to-one meetings, coming into a new community. Now this is all beyond meeting with one's congregation. I visited this whole congregation in their homes within a couple of months. Along side of this visiting, I met with maybe seventy-five or so community leaders, not members of this congregation. In each case, I asked them who they thought I ought to see and built on that geometrically. Agendaless, relational. A lot of them were clergy, and out of that began the building blocks for South Bronx Churches.[6]

Ed Chambers, meanwhile, was anxious to expand his New York base with its toe hold in Queens and its solid, expanding base rooted in Nehemiah in Brooklyn. He admits:

I had my designs on the South Bronx because it is the worst and most notorious place in the New York area. But I knew to do the South Bronx, minimally you had to have a top-flight organizer. Someone with a lot of experience in tough scenes. And, secondly, you would have to have a base in the midst of the corruption, one that was independent of the corruption.

Heinemeier was moving there and taking a parish and kind of ingratiating himself, becoming part of the woodwork, and that provided a base for the Protestant community. He went around and did hundreds of individual meetings, one-on-ones, so he got a relationship, and he starting calling me and sending me reports about it and whatnot.

I'm still bringing [the organizations in] Brooklyn and Queens to fruition. And it's important that they succeed because, if they don't, we'll never get to the South Bronx. He calls me, and so I say I'll come up. And I went there every four months for about a day at a time. Ran with him a couple of times, smelled around myself. And I said "okay let's try it."[7]

About his collaboration with Chambers, Heinemeier says:

He and I started to conspire together, and I started getting some focus on what some of the building blocks were. Meanwhile, he was being stimulated as well. And that is where it starts, a lot of individual meetings between myself and a number of others, clergy primarily. So that by October of '85 we signed contracts with IAF. There was an enormous number of meetings with individuals, and then there were more collective meetings.

In classic IAF style, South Bronx Churches began with modest fixed fights and worked its way up to more ambitious targets, including, most prominently, the entire local political establishment and its real-estate campaign contributors.

At this embryonic point, the biggest single impediment to the launching of a viable organization was the fact that the original charter congregations included no Roman Catholic churches, and a broad-based organization rooted in parishes needed strong Catholic participation to be viable. The reason that recruitment here faltered is that many of the Catholic pastors who were most inclined towards political activism were already affiliated with South Bronx People for Change.

Heinemeier says that, if it wasn't for People for Change, they would have gone right after the Catholic parishes:

> Tactically we left that as a special project, the appeal to the Roman Catholics. If it weren't for People for Change we would have gone after them immediately. We knew we had to have Roman Catholics in; we couldn't even keep going without Roman Catholics. Yet [South Bronx People for Change] didn't even have two-thirds of the Roman parishes in their organization. So that was silly on a power pattern. We were straight on that from the get-go. It was just when and how not to alienate People for Change. Or the Romans, because it was their little baby.

At this point Chambers made the decision to summon veteran organizer Jim Drake to the South Bronx to court the Catholic pastors. Chambers recalls:

> All this time, I know Drake is in Texas and wants to get out, and it's time to get him out for his own growth and development. And he is tough. Seventeen years of organizing with Cesar Chavez. He was Chavez's top man. Drake was the guy who dreamed up the grape boycott operation. He was the idea man on it, and one of the executors of it, making it work.

> So I told Drake in three or four months he had to come to New York and take a hot shot at the South Bronx. The problem was that we had twenty-three congregations but no Roman Catholic parishes. For two months I paid him out of IAF money, which we rarely do. *We* hired him for the first two months. I told the Protestants that, at the end of that time, we'd take the assessment, and, if there are enough Catholics coming on board, we'll then go to contract. We'll have a *bona fide* Sponsoring Committee and then we'll start the organizing.

> Drake came and did an outstanding job, saturating himself in ten, twelve individual meetings with Catholic pastors.

> John Flynn [the inspiration behind People for Change] was the first guy he met with. Peter Gavagan, MacNamara. Heinemeier tells us based on his one-on-ones, forget about John Grange, that's the guy at St. Jerome's; you'll never get him. That always bugs me when someone says that, it's a special challenge. So I'm telling Drake, I'm meeting with Drake pretty regularly, and I'm moving in behind Jim on some of these guys.

We got lucky on MacNamara. He knew us and Alinsky from Chelsea. When he heard it was us and Alinsky, he threw open the door. He wasn't going to operate with losers. He had some people dribbling about—People for Change—but his heart wasn't in it.

So the Catholic priests really checked us out. We told them come to Ten-Day Training. See what we are about. And some of them came. After that, we knew we had a Sponsoring Committee.

I had told the Protestants you won't see Jim Drake for the first two months he's here. First of all, he's not on your payroll so you don't got a fucking[8] say-so [about how he spends his time]. We've got to be an ecumenical, Black, Hispanic, Catholic, Protestant operation. He did a masterful job getting the Catholics and getting in some of the lay people. Clearly these guys were waiting for something that was real and had some depth to it.[9]

Heinemeier was impressed with Drake's work from the beginning:

I was in very steady communication with a lot of the priests but never with the intensity that Jim Drake brought. That became his baby. For the first three months he was here, that is all he did. Nothing else. He came about six months earlier than we ordinarily would have probably brought him on. He came in April or May of 1986. That was only eight months or so after we launched. Ordinarily, he wouldn't have been here for at least twelve months or maybe more like eighteen. He was brought in on IAF salary for the first two or three months he was here—we weren't even paying him—to bring in Roman Catholics, and he did it."

We were impressed by the vitality of the Valley Interfaith which he had created, still a very strong unit down in Texas. I was, by this time, very much conversant with national network people, and so I was able to ask questions about him. He was easy to get along with; it was easy to bring him in. We didn't have a lot of consternation about whether he would work out. Those first few months he was not on our salary, so we had a good chance to see him work. We did not hire him until after that, after we saw what he did with the Roman Catholics. We were very impressed.

The rivalry with South Bronx People for Change pitted two idealistic grass-roots groups of activists against one another, both vying for the loyalty, prestige, and money of the Catholic Church. Asked if there was any possibility of a compromise or any attempt to ally with People for Change, Chambers explained:

Well, we tried. I gave free scholarships, Ten-Day Training, for the executive director of People for Change. Met with him two or three times; Heinemeier met with him.

There was a strong tinge of Liberation Theology in People for Change, which was attractive. And they had a great priest by the name of Leo Connally, who was the heartbone of it. And I met with Connally, and I told him exactly what I was about. The Protestants were mobilizing and interested. And I said, "Well, what do you think? Should I continue this or drop it?" "Oh no," he said, "I think you should continue to meet the men and go around and whatnot." Well, that was at the same time they were getting ready to axe him, and they did axe him. They whipped him out of there and put him down on the Lower East Side. When they took Connally out, the heart of the movement was removed. He was the charismatic priest who could bring the priests together, and the Hispanics together, kind of around himself. Then Flynn was left isolated. Well, Flynn is a great guy, but he was not a Neil Connally; he was not an organizer.

So Drake just plowed ahead. We got four Catholic churches, then four more. Now we're up to, I think, thirteen. And another thing about People for Change was that the Black community would have nothing to do with them. Which really told us it wasn't broad-based. It was heavily Hispanic. Father Gavagan was a Liberation Theologian who spent some time in South America.[10] There was a real South American, Central American, constant overlay which just frightened the Blacks, just another Catholic thing. They did some good work. And in a vacuum, it looked pretty good.

Organizing the Pastors: Jim Drake and the Romans

Jim Drake was handed a formidable task, one that called for diplomacy, political sophistication, and the ability to inspire confidence. The way he signed up the most savvy Roman Catholic pastors permits a glimpse into the *modus operandi* of a top organizer reordering the priorities of politically sophisticated community leaders.

Of his effort to rally a critical mass of Roman Catholic pastors around the banner of South Bronx Churches, Drake explains:

> It takes about a year to get the pastors to do one-on-ones with each other. It takes a whole year to get them to trust the organizer and trust each other.

In the one-on-one encounter, Drake wants "to find out what makes them tick. What's interesting about them; what's in their self-interest. For instance, some are more interested in housing. I'm trying to find the ones who are relational, who haven't been burned too badly in the past by interfaith relationships, or cross-ethnic relationships. Have to weed out the nationalists. There is [sic] always some Black nationalist pastors. There is [sic] always the Hispanic nationalists. You have to weed those out because they are not going to be interested in diversity, in relationships with non-Hispanics, for example.[11]

Drake said that, in the Bronx, he arranged for one-on-ones with roughly one hundred pastors of all denominations and then worked more intensely with the "sixty who would keep appointments. And out of that sixty maybe fifty have come the whole way." These men "have all been to national training," the ten-day immersion into the ideology of IAF and its techniques for community empowerment.

Asked if the typical local pastor had volunteered to be in the South Bronx, Drake said, "Yes. Except for the Pentecostals, who tend to come to of the churches here." Was frustrated idealism a big factor in their ministries? "Yeah, there is plenty of that. Lots of cynicism about the political structure. You have to redefine politics for them. It is the business of the polity. It is not electoral business, it's not what Koch is raising money for, no, that's not politics." He then conceded:

> Electoral politics is the lowest form of political activity, but real politics is when you define for people very clearly what is possible. Remind them that this is their land. [The South Bronx] is now occupied territory. Teach people what you have to go through in order to get that land. Where we have to go. Who your allies are in order to get the money to build on it.

Teaching people how to build those alliances, how to seduce the Cardinal.

Among the pastors, we are looking for the ones who have been knocked down and keep getting up. Some don't get up any more; they stay down.

"Father Ryan from St. Luke's has been here forty years, still has got the spirit. Very skeptical," he said with admiration. Drake makes a distinction between cynicism and skepticism, with cynicism being corrosive and skepticism being healthy and warranted.

Why were pastors reluctant to meet?

They didn't want to meet with me, but I just wore 'em down. Some had been involved in People for Change and didn't want to do anything else ever again. Some of them have a pietistic approach. It would take them a whole long time to understand that there is another kind of politics. We make a strong distinction between the *World As It Is* and the *World As It Should Be*. This stuff that we have to do is in the *World As It Is*, not in the *World As It Should Be*. A lot of them are very trapped in just thinking about the *World As It Should Be*. They have given up on this one. They are going to wait for the next.

And, referring to the clerical leadership of the whole range of religious institutions in the Bronx, Drake claimed:

And some of them are just relatively successful at what they do. In other words, they pack their churches, make a good living. They don't see a need for any kind of interfaith power. Some of them have their own political connects already. Some of them are city councilmen. They got their little deals fixed. They *really* believe in the *World As It Is*.

There is [sic] only about ten of us that start organizations because you have to be on a peer level with all pastors. You have to have some history, some life in order to sit down with a guy who is sixty years old, and say, "We can put this community back together again." If you're a kid and say, "Try this," they'll say, "Oh, yeah? Come back fifteen years from now." That's why this whole process goes very slowly because it is a matter of building relationships, reconstituting relationships between very strong men, and some women. When you are forty-five, fifty you kind of figure you have seen it all. Somebody comes in to say there is a different way to do this, you don't always listen.

In some of those cases—guys I knew who were really talented— I had to have ten meetings with them before they would finally break down, and say, "Okay I'll go look at the Nehemiah." I was trying all kinds of things.

How did Drake get these pastors to talk? "I'd tell them real bluntly that I knew how to reorder the community. I knew how to do it. I had done it before. It is not that difficult. But I didn't think it could be done unless there were twenty or thirty men and women with a lot of vision." And, in the retelling, with a mocking sense of mischief at how he had stacked the deck, Drake said he locked eye contact with the pastor and innocently asked, "Are you one of them?"

You try to make yourself interesting. Almost all pastors get interrupted by the doorbell; they are giving away money or they are giving away food. They are like firemen; they respond to the alarm. And after about two times, I'd say, "Excuse me, but you don't value your time very much, do you?" "What do you mean?" "Well, I mean you just react. Do you react *all* the time? Or do you ever learn how to *act?*" You try to get into an argument, but with a sense of humor.

Asked how he would characterize the pastors politically as a group, Drake replied:

I'd say that anybody who chooses to be here, who's not here just to make a living, is an activist, and I think what they are involved in is *activism*. They confuse activism with action. But they would like to be involved in action; they think they are, but they are really just involved in activism. Activism is what you do in a movement, rather than what you do in a relevant power position. Movements are just activity, activity, activity to draw attention to the issues.

Power organizations are action and move an agenda. The agenda could be very broad: the agenda could be eight different issues at once. A movement is strictly just one issue. Activism is pouring blood on draft records because sitting-in didn't work. The newspapers are tired of taking shots of people sitting-in.

But this blood is kind of interesting, and they'll shoot that for about three times. And, after that, why, you got to cut your throat. It just gets more and more radical.

That's because you are drawing attention to the issues, which is valid, is a good kind of organizing, but eventually, if it hasn't succeeded, you get to the point where you probably have to go to court. And then struggle with the judge. That's the end of any kind of activity because the judge determines what is going to happen. All activity is frozen. There are a lot of activists who think that that is organizing.

Getting arrested is counterproductive in terms of power. And I am not saying that, for instance, the civil rights movement was not a good thing, or the antiwar movement. I spent my life there. However, it is easy to stop these movements. The way to stop those movements is to let the people win. So we'll give you the Civil Rights Act; now what the fuck are you going to do? You got it, now what are you going to do? [The movement] is disbanded. Or, I'll take your leader away from you; now what are you going to do?

It's an effective way to work if you are leading a guerrilla war, to win the war. Then you don't need broad-based power. You need a Ho Chi Minh, and people who will die for the leader. So it's a good strategy. But it does not work well in a democracy made up of diverse ethnic groups. I think it's great for Nicaragua. I don't think it works well here.

The specific skills needed to be a Lead Organizer are legion. Ed Chambers in a 1978 IAF-published pamphlet[12] offers this laundry list of essential leadership skills:

- how to make clear to yourself your self-interest;
- how to be an initiator rather than a reactor;
- how to listen to and affirm other people;
- how to distinguish between leaders and followers;
- how to identify and proposition current and potential leaders;
- how to run a meeting;
- how to hold members of your own networks accountable;
- how to hold other leaders accountable;
- how to raise money;

- how to analyze institutions (both your own and the ones you are up against);
- how to negotiate with other decision makers;
- how to run an action;
- how to run an evaluation of an action;
- how to pick issues so that you are not running into the biggest issues at the start;
- how to plan issue campaigns;
- how to develop realistic schedules;
- how to view and accept tension;
- how to live and grow with a *process* of dealing with issues rather than with the particular issue or task; and
- how to invite in new institutions and develop allies.

Nicholas von Hoffman, former *Washington Post* columnist and present muck-raking book author, was once an IAF organizer. In an article that was distributed in mimeographed form by Students for a Democratic Society (SDS) two decades ago and collected in a book of source material for community organizers by Eccklein and Lauffer, von Hoffman wrote of the perils of being an organizer, particularly a White organizer, entering a ghetto community:

Recognize the fact that the organizer who comes into the community for the first time is internally in a precarious position. He is afraid—or at least he should be if he has any brains that he doesn't want beaten out. . . . He is afraid because he is the bearer of a new idea. Mankind does not cotton to new ideas, in general, but especially not to the new ideas that organizers bring. This is so because they may mean trouble and because the organizer's mere presence in the community is a tacit insult. The organizer's presence says, in effect, "You are so dumb that you need me to think your way out of this mess you are in." Don't kid yourself about this. Nothing absolves the organizer of this sin.[13]

Jim Drake puts it this way:

The one thing you have to keep saying over and over if you are a good organizer is the organizer has no solutions. But he asks all the right questions. Do you want power? It's a good question. I can't tell you that I am going to give it to you, but, if your answer is yes, why, I'll tell you who you have to go see to get some. Who you have to go see is the pastor down the street. If you don't want to go there, I'll call him up, and we'll meet here. If you don't want to use your power, then fine, I won't bother you any more. I really don't care. I don't care about the South Bronx. I don't care if I'm here, or in Harlem, or in Watts. I don't care. I'm not going to be here four years from now. So why do I care about it? If you don't want to do it, fine, tell me now. It is a great liberating experience not to need to be anywhere. To know you got a job that is safe. Your profession is secure whether or not you succeed here. So you can take risks. As long as you are secure, you'll always succeed.

When Drake talks about his first action in the South Bronx, he is echoing Alinsky and Chambers and mirroring the strategy employed in the opening action of East Brooklyn Churches:

One thing I learned is that, when you start fighting with the city or whoever, make goddamn sure you are going to win, especially on your first fight. In fact, if I can fix it, I'll have a fixed fight first. I'll even do it with mirrors, so the people have the confidence that they are actually winning. The first fight we had [in the South Bronx] was to tear down a building. I wanted to make sure it could be done first.

Drakes believes that changes made by organizations like South Bronx Churches will become institutionalized:

SBC will be good for fifteen, twenty years. All our organizations have been around for decades. But the other part of it is we are very proud of the fact that our institution is an abstraction. It is not the real thing. The real thing is the parishes. The real power resides in St. Jerome's leaders becoming powerful enough to take on that public housing around their church. And we want to teach them how to do that. We are there to agitate them to do something about it. We are not going to do it for them. The power of SBC will be there for them if they need it; it's there. That is the *quid pro quo*. If they need forty churches to come to the support of St. Jerome's, well, forty will be there.[14]

7

South Bronx Civics: Morris High School

Before turning to a detailed account (in Part Three) of the successful drive to compel the city to surrender South Bronx land so that SBC could build hundreds of Nehemiah homes, it is worth pausing to review one other major SBC initiative. Of course, not all campaigns succeed; SBC's unavailing attempt to insert a foot into the door of local schools illustrates both its resourcefulness in mounting actions and, in this instance, its lack of ability to imaginatively build on early opportunities.

Morris High School dominates a hill in the heart of the South Bronx. From this commanding vantage point on clear mornings students who crunch through the bleak, rubble-strewn side streets on their way to school can look up and see gleaming in the sunlight the towers of the World Trade Center ten miles to the south in Manhattan's financial district.

Morris High, built at the turn of the century, is arguably the most impressive civic structure in the Bronx. This imposing gray brick, stone and terra-cotta building, the first secondary school established in the Bronx, was designed in the English Gothic style to resemble Trinity College in Cambridge. The soaring architecture fittingly reflects the grand aspirations Bronx citizens lodged in their schools.

Morris High School lies along Boston Road, which was once the principal stagecoach route from Boston to Washington via New York City. In 1990, the central tower of the school was shrouded in scaffolding because Morris, which had been slated to be demolished a few years before, was now in the midst of a multimillion-dollar refurbishing. Unfortunately, like other local efforts at rebuilding, the job became stalled, tangled in red tape and, it is rumored, corruption. All work on the rehabilitation had ground to a halt, leaving the scaffolding rusting in place, and the school roof leaking profusely, compounding the damage to the well-worn structure.

The immediate neighborhood surrounding the school offers a depressing and comprehensive display of urban ruin. Gutted apartment buildings with yawning holes instead of windows line both sides of Boston Road, One block away, seven hundred, previously homeless men live in an abandoned armory. There are five-story buildings with a few lower-rise structures interspersed with a forlorn little "vest-pocket" park and rubble-filled lots where more apartments and stores once stood. Most of the remaining red brick structures are battered but grandly detailed and encrusted with elaborate terra-cotta relief. Beautiful limestone carvings decorate the entryways and cornices, totally girding the buildings' entire first floor. Often the walls of the lobbies are encased in luxurious Carrara marble, the ceilings are patterned tin, and the now-chipped floors, mosaic tile. The tarnished mailboxes, punched-in and useless, are made of brass. It is said that practically all of these apartments were built by immigrant Italians, who were skilled masons and painstaking craftsmen. Now most of these once-splendid buildings have had their entrances bricked up and their windows shattered. Often the crude cinder-block barriers that seal the front doors have been punctured, offering convenient access for junkies or neighborhood children who might want to play inside the building.

Boston Road has a wide-open feeling that is not typical of most inner-city neighborhoods in New York. Expansive sky arches overhead, and traffic is curiously light on the wide street. Even buildings that look abandoned often have women with children sitting on the stoops. There are delicatessens, wash-and-dry places, a few bars, candy stores, a barber shop, a liquor store. Many of these businesses occupy the ground floors of otherwise vacant buildings. Most striking about the neighborhood, though, is the enormous number of store-front churches, almost one on every block.

The present scene of disheartening desolation would have been inconceivable to the builders of Morris High in the early 1900s. A sense of the unbounded optimism of the earlier time is vividly displayed in the dedication speech delivered by Nicholas Murray Butler, the President of Columbia University. The construction of Morris, the first high school in the Bronx, was a milestone for the borough. Speaking of the South Bronx in 1904, Butler gushed, "This community . . . is building slowly, little by little, a city beautiful, a city convenient, a city truly great and everlasting, intellectually and spiritually." His ambition for the Bronx did not stop there: "If our city is to be made great and memorable, it will be because we succeed in placing it by the side of Jerusalem, Athens, and Rome as an intellectual and spiritual capital.[1]

Since the deterioration of the South Bronx began accelerating twenty-five or so years ago, there have been a number of efforts, springing from both government agencies and local community development groups, to battle the devastation. Almost all of these initiatives deal with housing and drug addiction, which are the two most visible symptoms of the community's decay. Less energy is devoted to the schools, although the problems there are immense and the unmet potential staggering.

The systemic problems of New York City schools are legendary and are succinctly summarized by Richard C. Wade, the urban historian:

> The school system is in . . . disarray. Its physical structures are so decrepit that they compromise its educational mission. The Board of Education bureaucracy in Brooklyn has raised paralysis to an art form. Local boards, with few exceptions, are riddled with corruption and mired in mediocrity. Custodians and principals, hugging old regulations to protect old perquisites, mock change and frustrate reform.

> Conditions in the classroom make serious teaching almost impossible and discourage recruiting of the kind of talent that once made New York the nation's flagship school system.

> And outside the buildings, drugs, gangs and weapons threaten the safety of teachers and students. Even the most imaginative new chancellor will need billions of dollars to turn the system around.[2]

New York City is divided into thirty-two school districts, and the South Bronx encompasses parts of four of these subdivisions.[3] Each district is governed by an elected school board, which has responsibility for school affairs from K–8. The South Bronx districts regularly post some of the lowest reading scores and highest dropout rates in the city.[4] A number of the Bronx boards have been plagued with scandal, and it is widely acknowledged that the quality of educational leadership they provide has been severely compromised.

Although the community boards were created to foster decentralization and community control in the wake of crippling demonstrations and disruption by community activists in the late 1960s, only a tiny minority of South Bronx citizens participate in local control of their schools. In the 1989 local school-board election, fewer than 3 percent of the eligible voters in some districts cast ballots.

This made it easy for the highly organized teachers' union to dominate the local decision-making process.[5] This lack of genuine
community involvement opens a yawning power vacuum, yet surprisingly few grass-roots groups have been mobilized to exploit the
situation.

The high schools, which have a larger measure of autonomy,
are administered by the notorious Central Board of Education at 110
Livingston Street in Brooklyn. This means that any effort to improve
Morris High would have to win approval by the sitting principal and
administration of Morris as well as the central office.

In 1988 Rev. John Heinemeier was invited, along with a number of other clergy, to a meeting at Morris High. Acting Interim Principal Michael Simmons was attempting to reach out to community
people to see if they could assist in bridging the gap between the Morris professional staff and the parents of Morris's student body.
Though only three pastors attended, that meeting inadvertently
planted a seed that brought Morris High School to the attention of
South Bronx Churches.

Heinemeier, along with other leaders from South Bronx
Churches, hatched a plan to bring their organizing skills to Morris
and begin a formal collaboration between the school and the community. During the rest of 1988 and through the spring of 1989,
South Bronx Churches met perhaps a half dozen times with administrators at Morris in an attempt to secure permission to begin an initiative at the school. On 24 April 1989, they finally won the
opportunity to meet with Dr. Victor Herbert, Executive Director of
New York City's high schools. He was the one person who could
brush aside bureaucratic obstacles and allow the church group to
press forward. This was the opportunity they were waiting for. Confrontation is ordinarily one of SBC's most important and, perhaps,
indispensable tactics, but in this crucial meeting they wanted to seduce the central office decision maker, engage in what they called "a
dance of courtship," and win his approval.

The meeting with Dr. Herbert was held in the huge, peeling,
and antiquated office of the principal at Morris. Arrayed around a
battered conference table were Simmons, a former assistant principal in charge of the school for the 1988–89 school year but not eligible to be the permanent principal; Irene Fitzgerald, an assistant
principal who, in that September, would be appointed the new pro-
bationary principal; two other Morris administrators; and the contingent from South Bronx Churches. The church group was led by
Rev. John Heinemeier and included Jim Drake, SBC's Lead Orga-

nizer, two other full-time organizers from the group, and three community residents, one with a child presently at Morris.[6]

After introductions and opening pleasantries, Heinemeier drove straight to the point. He said that his group had been to many meetings with Morris officials through the previous fall and early spring and numerous times had patiently explained their plan to begin the process of revitalizing Morris. Looking straight at Herbert, he bluntly asked, "What we want to know now is, where does the buck finally stop? Here?"

Herbert, who appeared to be in his late fifties, was impeccably dressed and unfailingly polite and precise. His natty appearance and polished manner set him apart from most school people. He cautiously responded, "That depends on what you want." He said that he was familiar with the work of the Industrial Areas Foundation. He went on to mention that he had previously dealt with a half dozen community groups that were beginning to organize in high schools, principally around postgraduation job issues. He said he enthusiastically welcomed any employment opportunities that such groups could provide to youngsters in his schools.

He was referring to the fact that, in recent years, some corporations have "adopted" selected high schools by making available extra funding, supplementing the teaching staff by lending some of their own employees to the school, and capping the deal with offers of entry-level jobs to graduates who have met certain conditions such as faithful attendance and proficiency in math.[7]

Unfortunately, the results of these initiatives have been largely disappointing, principally because proffered jobs went unclaimed when graduates were unable to pass basic skills tests. Herbert also may have been mindful that a predecessor in his job, Dr. Frank Smith, was unceremoniously driven from office when corporations and newspapers loudly complained that the good-faith efforts of the private sector to help the schools had been thwarted by an almost comically inept central school bureaucracy which had been unable to connect youngsters with thousands of available summer jobs.

Edging away from an early commitment to jobs, Heinemeier responded,

> We are not positive that our principal concentration will be employment just yet. We want to start where we begin in all our organizing efforts. We propose to initiate two hundred one-on-one relational meetings with members of the Morris High community. We propose two hundred encounters between trained

SBC organizers, many of whom are local community people, and from the Morris community: eighty parents, eighty students, thirty teachers, and ten administrators. The meetings are with the purpose of really meaning it when we say "collaborative." It is a process of community people working for the betterment of a particular school. All elements have to be a party to these discussions.

One-on-one meetings are, of course, at the heart of SBC's *modus operandi.*

Undeterred, Herbert continued to press for more detail, but Heinemeier was evasive. He asserted, "We have to trust in that process [of one-on-one meetings]. Out of that process of really listening and engaging, a direction will be set for an enhancement of Morris." He said that to prejudge that direction now, to predict the results, would compromise the integrity of the individual meetings.

Herbert continued to probe. He asked, "Is there an instrument of some kind that you will be using. What is the purpose of the conversations?" Heinemeier, still doing all the talking for SBC, responded by saying that the two hundred encounters were not a mere survey: "that is not the essence of relational meetings. It is really two people trading energy, history, ideas."

Herbert remained unconvinced. Prudence dictated that he needed to know more about SBC's specific agendas, both overt and hidden, before he was going to allow the doors of one of his schools to be swung open to an aggressive and controversial political group.

At this point Tony Aguilar, a thirty-year-old, Black, full-time organizer for SBC, picked up the ball:

> I talk to people in public housing all the time, trying to organize them. I have learned that if you want to empower people, if you want to get them to do something, the people who are affected by the conditions must have a sense of ownership. This is where we differ from past community efforts to organize schools. Other groups had a focus, namely employment, and they went into the schools with that agenda. Now this may be one of our eventual focuses, but for now we want to try a different approach—one of listening to the Morris people first. What we will be doing is entering uncharted territory. Listening first, and then we will determine a direction. And, by the way, one of the things we will be listening for is to determine if there is enough *will* among the Morris community to become engaged. If there are not significant numbers who want to do something then we won't.

Herbert, who had once been a Jesuit priest as well as a teacher at Morris earlier in his career, then shifted gears. "Why Morris High School; why not begin in the earlier grades?" he asked plausibly. Heinemeier conceded, "From these meetings we may see that this is not the way to go." He reminded them, "The original impetus for this effort came from Morris itself, as an attempt to deal with the dropout problem. I was invited along with two or three other clergy to begin exploring how parental involvement with the school could be enhanced." He then elaborated on the importance of Morris:

Morris was the first high school in the Bronx and large numbers of students from our congregations go here. As you may know, we have forty-five congregations that are part of SBC. Morris will be a control school. For better or for worse, we want to see if we can learn from an engagement with Morris. We would learn more here than anywhere else. We want to try to work in a microcosm rather than tackle the macrocosm. Instead of working at improvement in all of Morris' twenty-two feeder schools, we want to see if we can do something significant for one.

Candidly, he continued, "The question really is what can we learn from a disciplined and systematic collaboration between the community and the school?"

Another SBC activist added that he didn't want to write off high-school kids and be forced to conclude that there was hope for students only if intervention is begun earlier. This struck a nerve, and Herbert cracked open the door, "I agree. This is not a lost generation. I certainly don't believe that it is. I welcome your desire to work with Morris."

Still, he hesitated and stepped back, "But how does it get done without being intrusive? The logistics are unclear. To what end will these meetings lead? You must have some intuitive feelings about the likely conclusions and their consequences." He returned to his central objection: "It is hard for me to accede without seeing where this process may take us." Mr. Simmons, the acting principal, apparently thinking out loud, began to try to fit the proposal into a bureaucratic schema: "When you compile information, will it go to some standing committee . . . and what would happen then? Where are we heading?"

At this point, Jim Drake reassured the group, "I understand your feeling. Your question," he said, "is what the pastors always ask me first. 'What is the program?' It's a hard question. The best answer is we really won't know until we have a relationship of trust, and out of that we can build something. He has to understand my interests, and I have to understand his."

Drake then shifted gears: "The present strategy is based on conversations with other activist groups who have attempted to broker the relationship between schools and corporations hungry for skilled entry-level graduates." Drake said he was told by these other groups that, in retrospect, "They wish they had more understanding of the parents and the kids before they set goals and made commitments. We need to hear from the creative people in this school. The banks are after us to get qualified young people. But we are holding them off until we understand more."

Aguilar summed up their position succinctly: "We want to get facts first, and then have a thesis." Herbert's resolve was melting, and he admitted, "That *is* novel."

Driving the point home, Maria Verona, another full-time organizer with SBC and the mother of several South Bronx high-school students, said with emotion, "I'm talking as a parent. There are few times that parents or kids are asked for their ideas. This is a way for all of us to listen to what people really think. We need to have trust with each other. We want to begin to establish that trust."

Wavering, Herbert asked about logistics and was told that the two-or three-week training for SBC organizers could begin in September. Heinemeier invited any interested teachers and other staff from Morris to participate in the training. Heinemeier said that the next round, the two hundred individual meetings, could be completed in perhaps two months. "We will have twenty of our best leaders each doing ten individual one-on-ones," he told Herbert and the other school people. "Out of our confidence in this process—the good faith in hearing each other out—will emerge some direction for the improvement of Morris."

As if on cue, another SBC activist, Sister Rosemary O'Donnell, a tiny white-haired nun, spoke for the first time and offered inspiring testimony. "I know that out of this process will emerge leaders— parents, students and teachers." Everyone who makes a career in the South Bronx recognizes that, in the late sixties and seventies when the neighborhoods turned dangerous, almost all who could manage to flee did so. Even bedrock institutions, such as churches and the YMCA, pulled up stakes. Among the few institutions that stayed the course was the Catholic Church. The central dioceses kept virtually all the churches and schools opened, heated, and lit. Among the heroic and committed people who remained for the two decades and more of the catastrophic devastation of the South Bronx were Catholic school nuns. This abiding fact gave weight to Sister Rosemary's words when she said with emotion, "I have never experienced ecumenism like I've found at SBC. Different churches who never talked with one another before have come together." The nun continued, "I know a similar thing can happen here. With this trust, beautiful things can come to light. I've seen it happen with the leaders of various churches combining their vision. My trust in the process has been affirmed."

By this point, SBC had won the day. The rest of the meeting was spent thrashing out Herbert's caveats, like cautioning against merely collecting teachers' "war stories" or precipitously going to the press with negative findings.

With everything beginning to sound so rosy, Heinemeier felt compelled to inject some *real politic* considerations. He reminded the group, "Trust does not stand or fall on a difference of opinion. We *will* have differences of opinion and perspective. Our collaboration can survive when there is good faith around the table. We have seen that in SBC with all its different denominations and ethnic and racial groups. All this makes for a lively encounter."

When Herbert concluded, "I don't think what you are asking is unreasonable," it was a startling breakthrough. The central office had given permission to an outside activist group to talk with the students, staff, and parents of a faltering ghetto school and presumably to stir up emotions and press for change.

Why did Herbert acquiesce to this risky proposal?

Given the complicated dynamics of the situation, the chances that a South Bronx high school could be improved significantly by enacting minor changes is vanishingly remote. Layering on another program (for instance, a bank-teller training effort financed by a local savings and loan) would not amount to much of a change. Indeed, Morris now offers a staggering array of overlapping programs and special projects.[8]

Despite this shotgun approach, the pupil performance statistics for Morris are disheartening. The average daily attendance hovers at 69.9 percent, although this is a huge improvement from a decade ago. Only a bare majority (56.3 percent) of the students pass the Regents Competency Test in Mathematics, a low-skills exam which is a requirement for graduation in New York State. A dismally low 57 percent of ninth graders are promoted to grade 10.[9] Morris' official annual dropout rate is 13.2 percent, but that number is deceptive. New York City has such a complex and obfuscating method of calculating its dropout figures that the numbers yielded are more misleading than illuminating. A perhaps more enlightening statistic in this regard is that, out of a student body of roughly 1500, only a mere 125 students emerge each year from their stay at Morris with high-school diplomas, their tickets to being integrated in New York City's economy.

It might be argued that, to make any real impact on the serious problems Morris High youngsters face in obtaining an education, only fundamental change in the school raises any realistic hope. Yet a push for such change might evoke bitter resistance from entrenched forces, especially if the impetus for such modification comes from outside the school. From this point of view, SBC's proposed intervention might be a recipe for disaster.

Yet, with conditions so bleak, it can be argued that Herbert has had little to lose by allowing an outside agency to take a crack at improvement. This certainly had not been a banner year for Bronx schools in general, as they came under unexpected and withering media scrutiny. The school district where Morris is located has some of the lowest reading scores in the city. According to the *New York Times* it is "a district with problems and recurring allegations of patronage and misuse of funds."[10] In 1989 a number of school board members were indicted by a grand jury on charges of bribery and for theft of school property. Also garnering grisly headlines was the jailing of Matthew Barnwell, a local principal, who was arrested for buying crack from an undercover narcotics officer. From this vantage point, it might seem irresponsible to turn away an indigenous group composed of the local established religious leadership which has volunteered to help the school by encouraging parents to participate in their children's education, especially when the group has a proven ability to engage widespread citizen involvement in community improvement.[11]

Alternatively, it is even possible that the decision to permit SBC to try its hand at reform may have sprung from the cynical calculation that the troubles of schools like Morris are so intractable that they inevitably wear down everyone, both sagacious insiders and idealistic outsiders, and, therefore, any effort presents little risk of fundamentally disturbing the school's inertia.

In any case, this effort, blessed by the director of New York City's high schools, to grant an assertive nonschool group the latitude to cultivate parent and student leaders and involve them in redesigning an historic inner-city high school in the South Bronx represented a novel approach to grappling with the failure of our urban schools to educate their students.[12]

Morris Outcome

Regrettably, the effort by South Bronx Churches to collaborate with parents, staff, and students at Morris High School got off to a stumbling start in the autumn of 1989.

In a meeting with the wary new principal, Irene Fitzgerald, during the first week of classes on 6 September 1989, a schedule was hammered out that called for training sessions for community residents who wanted to work with the Morris community to begin in late September, followed by the school's release of lists of Morris students and parents who would be likely candidates for the two hundred one-on-ones.[13] This effort marked a fundamental departure in standard IAF strategy. Instead of making the school a target and going after it like gangbusters, SBC was going to try to make an ally out of the school administration.

During the meeting, Fitzgerald asked if the training sessions would be open to any Morris staffers who might want to participate in the sessions designed to train volunteers for the one-on-ones. Seizing the opportunity to generate good will, Tony Aguilar, who was directing the Morris project for SBC, and Rev. John Heinemeier both enthusiastically welcomed the suggestion. Fitzgerald said she had told her staff that her goals for the academic year were to improve both student attendance and achievement, and she embraced any push that SBC could supply to "supplement, but not supplant those goals."

Later in the meeting Heinemeier identified "two new ingredients" in the proposed collaboration with Morris. "We seek a deliberate interaction on the part of the [local South Bronx] community with Morris." He reminded Fitzgerald that originally it was Morris that "sought out a community exchange. Now we will bring that forward in a disciplined way. Community leaders will be interchanging with the school family." He continued, "And secondly, professional organizers, who are at our disposal, can keep the newly trained local leaders at their task."

Fitzgerald seemed uneasy and reluctant throughout the meeting and finally blurted out her fears. "The use of the words 'professional organizers,' " she began slowly, "disturbs us most. Are these people coming from our kids' community? We have difficulty bringing in our students' parents to the school now. We are certainly not looking for people from the community who want to use the kids and parents for their own needs. And, let's face it, you are coming to us because you have your own needs." Aguilar tried to smooth the waters, asking, "Are you concerned that we are looking to run Morris? We certainly don't want to. We want to hear ideas from the Morris community and then help implement them. This is not a power play." Fitzgerald, perhaps protesting too much, countered, "I don't fear a power struggle. I'm not afraid of you usurping power I don't fear shared decision making. I just want to be clear about the direction this process will take." Then she conceded, "There is much that can be enhanced in regard to community involvement. We welcome more parent involvement."[14]

Heinemeier picked up the ball:

> "Our premise is not that Morris will be improved by an approach that merely asks the school community to be an information dispenser. Morris stands to improve significantly by a process that proceeds in trust. We seek a creative and effective role to play. It would be false to the process to predict its outcome before it begins. We want Morris to say to the community: "We invite you to work intensely with us on improvement of this school."

Heinemeier and his SBC colleagues were not being evasive about anticipated outcomes. They really did not have a clear notion of where they wanted to lead the school. In the preliminary strategy meeting of the organizers before the session with Fitzgerald, they asked themselves how they could best prepare for this experiment with schools. Heinemeier questioned the half dozen SBC leaders gathered in the basement of his residence behind St. John's Lutheran Church, "What kind of training and exposure do we want for this Morris task force? What reading should we do?" Should we be visiting model high schools? What educational leaders should we be having discussions with?" No one around the table had any real answers.

There was a sense that SBC would just proceed as it does in non-school organizing efforts. They would employ the one-on-ones to unearth leaders and fire the enthusiasm of participants. Initial discussion with the two hundred parents and students at Morris would pinpoint specific, concrete, short-range, accomplishable tasks that would be identified by the Morris community itself. In classic IAF fashion, they would then build on these modest improvements to earn credibility and amass power. Beyond that the future was cloudy; this genuinely would be an undertaking that broke new ground for them.

In late September and into October, SBC leaders Jim Drake and Tony Aguilar presided over three evening training sessions held at weekly intervals in the basement of St. Augustine's Roman Catholic church a few blocks west of Morris. In attendance were an average of twenty-five people including, surprisingly, almost a dozen Morris staffers. By the third session, many in the group were anxious to begin the one-on-ones and define a broader strategy. During the September 6th meeting, Fitzgerald promised to give Tony Aguilar lists of likely students and parents to contact, but, when the time came, she reneged.

SBC settled for beginning the one-on-one relational meetings with Morris faculty because SBC had ready access to teachers from the staffers in the training group. Quickly a perception grew that the one-on-ones were not generating much of a sense of momentum. Though some Morris teachers readily agreed to sit for them, they were puzzled by the encounter itself. This is partly because the meetings were without agendas and didn't build to a climax or seem to have a discernible purpose. Some teachers who had been contacted a number of times by different activists declined to participate in yet another meeting.

Fitzgerald's passive resistance flowered into ill-concealed hostility. By the winter SBC had pulled back and postponed formulating a new strategy specifically aimed at countering the noncooperation of the school administration.

SBC's forte has always been organizing large numbers of people to pressure various levels of government and sometimes the private sector into delivering needed resources. At SBC they knew even before the aborted one-on-ones began that the dilapidated condition of the school structure itself was a major concern of staff, parents, and students. In February 1990, SBC secured a commitment from the School Construction Authority to accelerate plans for the rehabilitation of the interior of Morris. Heinemeier contended that, in the early autumn, he had told Fitzgerald that SBC was going to intercede with the School Construction Authority but was cautioned by the principal that it would be fruitless. Despite the successful outcome, "Fitzgerald was miffed that we met with them."[15]

Although the interior of Morris is still shabby and Heinemeier asserts that it must be demoralizing for students to try to learn under such conditions, SBC's strategy does raise an important point. How, exactly, does the delivery of additional resources, as useful as they may be for many reasons, impact on student learning outcomes?[16] Clearly, Morris will be a more inviting place to attend when years of neglected or deferred maintenance are remedied. But is that likely to have a major impact on the education of its average student?

What would be the likely educational result for the average Morris student even if SBC is successful in delivering a windfall of additional resources?

SBC could no longer defer the basic question: Where do they want to lead the school? Indeed, what does it really mean to "turn around" a troubled ghetto school? A useful frame for thinking about this fundamental problem is suggested by educational scholar Mary Anne Raywid.[17]

Raywid looks at the last decade of school reform and argues persuasively that three distinct categories of educational change have emerged. She dubs them *pseudo-reform, incremental reform,* and *reform by restructuring.* Raywid does not define the first category, pseudo-reform in a pejorative way, because "some pseudo-reforms are very much needed and desirable." In this category, she places school building repair: "necessary and important, yes,: but reform, no. Fixing buildings may be essential, but it is a long way from transforming what takes place in classrooms."

The second, more ambitious type of change is incremental reform. "These typically represent serious efforts at changing classrooms for one group of youngsters or within one sphere of educational activity." Many of Morris auxiliary services, such as the jobs furnished by the privately funded office of New York Working at the school, would fall into this category. As welcome as these opportunities are, they tend not to make significant impact globally on essential student outcomes. The explanation for this, according to Raywid, is,

> Schools are notoriously difficult to change. One major reason is their interconnectedness. It appears, as several reformers have noted, that in order to change almost *anything* of significance in schools, a great deal must be changed.[18] The reason is that everything is connected to everything else. Schools are very like jigsaw puzzles with their interlocking pieces. It is impossible to modify any one piece without also altering all of those surrounding it—which in turn necessitates changing successive rings of pieces increasingly farther from where one began.[19]

After reviewing the evidence, she concludes that few researchers have found that this incremental approach has lowered dropout rates or raised test scores or made any other significant modifications to ghetto schools.

Absorbing the lesson that half-way measures would not make much of a dent took time for reform-minded practitioners, but around 1986 the Excellence Movement, according to Raywid, began to focus on the more systemic changes involved in restructuring schools. These more far-reaching proposals, in turn, can be divided into two further branches, Raywid argues: one focusing on site-based management, and the other on creating schools of choice. She is not optimistic about site-based management because "the research to date suggests that it often becomes just one more committee, involving only a small percentage of a school's teachers . . . nor does it appear to have much effect on instruction."

In Raywid's view, only genuine schools of choice hold out real promise. The heart of this strategy lies in

> officials freeing and supporting teachers to design and implement distinctive programs from among which families can choose. The roles of all teachers change immediately upon acceptance of the invitation (not the assignment) to become designers and innovators and to share responsibility with colleagues rather than working alone. The roles of families also undergo immediate and individual change, as they exercise the opportunity to select among a variety of programs.

Restructuring Morris by somehow transforming it into one or more schools of choice would at least increase the involvement of parents in schools affairs. Raywid offers direct evidence that suggests this would be a promising option.[20]

By 1990, South Bronx churches fell back in retreat. It was not merely that an obstructionist principal prevented progress—in truth having a clearly defined enemy is a plus in IAF-style organizing[21]—it was more that SBC did not have a coherent vision for schools. The pragmatic dream of affordable housing was created in alliance with trail-blazing building expert I. D. Robbins, and, at this stage of the school struggle, there was no I. D. Robbins of education.

Meanwhile, EBC in Brooklyn was further along in thinking about involvement with public schools. They had launched Nehemiah II, which was intended to be the next step after the homes were built, and a home-owning revitalized community began to sink deep roots. The original thrust was to work on motivating students to learn in school by offering them a job after they graduated. EBC was to act as a broker between corporations with available entry level positions and two of the worst high schools in the city: Bushwick and Jefferson. Criteria were established: good attendance and certain defined levels of academic achievement in exchange for jobs or college scholarships. In the end, so few students met the minimal standards that the program was judged a failure.

The inescapable conclusion drawn from this disappointing work with Morris and the two Brooklyn high schools was that, perhaps, working from within to reform institutions as complicated and inert as ghetto secondary schools was a fool's errand.

What kind of school would flourish in such devastated neighborhoods where so many students came from chaotic households?

The answer was hidden in the open. There are schools that work, that serve youngsters and families in the South Bronx, and that offer a future grounded in a solid education. They are the Catholic schools that have remained through all the wrenching changes of the last thirty years.

What is their secret? Researchers identify three bedrock components: Catholic schools are small, and each student is known by teachers; there is a consistent set of standards and accompanying high expectations for young people—all students take a demanding academic curriculum, with an emphasis on shaping character as well as minds; and the schools are run independently, without the smothering solicitude of a central bureaucracy.

What would happen if SBC took the proven principals of Catholic schools and established a new school incorporating these rules for success? Are these principles transferable to public schools?

Critics point out that comparisons of private schools with public schools are unfair because Catholic schoolchildren have, by definition, involved parents who sacrifice to pay tuition. Moreover, Catholic schools have the luxury of expelling troublemakers.

Involved, organized parents are no problem for SBC; they come with the territory. Expelling students from a publicly-financed school would be impossible. Yet the actual number of students thrown out of Catholic schools is tiny, and so perhaps that is not such a critical factor.

In point of fact, there is a widely heralded public school just across the Harlem River from the South Bronx that is based on the same principles as Catholic inner-city schools. It is Deborah Meier's Central Park East Secondary School which graduates 71 percent of its ninth-grade class in four years compared to the citywide average of 38.9 percent.

The core beliefs underlying the school are that: "smaller schools in which everyone knows everyone combat violence and lowers dropout rates while raising intellectual expectations, [and] students and teachers do better when they chose the school where they want to be."[22]

At the time of the derailed Morris effort, New York City hired a new School Chancellor, Joseph A. Fernandez, who lasted three years before he was fired in 1993, but who, as a parting legacy, cobbled together a plan for creating numerous small experimental high schools. Fernandez was aggressively courted by EBC from the day he began work in New York, and it was in collaboration with community groups like EBC (and unions like District Council 37 of the American Federation of State, County, and Municipal Employees and businesses like American Express) as well as educational theorists that the plan to extend the success of inner-city Catholic schools and public schools like Central Park East was devised.

In March 1993 the Board of Education approved the creation of an unprecedented thirty new high schools which opened with a ninth grade in September in 1994 and which will add a new grade every year after that until the schools reach the manageable number of 500 hundred students. The schools are based on themes and will have students studying science, for instance, by organizing a neighborhood measles vaccination campaign (El Puente Academy in Williamsburg, Brooklyn) or working with a curriculum based on the study of New York City's bridges, subways, and physical infrastructure. This latter project would be in conjunction with the School for the Physical City, a collaboration of Cooper Union and Outward Bound. Deborah Meier is heading the effort to replace the failing Julia Richmond High School in Manhattan with six smaller theme-based schools. East Brooklyn Congregations is collaborating on two new high schools in East New York and Bushwick, and SBC is backing a high school geared to community organizing in the South Bronx.

This collaboration with a new smaller-scale high school is another foray into uncharted waters for IAF, but it is a logical outgrowth of the effort to establish pockets of stability in areas like the South Bronx and allow people to participate directly in institutions that affect their lives.

This toehold in public schools is possible because there is a growing community of Nehemiah homeowners in the South Bronx. The struggle that touched success when the first proud South Bronx residents moved into their own homes in 1993 can be traced to a pivotal moment four earlier when the blasted streets of the Bronx were thronged with angry organized citizens.

III

✳

South Bronx Case Study

8

Here We Will Build!

At the convergence of three once-bustling streets in the heart of the South Bronx lies the ruined carcass of the Bronx Borough Courthouse. This elaborate Beaux Arts structure was built in 1906 when the Bronx was just beginning to prosper and civic pride demanded an appropriately grandiose seat of justice. The American Institute of Architects hails this structure as "a monument as well as a building." And notes, "In spite of many decades of smoke, grime, neglect and the rattling of the now-gone Third Avenue El,[1] it remains grand, even though its windows are missing, its metal work tarnished and its walls covered with soot."[2] Atop the huge arched entrance which, like all the ground-level windows, is crudely barricaded with cinder blocks and scrawled with graffiti, sits sculptor G. E. Roine's gleaming, white, twice life-sized, leaf-crowned statue of Justice which stares out blankly across Third Avenue to the equally impressive and ornate Church of Sts. Peter and Paul, built a few years before 1906. Hung on the grit-burnished limestone base of the courthouse is the familiar pink and blue sign of the Federal Community Development Program (FCDP), beloved by politicians because it gives them the opportunity to display their names and so claim credit for various municipal construction projects. In this case, instead of raising the hope that this powerful old building would be restored to splendor, the sign perversely boasts that the only change the City of New York is able to render to this magnificent landmark is the *"Seal Up* of Former Night Court." Without irony, the sign proclaims that this grand community development effort—bricking up the doors and windows to prevent enterprising junkies and (what are called in local parlance) "finishers" from stealing the pipes—occurred during the administration of Mayor Edward Koch.[3] Under His Honor's name is that of Stanley Simon, the former Bronx Borough President, who resides these days in federal prison, along with his political mentor, the previous Bronx Borough Democratic Leader, Stanley Friedman, who is serving time for conspiracy, racketeering, and mail fraud, and the senior Congressional leader from the Bronx, Mario Biaggi, also a prison inmate.

Across Third Avenue, adjacent to the church, on the weathered but immaculately clean limestone wall of the Catholic parish school of St. Peter and Paul is another sign. This one declares that this is a *"School of Excellence, 1985–86, U.S. Department of Education."* The striking difference between these two symbols, one of government neglect and ineptitude and the other of church-inspired hope and accomplishment, offers a vision of how the South Bronx can be resuscitated and also illuminates obstacles that must be hurdled before the process of renewal can slip into gear.

An examination of this struggle for revival perhaps best can be begun by recounting what happened in the three rubble-strewn, blocks directly across the street from the church in early April 1989. In this desolate setting the first pitched battle was waged over the future of this neighborhood.

In that month dozens of church-based groups, organized by South Bronx Churches and tempered by a number of fixed fights, clashed with the lethargic government of New York City that, after more than two decades of aloof disregard, was finally stirring. The war was over efforts to restore these blocks which once were filled with apartment houses, stores, and lively throngs of people. This barren stretch of the South Bronx is centrally located real estate, minutes from Manhattan by public transportation. In its present condition on the edge of a particularly malignant, crack-infested district, it is difficult to imagine a less promising plot, but the cycles of development make it inevitable that, at some point, this empty land will be restored to residential use. There is no disagreement that housing, which is in perilously short supply in the city and acutely so in the South Bronx, is the only sane policy goal for this land. The question in contention is, as it has seldom been before in the Bronx, *housing for whom?*

The city wants to build 350 condominiums in three- and four-story town houses on the 4.2 acres of these three cleared blocks. The municipal plan for this site is just a minor part of a startlingly ambitious renewal effort city officials have dubbed Melrose Commons, a development that the city projects will eventually blanket forty surrounding acres. This, in turn, is only one aspect of a mammoth ten-year, $5.1 billion citywide program to build and rehabilitate housing for low- and middle-income families that Mayor Edward I. Koch calls his "pride and joy."[4]

Rather than multistory condos, South Bronx Churches wants instead to construct ninety two-story owner-occupied rowhouses on the three square blocks behind the church. Former City Housing Commissioner Abraham Biderman argued that this is really a dispute about density and the most productive use of this vacant land: "Does it make sense to build 70 affordable homes when you can build 350?"[5]

To resolve that question, on a sunny April 2nd in 1989 the relentlessly efficient organizing efforts of South Bronx Churches filled these bulldozed stretches with thousands of people who gathered in knots under banners of forty Catholic and Protestant churches. The scale of the rally was unprecedented. As Father Jim Connally, the long-term pastor of Sts. Peter and Paul, said in awe a few days later, "The last time I've seen so many people out in the South Bronx was back in the seventies when the Pope came to Yankee Stadium."[6] The congregations of these forty churches, which only a few decades ago would have been almost entirely Irish, German, and Italian, are now exclusively Hispanic and Black. The tens of thousands of Jews who once lived in the now destroyed buildings are also only a memory on these streets.[7]

At the rally the angry crowd fanned out from the south facade of the Gothic church where a temporary stage and podium were set up and where fiery speeches merged florid religious imagery with blood-pumping class antagonism.

Perhaps the most electrifying speaker that afternoon was Rev. John L. Heinemeier, pastor of St. John's Lutheran Church, which is ten blocks to the north in the Morrisania section of the South Bronx.

Rev. Heinemeier does not fit the stereotype of a fire-and-brimstone ghetto preacher. Indeed, main-line Protestant denominations like the Lutherans are frequently derided as "the Frozen Chosen" by Black Baptists and others who specialize in igniting powerful emotional response in their worship services. Yet earlier that day, he warmed up for the rally with a stem-winding sermon that shook the rafters. His church is in a particularly bleak section of the South Bronx, squeezed near a recently built, utterly disconcerting windowless junior high that, in its 1960s Brutalist style, resembles a maximum-security penitentiary, as well as Bronx Lebanon Hospital, where 1988 random blood testing of emergency room patients revealed that a staggering 23 percent were infected with the AIDS virus.[8]

At his 11:00 A.M. service, roughly seventy Black parishioners of all ages were galvanized as he railed against city officials and painted a vivid vision of the housing that South Bronx Churches wants to build on the parcel, designated on city maps as Site 404. He began slowly, almost softly: "South Bronx Churches wants to build homes on Site 404, not apartments. *Single-family homes.*" he emphasized with exaggerated deliberation, savoring every word. "Homes that have a front yard where you can park your car and a backyard where you can barbecue. Homes that have a full basement that you can fix up and party in." His pace accelerating, he continued to sketch out the dream: "Homes with two [*pause*] even three bedrooms. And these homes will sell to our people for a little over $43,000. You have to put about $5,000 down, and the monthly payment would be about $380."[9]

His voice rose and, in an abrupt shift in tone, dripped with contempt as he continued,

> The leaders of this city, just like the Pharisees and Sadducees are extremely jealous of that. Because it shames them. *Their* developers, the ones who build *their* apartments, are the ones who contribute more as a single group to their reelection campaigns than any other group in the city. Their developers receive $20,000 to $25,000 on each apartment they build. Our developers will receive $1,000 per single family home. And they are grabbing the best piece of land on which to build, Site 404.

He pounded home a class-driven analysis to his parishioners, most of whom live in the mammoth and dangerous Claremont Village public-housing project which sprawls through a large section of this neighborhood.[10] And to this audience, keenly receptive to any hope of improved housing, he continued, "And *they* asked The Partnership, that's Chase Manhattan Bank, American Express, and the Rockefeller Family and folks like them to build *condos* on Site 404 to sell for over $100,000 each!" Gesturing dramatically, with his robust voice echoing off the vaulted ceilings, he roared, "Condos, not homes. Apartments! People on top of you; people below you; people over here; people over there; in front and in back. They are *telling* us; giving us strict orders not to give them any more grief about that site. They are saying it's settled. You folks in the South Bronx: Be still!"

He was referring to The New York Housing Partnership, a nonprofit housing development organization that secures private funds through its connections with some of New York's most prominent businessmen and blue-chip corporations and then supplements that with public subsidies to construct affordable housing in areas where private developers are reluctant to build. The Partnership works in close collaboration with the city and, in the case of Melrose Commons, actually awards contracts to builders who must confirm to guidelines and zoning regulations that The Partnership helped create.[11]

According to the *New York Times* The Partnership's plans for this section of Melrose Commons depend on the city's contributing "$10,000 and the state $15,000 for each apartment. The condominiums will start at $95,000 and would be affordable for families with an income of $36,000 a year, housing officials said."[12] By contrast, the enterprising South Bronx Churches leaders depend on interest-free loans from a $5 million revolving fund they raised from various New York City church hierarchies. Additionally, they rely on donated city-owned vacant lots, ten-year property tax abatements, and city subsidies of $10,000 per house, repayable by the owners when the homes are resold. (The subsidies on the Melrose Commons sites go directly to the builder and are not paid back.)

In his church service, Rev. Heinemeier underscored his central message: a rally was planned for that afternoon, and all parishioners were most emphatically urged to attend. A community dinner would be held in the church basement right after this service, and then school buses (furnished by South Bronx Churches) would ferry St. John's congregation to the housing site for the rally. At that moment the organ boomed, and the whole congregation was on its feet spiritedly singing, "Onward Christian Soldiers," with Pastor Heinemeier's passionate baritone booming the loudest.

After that rousing warmup, Heinemeier was ready to spark the eight thousand demonstrators at the afternoon rally with stirring oratory. He was one of four principal speakers, and his job was to contrast dramatically the housing goals of South Bronx Churches with that of the city's Department of Housing Preservation. He explained to the crowd that South Bronx Churches was not striving for implausible dreams; groups like South Bronx Churches had a track record, and so their claims could be substantiated.

The crowd was reminded that a sister group, East Brooklyn Congregations, had built across the river in Brooklyn the same kind of affordable housing now being advocated for the South Bronx.

As Rev. Johnny Ray Youngblood, of Brooklyn's St. Paul Community Baptist Church and a principal leader of the sister group, East Brooklyn Congregations, later explained to the crowd, Nehemiah was the Old Testament figure who rebuilt Jerusalem with a trowel in one hand but with a sword in the other. "We are ready now to wield the sword," he warned.[13]

At the demonstration Rev. Heinemeier was introduced as the man who would tell "how the city stole the land from the people of the South Bronx." He began with understated drama: "Ten days ago four of us met with Mayor Koch. On Site 404. It turned out not to be a meeting at all, but a lecture. Koch said, 'I decide; you listen. I command; you jump.' It was a meeting that bordered on disrespect,"[14] At this, the audience began murmuring, many apparently thinking that these were Koch's actual words to their religious leaders, their esteemed representatives—a shocking, almost blasphemous affront. "He was saying, 'I have made up my mind on 404. And I don't care what you think or what you say, or what you do even on this April 2nd. It has been decided.' " The throng booed loudly, shouting, "No!" "He said, 'I have got Freddy Ferrer in my pocket on this,' " Heinemeier told the crowd, alluding to the Bronx borough president and the only Hispanic in New York City perched in a high government post. He then described the "six-hundred houses" that SBC wants to build in the South Bronx with Site 404 as the heart. "It will be a community of homes, of families who own their own place for a change. . . . For a Nehemiah home, your family needs to earn no more than $18,000 a year. For one of Koch's condos you need to have at least $35,000 per year. Can you afford $1,000 a month payments?" The crowd chanted, "No!" "Is there any difference between Koch's condos and Nehemiah Homes?" The crowd roared back with even more vigor, "Yeah!"

Now warming to the enthusiasm of the crowd hanging on his words, Heinemeier began to ratchet up the volume. "The Nehemiah homes are for *our* kind of people. Koch's condos are for *a whole different crowd,* who want to move back into the Bronx on the basis of our tears, and our sweat, and our agony."

By this time, though his voice was a hoarse shout, he kept punching up the urgency, thundering, "Come on, Mr. Koch. Come on, Freddy! This land is *our land.* Here we have cried. Here we have worked. Here we have struggled. Here we have prayed. and, HERE WE WILL BUILD!" The crowd was now cheering lustily. After Heinemeier's rousing invocation another clergyman delivered an equally emotional speech in Spanish. His refrain was What a shame! "*Que Verguenza!*" The crowd did not have to speak Spanish to be riveted by the recurring power of *Que Verguenza!*

This sharply pointed, but scrupulously nonpartisan thrust was a consistent theme throughout the rally. Striking a delicate balance was essential: SBC wanted to keep all politicians at arms' length but, at the same time, strived to have proper, respectful alliances with those who we are shrewd enough to respect SBC as a powerful force in this community. A genuine grass-roots independent political entity would be a novelty in this neighborhood, which has had in the last twenty years only sporadic and venal leadership. The rally occurred more than six months before the 1989 mayoral election, and the contest was already heating up by the early spring. At the time of the rally, it was anticipated that three-term Mayor Edward Koch would battle his party's nomination against at least three other Democrats, including Manhattan Borough President David N. Dinkins, a Black politician who was expected to be invincibly popular with the large but politically inert Black population of the city; Harrison J. Goldin, a four-term comptroller; and dark-horse businessman Richard Ravitch.

Koch, who had dominated the political life of the city for twelve years, was considered vulnerable, and many in the leadership of SBC regarded his possible reelection as an unmitigated disaster. On the Republican side, there were two unannounced candidates, the more muscular of whom was Rudolph W. Guiliani, the enormously popular former federal prosecutor in Manhattan who sent Mafia bosses, corrupt city politicians, and Wall Street white-collar criminals to jail in impressive numbers.

All these candidates were invited to the rally, including the mayor. Koch, who perversely often relishes a hostile audience and prides himself on his dexterity in these tense situations, did not show, perhaps because the prospect of facing thousands of sorely vexed citizens in an empty lot in the South Bronx would cool all but the most foolhardy of their ardor for reelection combat.

The only candidate who attended was Mr. Guilani, who was given a respectful welcome but was told that he would not be permitted to make a traditional stump speech. Instead, a pastor from a Methodist church in the Tremont section of the South Bronx would ask him questions. He was informed that he would have a minute to answer each inquiry and then would be permitted two more minutes to add any further comments. The message was unmistakable: as much as his presence may have been appreciated, SBC would not be coopted by publicity-hungry pols.

Guiliani was asked in both English and Spanish what he would have done if he were the mayor during the meeting that Rev. Heinemeier had just described to the audience. The former prosecutor, who was running for office for the first time, was widely expected to be an inept campaigner, and even his supporters publicly worried about his shooting himself in the foot when dealing with complicated local ethnic disputes. Though SBC put him on the spot, he deftly responded that he had grown up poor in his parents' modest home which was very similar to the Nehemiah structures and that he had visited the Nehemiah homes in Brooklyn and regarded them "as one of the best answers in America to the problem of affordable housing." He went on to express puzzlement about "why the city keeps blocking expansion of Nehemiah housing in New York City when it works so well. Why?" Later, he said that good housing in this neighborhood was deserved and, adroitly echoing the central theme of SBC's ideology, elicited cheers when he proclaimed, "It's your right. You have to go out and get it for yourself. And I have tremendous respect for all of you, every single one of you because you are not letting people tell you how to lead your lives. You are determining how to lead your lives."[15]

Another major purpose of the rally was to mete out stinging political punishment to Fernando Ferrer, the borough president, who, allegedly at the behest of Mayor Koch, contacted Democratic candidates Dinkins, Goldin, and Ravitch and urged them not to attend the rally. Ferrer's power stems from the fact that he is the highest-ranking Hispanic elected official in the city, and so all Democratic aspirants are hungry for his blessing. When the demonstration commenced, a representative from each of the forty congregations stepped up to the microphone. Each announced his parish affiliation, the number of parishioners in attendance (some with ringing hyperbole), and all added some colorful version of "We are here; but where is Freddy?" One woman announced with mock urgency, "I ask you people. We have a problem. When this rally is finished over there is the 42nd Precinct," she said, pointing two blocks north to a forlorn-looking structure, one of the few standing buildings remaining in the area. "Tell them we have a missing person!" After a pause to let her words sink in, she shouted with indignation, "Where is Fernando?" Consistent with this pitiless line of attack, Guiliani was asked why he had not stayed away like the other politicians who had heeded Ferrer's warning. Glossing over the fact that he is a Republican and therefore not likely to attend to advice from an incumbent Democrat, he replied, "Because no one tells me what to do," thereby striking a harmonic chord.

The rally unfolded like clockwork. Two Protestant bishops spoke, including a surprisingly wound-up Lutheran, Bishop William Lazareth, a bespectacled white gentleman in his late fifties who looked every inch a dignified bishop. Bishop Lazareth startled the crowd by sounding like a fervently inspired Mohammed Ali, bellowing in verse, "Remember this: I don't know where is Freddy; but I do know God is ready!" At one point he was so transported that he quoted God as proclaiming, "Nehemiah Now!"

Near the end of the rally everyone was summoned to pick up a rock or a piece of rubble as a memento of the dream here of transforming this desolate stretch of land into a vibrant neighborhood of minority homeowners. People then spontaneously raised their pieces of debris aloft for a blessing; although Guiliani clutched his assigned rock stiffly at his side, even he later joined in when everyone linked arms and sang, "We Shall Overcome."

In fact, imaginative symbolism was the signal aspect of the afternoon. Rev. Johnny Ray Youngblood, the charismatic preacher from East Brooklyn Congregations, is a master of this oratorical device. At one point during his speech, he stopped short and looked around, as if suddenly jarred: he marveled at the surrounding abandoned buildings and leveled blocks, musing, "This place looks like a bunch of dinosaurs came through here," After a pause he continued. "I saw their trail. I even discovered some of their names. The leader's name was Kochwrecksosaurous." The crowd went wild. He pressed on, "This land is our land. If our *leaders* thought they nailed us to the cross Friday," he continued, referring to the just observed Good Friday, "we need to remind them that Sunday is always coming after Friday." This was followed by much rhetorical linking of Koch to the cruel Pharisees, and the rocks people were holding were compared to the rock that blocked the tomb of Christ before the Resurrection.

In the end, people were assured that the fight would continue, that from now on every Wednesday was declared to be *Nehemiah Wednesday*. A polished, impeccably tailored young Black man raised in the South Bronx, Tony Aguilar, who was once a corporate banker but had been a full-time organizer with SBC for almost two years, told the gathering, "This is not a one-day war. This is a long-term war! We want people back here on Wednesday. We are planning a sneak attack of our own. We have declared: *War on 404*. It's wartime!"

Directly after the rally, seventy leaders, clergy and lay people, convened in the basement of Sts. Peter and Paul Church to evaluate the action. Jim Drake, the master strategist and principal architect of SBC, told the leaders that "evaluation is of equal importance to the action itself." For the previous ten days, Drake and his key organizers had worked literally without pause to pull off this demonstration, and the collective assessment was clearly important. The perception that evaluation is absolutely fundamental is vintage Industrial Areas Foundation ideology: Larry McNeil, a senior IAF organizer who operates four groups in East Los Angeles like South Bronx Churches, says,

> You must analyze the action. You have to look at its implications and explore what could have been done differently. You have to give it some time to sink in, and you have to ask people how they are *feeling.* There is a need to collectively embrace the lessons learned in the action. In fact, a bad action can often be saved by a good evaluation.[16]

Drake told the leaders, "Let's take some time for serious evaluation. I want your feeling from your heart, not your head." For most of the organizers, it had been an exhilarating afternoon. They felt that this action put them on the map, that they proved themselves to be up to the task, and that now anything was possible. Drake good-naturedly cautioned against arrogance. Sitting at cafeteria tables in the dingy church basement, the leaders went on to evaluate each speaker's performance, finding, for instance, Heinemeier's presentation powerful, clear, and one that "educated as well as animated" the assembly. They assessed the turnout, seeking to correct mistakes or congratulate organizers who brought out large numbers.

Drake commented that he and the SBC Strategy Team envisioned four goals for this action:

1. Significant turnout;
2. Clear demonstration to the city of "the cost of not doing business with us;"
3. Cementing a public relationship with the candidates for mayor;
4. Successful launching of a campaign that may have to go until the election, six months down the road, if necessary.

They felt they did well on the turnout and claimed eight-thousand protesters. Newspaper accounts differed, pegging the count at anywhere from a low of thirty-five hundred to a high of eight-thousand.[17] In terms of illustrating the risks to politicians of defying SBC, most felt they had made that point vividly. Drake revealed that, during the action, a nervous representative of Bronx Borough President Ferrer's office approached him; but Drake had brushed him aside, saying he was too busy to talk now but that Ferrer's office should call SBC on Monday. That television coverage was sparse was a major disappointment, given the fact that most South Bronx residents get their news from TV and politicians can be extremely responsive to ideas neatly packaged in television sound bites. There was a mixed reaction to the handling of Guiliani, with most content that they had not gone overboard in embracing him and others disappointed they had not nailed down his support for Nehemiah housing on 404. Most of the organizers did feel that they had positioned themselves well for a long drawn-out campaign and anticipated that perhaps two-hundred people might show up on the following Wednesday morning for the first Nehemiah Wednesday. The criticisms were minor: the school chorus arrived late and bungled the opening, some people could not resist making speeches during the roll call, which unnecessarily slackened the pace of the demonstration; and there was some dispute about whether the translation into Spanish of most of the proceedings amounted to too much or too little.

9

War on 404! The Reaction to the Action

The first Nehemiah Wednesday, three days after the April 2nd rally, found churchgoing protesters crunching through the pulverized debris on Site 404 to the middle of one of the bleakly empty blocks where two-hundred people stood in a semicircle around a huge white pad of paper precariously propped up on a portable tripod. Squinting in the bright sunshine, the gathering listened as a number of speakers brought them up to date on the political reaction to the Sunday rally and mapped out actions planned for the following week.

As in all their rallies, they opened with a prayer. Protestant minister John Collins read a scriptural passage and invited anyone in the crowd "to lift up a sentence or a word of prayer in English or in Spanish; God understands all languages equally well." One older Black man, demonstrating the media sophistication of many in the crowd, first thanked the press "who found time to come out and give us the coverage, for they too know what we are trying to do." John Heinemeier, piping up from the back of the crowd, prayed, "We ask for your blessing, Lord, upon our mayor and on our borough president. We ask you, Lord, to soften their hearts and to share with us at this moment of great promise in the South Bronx." He beseeched with passion, "Work on 'em, Lord!"

Jim Drake made the introductions at this brief rally, which was unusual because he customarily makes a point of staying in the background. True to form, the meeting started on time, was fast paced, and the focus leapfrogged among a half dozen clergymen, so that no one leader would dominate.

A young representative of State Assemblyman Jose Serrano (D-Bronx) nervously read a letter sent to Borough President Fernando Ferrer, in which Serrano pointedly reminded his fellow Hispanic political ally that, in the past, they had both solidly supported the building of affordable housing and encouraged him now to support the surrender of Site 404 to South Bronx Churches.[1]

John Heinemeier good-naturedly began by alluding to the press coverage of the rally, which highlighted the section of his speech where he talked about Nehemiah homes having a front lawn and driveway and a backyard where people could cook outdoors. He joked that since last Sunday, "I am now known as 'The Barbecue Preacher.' " Defiantly, he then affirmed, "I accept that title! *Downtown* they don't believe we want backyards. *Downtown* they don't believe we deserve backyards." The crowd picked up his cadence: "Yes we do!" He went on to say that, on the coming Monday, there would be a meeting with Fernando Ferrer. "We will meet at his office. With five-hundred people." He concluded with hope, "It is possible that he is seeing the light."

Drake wrapped up the meeting by asking representatives of each church to estimate how many of their members would attend on Monday. He scribbled a loose running count on the large paper pad, and when he finished the total hovered near seven-hundred. Drake then singled out three clergymen to meet separately with the three announced candidates for mayor (David Dinkins, Harrison Goldin, and Richard Ravitch) to invite the candidates to the meeting with Ferrer. Each churchman signed up no fewer than fifteen community residents to accompany him to these meetings. Although the chance was remote that any of these politicians would attend the bargaining session with Ferrer, the encounter to solicit their participation would put the politicians on notice that pressure was mounting for them to take a public stance on Site 404.

In an interview afterwards, Pastor Heinemeier was asked if there had been any response from politicians to the April 2nd rally. "In our organization, all actions are measured by the reaction," he claimed. With satisfaction, he added, "We have gotten reactions from just about everybody." He conceded that there as yet had been no forward movement on the city's part, but "we will see next week, as things heat up in the borough president's office, whether he is going to be wise or foolish." Heinemeier remained adamant on Site 404: "The city has just offered us sites for six-hundred homes, but not a single one of them is on a cleared block." The economics of building large numbers of attached affordable homes demands contiguous land, where, for instance, hundreds of foundations could be dug at once. "They offered us scattered sites. We will take those six-hundred. But we want to *begin* in a place that is clearly feasible. Our builders are willing to take some of the bad, but they want to begin in a place where there is no demolition needed. We could begin here by July 4th." Returning to his standard explanation for the intransigence of the city, he suggested, "The city also sees this as an attractive site, possibly because developers are among the main contributors to Mr. Ferrer and to Mr. Koch. The city, possibly, has some kind of arrangement with developers. Their developers will get $25,000 to $30,000 profit per unit, while our developer will get only $1,000 per unit. There is kind of a picture emerging in that contrast."

Asked what impact it would have on Koch if Ferrer changed his mind and supported Nehemiah housing on Site 404, he said, "I think it would be an embarrassment to Mayor Koch if Freddy turns coat in this. But locally he needs us more than Koch does." Was there any possibility that Koch would ever change his mind? Heinemeier speculated, "It's hard to say. Some in our organization are saying that he has a death wish. I have never known Mayor Koch to be quite that dumb, but I can't predict what he will do."

The day after the first Nehemiah Wednesday, twenty members of the Strategy Team convened in the South Bronx Churches office, which is in a room over the chapel in St. Jerome's Church, near the lower tip of the South Bronx. They assessed their present situation, shared reactions in the wake of the rally, and mapped strategy for the upcoming April 10th confrontation in Borough President Ferrer's office.

Predictably, Mayor Edward Koch "came out ferociously against us," Drake reported, Koch was quoted in news accounts as taunting, "Nehemiah doesn't tell the truth." According to that day's *New York Newsday*, Koch also strangely "blasted Nehemiah developer I. D. Robbins for collecting $1,000 for each completed home."[2] Since no one expects a developer to work for free and since the city's developer, The New York City Partnership, will allow rates of profit which are at a minimum eight to ten times that amount per unit, this seemed like a particularly anemic criticism. Koch charged that the actual construction cost was not the $42,500 that South Bronx Churches claimed but was actually more than $50,000. I. D. Robbins, the developer who at that point had built fifteen hundred single-family Nehemiah homes in Brooklyn, confirmed that the actual construction cost was now estimated to be $49,000 for each two-or three-bedroom home but that this still represented a huge savings over what the city could expect from any of its builders. The Partnership, for example, reported that its condo apartments (which would cost $125,000 to build) would have to be heavily subsidized to be affordable to local residents.

Curiously, Koch, in his recently published *His Eminence and Hizzonor*, praises the Nehemiah concept of housing, calling the

Brooklyn effort, "a miraculous . . . rebuilding of a community . . . that had [become] one of the most blighted, and some would say god-forsaken, ghettos in all of urban America."[3] Koch adds wistfully, "Space permitting, we have every reason to hope that Nehemiah can accomplish throughout New York City what it has already done for its first eight hundred homeowners."

At the planning session, Drake told the group that a political reporter friendly with Ferrer had contacted him informally to try to persuade the Borough President to change his mind. The newsman then promptly called Drake to report on the conversation, noting that Ferrer "was beside himself with anger, and was reacting like a whipped puppy." Drake took some solace from the fact that Ferrer's mild comments on the record were "not caustic. He's claiming he is all for more Nehemiah homes, just as long as they are not on Site 404."

Unexpectedly, another prominent South Bronx churchman and successful builder weighed in with accusations. Father Louis Gigante, the controversial Catholic priest who has rehabilitated many apartments in the Hispanic Hunts Point section of the South Bronx, took what Drake characterized as "a dumb swipe at us. He accused South Bronx churches of not representing all of the [South Bronx] churches." Drake continued, "We never said we represented all churches, although [admittedly] we may have acted as if we do."[4] At this time Gigante was under a cloud of suspicion prompted by a lengthy investigative exposé in a recent issue of the *Village Voice*[5] which documented his extensive and long-time ties with the Mafia, particularly his dealings with various mob-controlled construction companies. Arguably, the most powerful figures in the South Bronx are Father Gigante, Ramon Velez (a formidable figure who controlled millions in federal dollars earmarked for antipoverty programs, and who also attacked South Bronx Churches), and Fernando Ferrer. Both Valez[6] and Gigante rose to power during the sixties when they successfully garnered huge amounts of Federal money which briefly poured into the borough in a futile attempt to stem the tide of apartment building abandonment. Koch was with Father Gigante the day before the SBC meeting at a political function and praised him, according to the report that SBC received, as "the only man in the Bronx who knows about housing."

In other reactions to the April 2nd rally, one board member of The New York City Partnership, E. Thomas Williams Jr. sent a long emotional telegram to his board colleagues urging them to withdraw from their contract to build on Site 404.[7] Democratic hopefuls Dinkins, Ravitch, and Goldin all had been in contact with SBC, although not one had as yet gone on a limb and defied Borough President Ferrer. SBC was in frequent communication with these politicians, well as on its way to establishing ties with the candidates as well as cultivating key members of their staffs. They were making it impossible to deny that SBC was a major player in the Bronx; politicians now would have to cautiously assess the risk of incurring the wrath of their efficiently mobilized, churchgoing constituents (who, not incidentally, we are among the minority of South Bronx citizens who voted consistently).

The session then shifted gears to the crucial business at hand: how to get Ferrer to change his mind on Site 404. The group of twenty activists had a delicate problem in that the borough president had publicly, and perhaps inextricably, tied himself to Mayor Koch. Unless they could pry Ferrer from the smothering embrace of Koch, there was no chance that Koch would feel isolated enough to back down and relinquish Site 404.

Drake called for suggestions. A perennial danger in all activist political groups is that, when many forceful leaders squeeze into one room, infighting and rhetorical posturing can easily overwhelm the agenda and thus unintentionally torpedo critical problem-solving efforts. In this group dominated by strong-willed pastors, men who are customarily deferred to, the hazard of derailment is even more acute. Add to this volatile mix all the long-simmering antagonisms that boil just beneath the surface in any nominally ecumenical group. Then, for good measure, include the long-percolating tensions that exist between Black and Hispanic inner-city decision makers and White "outside" leaders. Yet, conforming to IAF's collective leadership principal, this discussion was soberly businesslike, a straightforward problem-solving session in which all parties struggled to discover a common strategy.

The first suggestion, born of frustrated anger, was to confront Ferrer with Koch's arrogant boast that Ferrer was in his pocket. Drake instead asked, "If you were Ferrer, what would you want to hear in this meeting?"[8] That realigned the discussion; ideas to make Ferrer look good began to surface. One participant who had dealt with Ferrer in the past suggested that the borough president perceived himself as a "fixer. And we can play to his [perceived] strength by giving him a way to fix this impasse."

Throughout, however, they never wavered from their bottom line: there could be no compromise on Site 404. That land was deemed crucial for the success of the Nehemiah enterprise. There was much loose speculation on what lay behind Ferrer's reticence in allowing Nehemiah homes to be built there. What was in it for him? They kept lighting on the fact that allegedly 80 percent of his November election campaign war chest had been financed by real-estate developers, and developers were presumably terrified that the economically sound and virtually profitless Nehemiah concept might gain a beachhead in the Bronx. They examined in detail Ferrer's public justification for his opposition, a justification which has shifted over time. At first Ferrer was opposed because the 4.2 acres of Site 404 was part of the larger forty acres of the proposed Melrose Commons project and, therefore, not subject to independent development. The city subsequently backed away from that position and now said that, although site 404 was not part of the grandiose Melrose project, the low density of single-family rowhouses on this site was wasteful and inappropriate. There is clearly some merit in this stance, although the most celebrated housing initiative in the South Bronx during the previous twenty year was the aforementioned rebuilding of Charlotte Street, a dozen blocks to the north, in which less than a dozen houses prodigally sprawled across each acre.

Drake let the discussion take its course, and, when new ideas began to sputter, he said, "Well, if Ferrer is stuck on the question of density, let's explore how we can solve his problem," When no one could come up with any striking suggestions, Drake admitted that he had been thinking along these lines the night before and proposed that South Bronx Churches counter the city by offering to build three-hundred new *rental* apartments in any location in Melrose Commons, excepting Site 404. What made the deal seemingly irresistible was that SBC could "build them at no more than 70 percent of the cost that The Partnership can. This way Ferrer can come out and say his worry over the density problem is met," Drake concluded. The idea was classic in its beauty. It would seem that the city would be hard pressed to reject an offer that essentially met its stated concerns about density; although it was still only 50 percent of what the city proposed, this project could be brought in at a price that was more than competitive with any the city could expect from its builders.

Much nuts-and-bolts talk ensued about where they would get the money to begin construction and how to configure rental apartments, and then Drake offered to get I. D. Robbins, the builder of Brooklyn's Nehemiah houses, to the office on the following Monday, hours before the meeting with Ferrer, to give the group a lightning-quick seminar on adapting the single-family Nehemiah concept to low-rise rental apartments.

Pastor Heinemeier pointed out this new shift in thinking did not really mark a departure from their original plans: "We have always had a three-pronged housing strategy. We have intended from the beginning to build owner-occupied single-family row houses, and low rent apartments, and also to begin to rehab existing structures. All we are offering now is to push forward our original plan at a faster pace," he reassured the group.

Drake suggested that they might even want to sweeten the pot by offering to house the first three-hundred people who would need to be relocated from the proposed Melrose Commons site. Although the area had been largely cleared, there remained a number of inhabited buildings. These residents inevitably would be displaced during the demolition that would precede new construction. "We then regain the initiative," Drake suggested, "and are not just reacting to [the city], but actively making it less reasonable for them to say no." Someone objected that this proposed enhancement inadvertently would "give some value to the notion of relocation," and, after a bit of discussion, Drake responded by taking his proposal off the table. The issue of relocation is a thorny one in the South Bronx, as it is in many inner-city areas. City and federal authorities have a distressing, largely disastrous history in "urban renewal," a process which has been characterized by the wholesale bulldozing of viable neighborhoods. Some once-bustling, albeit run-down, communities have been replaced by poorly planned, often sterile public housing projects; even worse, many times leveled neighborhoods have remained fallow for decades, like Site 404.[9]

The fast-paced meeting concluded after a mere hour and a half, deviating from the usual practice among political activists of insensitivity to punctuality and brevity.

Clearly the battle to win over Ferrer on Site 404 was the crucial first step in gaining clear title to that key parcel for Nehemiah building. Hours before the meeting with Ferrer on April 10th, twenty members of the Strategy Team caucused to fashion negotiation tactics, to design the logistics to marshal hundreds of demonstrators who would descend on the courthouse, and to hear from Nehemiah builder I. D. Robbins who would give them a densely textured tutorial on the economic realities of real-estate development in the inner city.

The first issue tackled was Housing Preservation and Development (HPD) Commissioner Abraham Biderman's counterattack over the weekend, intended to increase the allure of the city's development plans. In an ironic choice of Pentagon Vietnam-era jargon,

Drake dubbed this initiative a "preemptive strike." The Koch administration had issued a press release on that Sunday offering to beef up the subsidy for The Partnership's homes and further tried to appease South Bronx Churches by dangling another two parcels of land—each 1.5 acres—in front of the group if it would abandon Site 404. The magnitude of the additional subsidies was astonishing. According to the press release, "Under the subsidy plan, the homes will be sold for prices ranging from $70,000 to $75,000, affordable to families earning $30,000 a year. Under the original plan, these homes would have been affordable to families with an annual income of $36,000 at prices between $85,000 and $90,000.[10]

Keeping track of the math in the myriad of proposals and counterproposals is a bit tricky because the numbers tended to float week by week. For instance, only one week earlier (on April 3rd) in response to the huge rally on Site 404, the city contended in the *New York Times* that "The condominiums will start at $95,000 and would be affordable for families with an income of $36,000 a year, according to housing officials."[11] For these homes to come in at that price, the city offered to contribute $10,000 and the state $15,000, making the total government subsidies $25,000 per apartment. Now, with the extra subsidy, the city maintained that it could sell the same apartments for $70,000 to $75,000. Or, in other words, to the initial $25,000 bankrolling of each apartment, the city now claimed it would ante up another $25,000. This would appear to make them, at $50,000 per apartment, the most heavily subsidized condos in local history. Taking the city at its word, always a risky proposition in an election year, it was hard not to be impressed by the lengths the city claimed it would go for the sake of preventing Nehemiah housing from arising on the empty stretches on Site 404 which had previously languished in desolation for over twenty years.

Drake reported to the group that the city's offer was fraudulent and they were merely "negotiating through the press," since the city had not, in fact, even contacted South Bronx Churches. Manny Cologne, another full-time organizer at SBC, was dispatched to Ferrer's office to pick up the text of the release which had been faxed that morning to the borough president, who presumably was also seeing it for the first time. On the positive side, the city did concede that Site 404 was, in Drake's words, "no longer the crown jewel of Melrose Commons," and now its only remaining problem was one of numbers of units per acre. "We will now take care of the density issue by building three-hundred apartments elsewhere in the neighborhood,"[12] Drake declared.

"Let's Do Some Strategizing"

With that, Drake turned the meeting over to I. D. Robbins, the man who made family rowhouses in East Brooklyn an affordable reality and wanted to duplicate that achievement in the South Bronx.

Dapper in a tailored gray suit and vigorous-looking, he began authoritatively: "Let me give you a picture of what we have done."[13] Lapsing momentarily into the rosy rhetoric one associates with all real-estate entrepreneurs he continued, "We build a better house— brick and block—at less than half the price of other developers." He recounted a dispiriting chronicle of the city's blocking his attempts to build from three-thousand to six-thousand Nehemiah-type homes in Rockaway, a barrier island oceanfront community on the southern tip of Queens. There another huge site has, like Site 404, remained desolate for twenty years after the previous housing was flattened in anticipation of urban renewal high rises which were never built.

Robbins tackled the issue of density directly. "Density is just a political issue," he said dismissively. "High density [in these neighborhoods] is not socially desirable. And besides the city has literally a thousand acres in the South Bronx they could develop, but don't. Your difficulties," he contended, "are that you are an independent group, and you don't truckle; and they hate you for that."

The density argument had to be considered in light of the fact that Site 404 had been vacant for almost two decades and, according to Robbins, the city had been tying itself in knots for years trying to figure out what to do with it. "This site," he said, "has been the subject of numerous studies by New York City. I remember one in 1970 under [Mayor John V.] Lindsay. They got," he continued, still incredulous after almost two decades, "some guy from Lithuania to come up with a plan. I personally know of twelve different studies on this site."

When the city built on Charlotte Street, the blasted few blocks that had become a national symbol of the impotence of urban government, "All the politicians were beside themselves with happiness," Robbins pointed out. The Nehemiah plans call for more than triple the density of the detached, suburban ranch-style houses, which presently give Charlotte Street a macabre otherworldliness. The Charlotte Street pastel-colored houses, which sit in the center of green lawns and are bordered by white picket fences, stand in splendid isolation from one another as abandoned tenements loom in all directions. "We will build twenty to twenty-two homes per acre, and now all of a sudden density is the big issue," Robbins charged.

Driving to the heart of the controversy, Robbins asserted, "Our theory [of community] is the correct one. We want to build a stable community. To do that you need a critical mass of people with a community attitude." This he defined as people who were committed to their homes and their block. They are people who take an interest in the schools where their children learn, who will be a stable presence dedicated to their churches and other neighborhood institutions, the kind of community-minded residents who were the norm in these streets before the deterioration of the sixties and the fires of the seventies shattered the neighborhood.

With exasperation he claimed, "[City Housing Czar Abraham] Biderman has never visited Nehemiah in Brooklyn. Ferrer has never come over to see what a healthy community is like. I would pay them to come over and look." Site 404, since it is a contiguous expanse and forms the western border of the other land that South Bronx Churches intended to build on, is the perfect cornerstone of a stable community. This really is the preeminent point of the Nehemiah experiment: SBC intends to build not just housing that many current community residents can afford, but they plan to lay the foundation of a robust, multiracial and highly organized community which can revitalize itself and evolve in its own independent directions.

Bronx history is filled with depressing failures which demonstrate conclusively that it is not enough to build affordable housing. The South Bronx is littered with examples of abandoned housing gut-rehabilitated at great expense and made available at subsidized rates and were subsequently destroyed by some of its own residents in a matter of years. Robbins pointed to a location only a dozen blocks south of Site 404, "rehabbed buildings, on St. Mary's Street, that lasted only five years" before they were rendered unlivable.

Indeed, just two blocks east of St. Jerome's where they were meeting, the ill-fated Mott Haven Housing Development serves as a stark reminder of soured good intentions. From 1969 to 1972 over $4 million in public money was poured into rehabilitation of two squalid blocks of twenty five- and six-story buildings.

A few years later the *Times* concluded:

Today the completed project is a nightmare of dashed hopes and redevastated buildings, of apartment houses once more abandoned, and again housing people amid dilapidation.

With half the 20 buildings entirely empty and ravaged, and the others only partly filled, Federal officials are seeking to consolidate the remaining 100 families in seven of the least ruined buildings and wondering what to do with the other buildings. Demolishing them is being considered.[14]

Robbins said that he had already constructed in Brooklyn three model Nehemiah homes, specifically designed for the South Bronx in order to refine the costs of the project and, crucially, to secure the necessary building permits in Brooklyn, thereby making an end run around the housing department bureaucracy in the Bronx. "We know the costs. We are ready to hit the ground running, as soon as the green light is given," he flatly asserted.

A give-and-take discussion ensued to flesh out the details of apartment construction which was the centerpiece of the South Bronx Churches counterproposal. "We can build apartments for rent, for selling as condos, or as coops," Robbins speculated. He insisted that SBC should build the apartments, then immediately turn them over to the city or some other management entity. "We know it makes no sense for citizens' groups like ours to be landlords. I remember when the Presbyterian Church built rental apartments in Patterson, New Jersey," he reminisced, "They quickly became known as landlords. It was disastrous. You need very able management to handle rental buildings; otherwise, they tend to deteriorate quickly. Volunteers should not get involved in management." Another drawback, he said later, was that rental buildings need, not only skillful managers, but maintenance men and other support staff, all of which can add 25 percent to the rent.

Robbins was asked to talk specifically about the details of apartment building. He began by saying he could build whatever is wanted but firmly advocated a more dense version of the familiar Nehemiah single-family housing. He suggested constructing garden apartments. These would roughly double the density of the single-family Nehemiah scheme by building two-story buildings closer to the sidewalk, eliminating the driveways, and arranging the buildings to accommodate four families per entryway. He would built "deeper into the lot, and put parking and the common areas in the back."

"We are prepared to build; you pick the sites, and we'll put up one-hundred or more units per site," he claimed, but he cautioned that there would be a problem with scattered sites. The cost in that kind of building is elevated because there are expenses associated with setting up each site, maintaining security, moving the construction equipment to new locations, and shifting the on-site contractors' office from place to place. All this cuts down on the interlocking efficiency that is necessary for the state-of-the-art construction methods he employs.

Although the rental apartments sounded very similar to the Nehemiah single-family homes, Robbins noted an important difference besides the doubling of density. Owner-occupied housing needs a critical mass of like-minded residents in order to establish a sense of security that would encourage families to sink their life savings into dwellings situated in a shaky neighborhood. "Rental apartments were never secure, and no one really expects them to be" at this stage of the game, he implied, and emphasized again that once the apartments were built, SBC should consider its work done and turn the apartments over to the city.

Returning to the economics, he alleged that The Partnership planned on a $9,000 profit per unit. "There is not profit in mine, nothing but a $1,000 fee. I left that business [lucrative real-estate development] behind, a while ago. I also carry the job until *after* the units are occupied." A question was raised about where SBC could get the startup money to finance such a large-scale project. It was thought that they could perhaps borrow from the city's construction finance pool at no interest, or perhaps from banks, but tapping the resources of commercial banks would add substantial interest costs. Robbins conceded, "You could borrow from the city, but remember you now have absolute control of your money," and that is a powerful advantage. The city's comptroller holds the purse strings and pays out disbursements at his own pace, a pace sometimes infected by politics. An important economy of the Nehemiah plan is that prompt payments, within a week and a half, insure timely and cooperative relations with subcontractors and vendors. To begin Nehemiah housing construction, SBC raised $4 to $5 million from various church hierarchies in no-interest, repayable loans. But getting further commitments from churches now, with nothing actually built in the South Bronx, would be problematic.

As the discussion began to bog down in financial intricacies, Robbins warned, "Don't get into specifics with Ferrer; don't contract with the city under any circumstances, and don't get maneuvered [today] into making a business proposal to the city that we can't handle."

Drake, attempting to cap this part of the discussion, asked if anyone could craft a five-sentence statement to the press boiling

down the essence of their proposal to Ferrer. Robbins, going one better, distilled their offer into one long sentence: "SBC proposed today
to Fernando Ferrer that, if it were permitted to build on Site 404 as
the cornerstone of a new eight-hundred-family affordable home community, it would, in turn, build up to five-hundred units of rental
garden apartments at a minimum of 30 percent less than anyone else
could do it."

Just as the city's numbers tended to get fuzzier over time, SBC
was not immune to the same inflationary impulse: The six-hundred
proposed Nehemiah homes of the April 2nd Rally were now eight-
hundred, and the $43,000 price was inching up to $50,000.

After an hour of fleshing out details, Robbins left and John
Heinemeier said, "Let's do some strategizing." The rest of the
meeting was absorbed with sketching out logistics of how to maneuver the hundreds of demonstrators expected that afternoon at
the courthouse where Ferrer has his office and with planning their
negotiation tactics with the borough president. The decisions were
all made by consensus. After a detail such as deciding who was authorized to speak to the press on behalf of SBC, John Heinemeier
typically would nail down the decision by declaring, "Okay, I hear
us saying . . . "

They designed the meeting with the borough president so that
Ferrer could feel free "to vent his anger." They vowed not to react
to any expression of indignation but to press Ferrer firmly into reacting to their "enhanced proposal" of building garden apartments
in addition to the Nehemiah rowhouses. Drake cautioned that
"nothing is going to be settled today. We want to get his imagination working so that he will act more like a politician than like a
whipped puppy."

Although Ferrer had not endorsed any candidate for mayor at
this point, it was widely thought unlikely that he would throw his
support behind Koch. Accordingly, Drake counseled that they
should be relentless in challenging him: "Why are you with Koch on
this instead of us?" Drake didn't expect that Ferrer would cave in on
the spot but suggested that the best outcome of this confrontation
would be for the borough president to relent and say, "I'll talk with
the mayor on Site 404. Let's get together tomorrow and iron out the
difficulties."

It was clear that Koch had dug in his heels, and there were probably only two people who could get him to back down. One was his
coauthor and friend, John Cardinal O'Connor, who had verbally
committed $2 million of diocesan funds for interest-free loans to

Nehemiah home buyers in the South Bronx, but who had also, according to Drake, "opted out" of the controversy, although O'Connor was still deemed to be a last-ditch potential ace in the hole. Ferrer, because of his standing in the Bronx, would leave Koch isolated if he reversed gears and backed Nehemiah homes on Site 404. The group then fine-tuned its presentation by role playing in which Drake impersonated a shrewd and unbudging Ferrer.

A few hours later at the courthouse, amidst the chants of 250 demonstrators, the well-rehearsed drama was played out, but the result was disappointing.

On the courthouse steps, 250 South Bronx residents carried "Nehemiah Now" signs and marched and shouted fervently. Five floors above, a dozen SBC leaders, (Black, Hispanic, White, Clergy and lay people) negotiated with Ferrer and a few members of his staff. SBC staffers were sent down periodically to keep the crowd abreast of the progress of the meeting. The first report to the crowd was relayed by SBC organizer Tony Aguilar who stayed at the rally and led cheers through a bullhorn. After about forty minutes, Aguilar gathered the assembly around him and reported: "Ferrer is trying to hold on to Site 404 for Melrose Commons. Right now he is looking at a map. He's going around the map to try to find other spots. You need to tell him; you need to be much louder; it's 404!" This fired the crowd, who were mostly women, perhaps reflecting the fact that it was late afternoon and many other family members were still at work. Aguilar's report was then translated into Spanish, and the reaction was even more vociferous.

This scene was repeated a number of times during the next hour and a half. It was sunny but extremely blustery, and the SBC supporters were buffeted with swirling trash as they marched back and forth in front of the courthouse on the heavily-trafficked Grand Concourse. They heard their leaders tell them, "We are negotiating. It is rough. It is up and down. But it doesn't look completely negative."

The ranks of protesters were considerably thinner when, hours later, the SBC negotiators descended the courthouse steps to report that they had failed to win over Ferrer. John Heinemeier, putting the best face on the grim outcome, told the crowd through the bullhorn:

> We made our offer to Mr. Biderman [the city's chief housing official] and the City of New York. And we will be meeting with them again shortly. Hopefully, this week. We feel he needs more of what happened today. More pressure. More visits.

More heat from the people of the South Bronx. And we are going to meet on our site, Site 404 at 10 o'clock Wednesday morning. Like we said we would. I'll tell you one thing. Sitting up there around that table, it made us feel very strong to hear you down here. We could hear you loud and clear!

10

Digging in for the Long Haul

From the beginning, SBC strategists defined the skirmish for Nehemiah housing as essentially the Battle for Site 404. They vowed not to build in the South Bronx until the city surrendered this cleared, flat, and centrally located 4.2 acres.

Before the public dispute caught fire in April of 1989, SBC had painstakingly built its assets and courted allies. It had on board master builder I. D. Robbins and his proven ability to deliver sound, affordable housing. It had the potent and loyal affiliation of forty-five South Bronx congregations—Black and Hispanic, Protestant, and Catholic, with influential pastors and a core of committed church activists. It had the superb, seasoned leadership of veteran organizers like Jim Drake, and, in the wings, the wily Ed Chambers, as well as inspiring church leaders like John Heinemeier and a host of others. It also had an ample bankroll to finance day-to-day operating expenses, and it had access to the deep pockets of the major church hierarchies that would lend the millions needed to finance construction. SBC had political allies like influential State Assemblyman Jose Serrano and leading mayoral hopeful Rudolph Guiliani. Less tangibly, but equally importantly, it had a compelling logic on its side: for two decades the city had proven utterly incapable of building anything on Site 404; in truth, it had been unable to arrest the slide of the South Bronx for even longer, and, at best, it would be years before municipal authorities could erect anything. Meanwhile, it was conceded by almost all that what the city would build certainly would be more expensive for taxpayers and less affordable to the present residents than SBC-sponsored housing.

Arrayed against SBC was the power of the city, if not to build, then at least to obstruct. In Mayor Koch, they had a sworn and vindictive enemy of a dozen years' standing, dating to the first confrontation with him in Queens that left the mayor feeling he was confronting belligerent Nazis. Luckily for the project, Koch was pragmatic enough to bend if it suited his purposes, and now in an election season he was desperately fighting for his political life. More serious was SBC's inability to win over Borough President Ferrer, whose vicious mocking at the huge April rally had cemented poisoned relations. An IAF axiom is that there are no permanent enemies and no permanent allies. So, even at this late date, SBC had no qualms about allowing Ferrer to claim credit for Nehemiah if he would persuade Koch to release 404. Ferrer, on the other hand, seemed, understandably, to take the vilification much more personally.

As the opening phase of the Nehemiah campaign drew to a close in the late spring of 1989, SBC had decisively proved that its support was widespread by turning out eight thousand angry citizens and gathering petitions with one hundred thousand signatures. Now the deadlock with Koch and Ferrer called for new tactics, and so pressure was brought on other allies and enemies.

Si Kahn makes a useful distinction between strategy and tactics in his 1982 book, *Organizing: A Guide for Grassroots Leaders.*

> Strategy and tactics are often talked about at the same time, and sometimes as if they were the same thing. But they are really very different. Strategy is the overall plan for how we are going to get where we are going. Tactics are the specific things that we do to help us get there: petitions, picket lines, marches, demonstrations, hearings, publicity and pressure campaigns. Tactics are important because they move the issue along and also build the organization.[1]

In this case, the strategy was clear: reject the city's tentative offer for six hundred noncontiguous sites and bet the ranch on winning Site 404.

A specific tactic was to assemble activists and attempt to drive a deep wedge into the forces blocking Site 404. An early quarry was The New York City Partnership, the group designated by HPD to bid out the contracts on Site 404. To personalize the prey, the Chairman of both American Express and The New York Partnership, James Robinson, and his deputy for housing, Kathy Wylde, were chosen to be the hot foci of wrath. the goal was to make The Partnership skittish about building on Site 404 and therefore throw a monkey wrench into the city's plans. Like the previous battle to shoulder aside Ferrer, this too sputtered out when, on June 14th, two hundred South Bronx Churches demonstrators gathered in a light drizzle in the shadow of the World Trade Center, the symbolic central nervous system of world capitalism, to rail futilely at a mute symbol of power.

A month before the last-ditch demonstration, Melrose State Assemblyman Jose Serrano wrote to James Robinson and urged "cooperation over Site 404 [which] can begin with discussions between yourself and representatives of SBC."[2] The respected minority politician also once again solidly backed SBC plans for Site 404, calling it "a necessary component in SBC's home ownership plan in my district. I request that your organization relinquish Site 404."[3]

In a series of feverish meetings in the days before the planned June 14th show of strength, Jim Drake telephoned the offices of Jim Robinson, the head of The NYC Partnership, eleven times, trying in vain to arrange a meeting with him. As Drake later told the crowd at the rally, "And eleven times, his staff said no." Trying to recoup from the snub, "We tried for six times to get a meeting with Virgil Conway, who is the Chairman of the Subcommittee [for The Partnership] on Housing, and six times Virgil Conway's staff said no." It is standard practice for IAF groups to go right to the top, slicing through layers of bureaucratic insulation and grappling directly with decision makers. When stonewalled, they resort to confrontation to "increase the cost of not doing business with us," in the words of Jim Drake.

A few days before the planned rally, SBC fired off to Robinson a harshly polarizing letter signed by a dozen local pastors, which ostensibly was intended to badger The Partnership's chairman into meeting with SBC leaders. It charged in part:

> You are always ready to accept the public recognition awards, why can't an hour of your entrepreneurial skills be applied to a thorny problem your staff of the New York City Partnership got its Chairman in? Your representatives have conspired against our South Bronx Churches organization and we will not be kicked and pushed around by your surrogates.
>
> Wealth is one form of power in New York City; organized people with a just cause is another.
>
> Don't tell us about abstractions and legalisms. The reality is the Koch administration and the culture of corruption [Stanley Friedman, Stanley Simon, Mario Biaggi, etc.] with whom the Partnership conspires.

In an interview directly before the rally Rev. Dr. Shelley Sampson, the dignified Black pastor and chairman of SBC's education committee, speculated on why Robinson hadn't agreed to sit down with SBC representatives. Rev. Sampson noted, "Everyone else from

Koch on down has negotiated with us. Robinson probably didn't agree to see us because there is a lot of symbolism involved with meeting with us on equal terms. Things are apparently different in the corporate world."[4]

Drake had warned Robinson's staff that, if he refused to meet with SBC leaders, 750 provoked South Bronx residents would descend on American Express's headquarters and turn up the heat. John Heinemeier was baffled by Robinson's readiness to duck the meeting and suffer the embarrassment of a public display of anger. In an interview he candidly conceded that, if Robinson would agree to sit across the table from them and merely hear them out, Robinson could then decline to abandon Site 404 and, in the process, avoid the irritation of a rally on his doorstep.[5]

Kathy Wylde, the housing specialist for The Partnership who was crucified by speaker after speaker at the American Express rally as the embodiment of the problem over the Site 404 deadlock, said in an interview a few weeks later that Robinson had never seriously entertained meeting with SBC unless they agreed first to meet with his staff for some preliminary ironing out of details. She charged that Drake rudely *demanded* a meeting and that his self-important bluster and crude confrontational style further convinced Robinson's staff that they were not dealing with a seriously professional opponent.

The rally itself was a dispiriting, somewhat lackluster affair. The demonstrators arrived in four chartered buses at the steps of Three World Financial Center, a looming, recently completed skyscraper clad in marble with a polished brass entranceway and sleek maroon metallic trim. Although the event was billed as a press conference, there appeared to be no reporters, causing the rally to resemble the proverbial tree falling silently in the forest for want of a pair of ears to detect the noise.

The crowd, numbering some two hundred residents and clergy, carried homemade signs blasting Robinson personally: "Robinson III: Come Down From Your Tower" or "Robinson III: Greed."

As late as the night before, some SBC leaders held out the hope that the demo could be averted if Robinson made a gesture toward hearing out SBC, since they concluded that it did not really serve anyone's purpose to further polarize the situation. In truth, it appeared that the rally squandered an intimidating show of strength, and perhaps even depleted strength, for a fish that could not be netted. Yet, in light of the discouraging lack of measurable success so far in the battle for Site 404, fielding two hundred demonstrators on a rainy weekday in Lower Manhattan showed considerable organizing muscle and healthy community loyalty to SBC.

The rally opened with a Black priest, Father Bert Bennett of St. Augustine's, telling the crowd huddled under a sea of umbrellas, "It is good to see so many people here who are dedicated, committed, and are ready to go wherever it is necessary to go to meet the needs of the people of the South Bronx. Give yourselves a hand." Before the improvised opening prayer, he reminded the activists, "It is not over until it's over," and threatened, " We are ready to do everything necessary for Site 404!"

Jim Drake, shedding his customary behind-the-scenes reticence, stepped forward and, in a belligerent tone, harked back to the "Sign Up and Take Charge" petition campaign SBC had launched a year earlier. He instructed two men in the crowd to hold up the stacked and boxed petitions with 102,000 signatures, a number that he later claimed represented over 50 percent of the adult population of the South Bronx. That opening shot in the campaign to organize the South Bronx focused on establishing name recognition for SBC, stirring up discontent on various pressing local issues, and demanding a number of immediate reforms, including the building of affordable housing. He told the crowd that this huge roster of names was solid proof that the vast majority of South Bronx residents want Nehemiah housing.

He then briefly recapped the dispute on Site 404, ticking off the highlights of the struggle. He reminded the crowd of activists:

> Two and a half years ago, the first survey was made of the land in the South Bronx. The organization was in its very infancy. But, at the very beginning, it was decided that some kind of housing should be built on that large piece of land next to Peter and Paul. This isn't something we dreamed up yesterday just so we can stand in the rain in front of American Express.

> The same organizers who collected the 102,000 signatures—with all of the volunteers—took one week out and went block by block and surveyed the land. That was a little more than a year ago, and we drew a map. And that map we took to Fernando Ferrer. And we told him we wanted the land between Park Ave. and Prospect and 163rd and Westchester.[6] So it was no surprise when we went back later with a very specific map and pointed out the exact sites.

Last November there was a meeting with Cardinal O'Connor. In that meeting, for the first time, The Partnership raised its head. They came to that meeting in the person of Miss Kathy Wylde. And she came hand in hand with Mr. Crotty, who is the campaign manager for Mr. Koch. They came to try to convince the Cardinal not to take the position that was being asked. And that was the first time that we got the idea that The Partnership, The NYC Partnership which is part of the Chamber of Commerce, was going to oppose us.

And then last January, February, March, we had our meeting with [HPD Commissioner Abraham] Biderman, and Biderman made it very clear, that that land, Site 404, had already been suggested to be given to somebody else *secretly*. And in secret the land that we asked for publicly was stolen from the people of the South Bronx.

Four days before our massive action of April 2nd, with eight thousand people on the land at Site 404—four days before that, Mayor Koch held a public press conference with people from The Partnership, and the city turned the land over to The Partnership, four days before they knew that we were going to stand on that land. So this conspiracy, this collusion between The Partnership and the city, Mayor Koch and the borough president, has been working now for almost six months.[7]

Drake outlined his failed efforts to arrange a meeting with Jim Robinson. He said Robinson's staff told him, " 'If you want to meet, meet with Kathy Wylde.' " But Drake charged, "Kathy Wylde was the one who was conspiring with the city. *She's* the problem. So we are here today as part of a history that has gone on for almost two and half years and will continue to go on for another two and half years if necessary."

Next up was Dorothy Walls, an elegant Black lay leader in Tremont United Methodist Church, a parish that was sliced to ribbons two decades earlier when the Cross Bronx Expressway steamrolled through it and many other Bronx neighborhoods. She evokes the refugees from Tremont who yearn to return to their community. Poignantly addressing an absent James Robinson, she said,

I, like many others in Tremont, have walked the quiet streets of Nehemiah homes in East Brooklyn. It is like a dream to us. It is what we have dared not even dream for. Family homes with a little yard, and all for about $380 each month. Our church and our people have clung like moss, waiting for a spring rain. And we sense that the moment is now. And I must tell you, Mr. Robinson, we will resist with every ounce of our energy, any outside effort to destroy our dream. We will resist.

Then, assailing him for having delegated authority to an obstructionist staff, she somewhat patronizingly pointed out,

Your employees in The New York City Partnership have been going hand in hand with Mayor Koch's campaign chairman, undermining SBC and Nehemiah homes. You are responsible for the actions of your staff. They are like children playing with fire. It is the job of the parents to discipline them. Why do you demand that we meet with the very ones who want to do us harm? When will you meet and hear us out?

She concluded with a stark warning: "You do not understand what you are getting into. Site 404 is our Tiananmen Square![8] We are not going to stand back and see it stolen for a second time. Do not try to build there! Your builders will only be met with hostility. We of South Bronx Churches will *resist!* We will resist! We *will* resist!"

Mrs. Walls' speech was the most fiery of the morning, but it failed to truly inflame the crowd. Even the chants which usually provide an enthusiastic release for the spectators were particularly muddled that day. At various points between speakers, an organizer at the podium would somewhat ambiguously shout, "Okay, what do we want?" And some of the crowd would roar back, "Nehemiah Now!" while others drowned them out chanting, "404!"

The last principal speaker was Father Sal Ros of St. Margaret Mary Catholic Church near the Concourse. His speech, which sounded like an angry letter to the editor, further subdued the crowd who had no opportunity to raise their voices. Father Ros said, "I want to attest firsthand to the difficulty South Bronx Churches has with dealing with your staff—the ones you want us to work with. Just yesterday I had a long conversation with Ms. Kathy Wylde from your Partnership office. As fifteen members of SBC can attest, she did not listen to one word I had to say." Intensifying the personal attack the priest sarcastically alleged, "She couldn't because she talked nonstop. So, please, Mr. Robinson, do not direct us to solve our difficulties through your staff." Kathy Wylde, in an interview two weeks[9] later, couldn't recall having talked to Father Ros. When showed a transcript of his remarks, she said that she did remember that once when she was talking with Jim Drake on the phone he put a number of people on the squawk box, and presumably that was the conversation to which the priest was referring.

SBC backed off a bit from its reluctance to talk with anyone but Robinson as Father Ros offered Robinson the option of telling "us with whom you want us to meet to prepare the agenda for our [subsequent] meeting with you. We will work with whomever you appoint, once we know it is in preparation for the more critical meeting, the one with you."

At this point the scheduled speakers were finished, and there were no reporters around to have a press conference with, and so the crowd treaded water, bellowing "Nehemiah Now!" Some of the activists wore "Nehemiah Now" baseball caps and held aloft placards with blowups of a recent *Daily News* editorial. The tabloid newspaper, long identified with blue-collar New York and not noted for racial sensitivity, has a colorful history of incredibly blunt, bareknuckles editorials and snappy, brash headlines.[10] This tradition has changed in recent years as *The News* has attempted to court the more affluent suburbanites and still maintain its base in the city where the average subway rider, and morning newspaper reader, is increasingly Black or Hispanic.

The editorial, titled "South Bronx Fight: The Locals Are Right,"[11] is conspicuous for its wholehearted embrace of every detail of SBC's position. It undermines the city's strongest point, that the heavier density of the condos, three hundred units for Site 404, outweighs any other social advantages of the smaller ninety-unit scale of the Nehemiah plan. The editorial says, in part:

> Koch and Housing Commissioner Abraham Biderman argue that arithmetic makes their case: three hundred units are better than ninety. If those were the only numbers involved, they'd be right. They are not—much more is at stake. South Bronx Churches is proposing an ambitious construction and rehabilitation plan to produce some twelve hundred moderately priced apartments, starting at Site 404 and spreading through the surrounding area.

> Site 404, the largest vacant tract in the South Bronx, is the heart of the plan. It cannot proceed without the site, SBC argues, because there will be no center, no anchor, for the new community. The Nehemiah experience in Brooklyn proves several things. At the top is the clear truth that only when a large, de-

fensible community is created does new housing have a chance of withstanding decay and vandalism.

So the argument isn't really ninety vs. three hundred—it's three hundred vs. twelve hundred. Which is to say, if Koch insists on putting his three hundred apartments on Site 404, he's going to blow the opportunity for twelve hundred units from Nehemiah South Bronx Churches.

The reasoning in this editorial sounds like it is straight from I. D. Robbins, and the suspicion lurks that perhaps Robbins influenced the editorialists at *The News* where he was a popular columnist for many years.

With no questions from the press, the rally was drawing to a premature close, and so, with an air of improvisation, a few other speakers took the mike and tried to whip up the gathering.

A hoarse-sounding John Heinemeier exhorted the group, explaining why they were attacking The Partnership: "A home for each of our families who can afford it. For the working class, for the working poor. That's why we're here. James Robinson we believe is a good man. We believe all he needs to do is to stop listening to his staff, and start listening to the people of the South Bronx."

Then, in a wonderfully theatrical gesture, Rev. Heinemeier in his black clerical clothes, white collar, and black beret, cast his blue eyes heavenward at the gleaming corporate edifice and yelled, "Come down from your tower, Mr. Robinson! Come down to the streets where we live. Come down and talk with the South Bronx; we want to talk with you. So come on down!" Built into his speech were plenty of opportunities for the call and response style of public discourse that is so emotionally powerful in minority communities. But by this time the soggy weather had seemed to wilt the crowd, and its sense of outrage was uncharacteristically sapped.

There followed some lame attempts to parody American Express's ubiquitous slogan. One speaker held up Jim Drake's American Express credit card and said, "Don't leave us without our homes!"

In an eloquent closing prayer Father Peter Gavagan celebrated "the courage of the poor to confront the mighty. We ask the leaders of this city, Mr. Robinson, to hear the cries of the people of the South Bronx. We do not want two cities, Our Lord, a city of the rich and a city of the poor. . . . And we thank you, Lord, that we live in the South Bronx. Amen."

The rally unfolded invisibly in the bleak, pedestrian-free landfill block of Battery Park City with only a passing few autos taking note of the sign-carrying activists. It had no discernible effect on budging The Partnership, and perhaps Robinson's ability to easily roll with the best punch SBC could muster may have even encouraged The Partnership to remain adamant. It is hard not to be impressed with the aloof, confident disdain corporate officers apparently can afford to exhibit when confronted with alarmed citizens.

At the last minute, the huge effort involved in turning out all the residents and transporting them to Lower Manhattan was partially redeemed when a local television-news camera crew taped a few of the organizers, using the American Express corporate logo on the building as a dramatic backdrop.

Meanwhile the city's gears churned. A call for bids invited developers to submit proposals to build on Site 404. The specs detailed higher density three- and four-story buildings, thus freezing out SBC with its lower density Nehemiah homes.

On the decision not to bid on Site 404, Chambers was adamant:

> Why bid on something you don't believe in? You have to bid according to specs. The specs call for three- to four-story buildings. There is no indication that it is going to be owner-occupied.

> That's bullshit. They are going to have to subsidize the shit out of it. Whoever builds that is going to get about $70,000 per apartment, in order to force the price down near to Nehemiah. The subsidy is just going into the pockets of one of the developers. Nehemiah is dead in the South Bronx if we don't get 404.[12]

11

Armistice in the War on 404

On April 27, 1990, a little over a year after the War on 404 was solemnly declared at the massive April 2nd rally, the leaders of SBC agreed to a peace treaty with the city that, although it all but ratified their loss of that crucial, cleared three-block stretch of the South Bronx, swept away the most serious barriers preventing construction of the long-awaited Nehemiah homes on nearby sites.

At 8:30 A.M. in the basement of St. Jerome's a few flights below the offices of SBC, eighteen leaders of SBC (ministers, lay people, staff organizers and Ed Chambers) gathered around a long oak table to weigh their options.

Hanging over the discussion was the slow-grinding history of the past year. The euphoria of the April 1989 rally had been abraded by the frictional wear of battling the turtle-paced city bureaucracy. The year was filled with spirit-pumping rallies, modest meetings in parish basements, confrontations with elite city decision makers, and the slow, deliberate building and maintenance of an indigenous South Bronx power base. The long year, however, was punctuated by two major events: the most important was the defeat of Edward Koch by David Dinkins and the subsequent replacement of HPD Commission Abraham Biderman with Bronx-born Felice Michetti; the other was the radical switch of tactics, born of irritated vexation, embodied in the launching of a lawsuit against the city—a startling maneuver which violated a longstanding IAF taboo against wading into legal swamps.

SBC's relations with David Dinkins had never been cordial, although none of the activists doubted that he was a vast improvement over the belligerent Koch. Throughout the spring and summer and into the fall of the 1989 mayoral campaign, SBC and the two other IAF New York groups assiduously courted Dinkins.

The candidate, overconfidently calculating that the IAF groups which represent a mostly minority constituency had no place to go other than him, took their support for granted. Perhaps unintentionally, he deeply offended their leaders by ducking meetings that other candidates readily sat for, and then, when he reluctantly agreed to an encounter with major IAF leaders, he arrived late. He outraged them further when he distractedly ate his lunch during the abbreviated session.

Still, with Koch gone, new opportunities were in the wind. Why would the new administration not want to do business with South Bronx Churches? Clearly SBC was a group that could deliver on its promise to build new housing, *at no real cost to the city!* in areas where municipal authorities had been unable or unwilling to move construction forward. Since the church group was willing to share the credit with the new mayor, turning over the vacant land seemed like a win-win situation for all concerned. However, there was still the Ferrer roadblock and the potential foot-dragging from HPD staffers. It was clear that a lot was riding on the politics of the new HPD commissioner.

IAF's relations with HPD commissioners had been stormy even before Biderman. His predecessor, Anthony Gliedman, now an official of bankrupt casino operator Donald Trump, had a classic IAF baptism of fire with the Brooklyn group. Heinemeier recalls:

> We were trying to get Gliedman's attention on Nehemiah. We scheduled a meeting with him. It was at City Hall, not at [HPD's headquarters on] Gold Street. He decided to meet with us in one of the hearing rooms in City Hall. Why, I'm not sure. It was a very inhospitable, cold, judicial-type of room.
>
> The day before the meeting we sent one of our staff people down to look over the room where we would be meeting. It was a hearing room with a horseshoe-shaped table, a big, big table. I think we decided how many to take based on the number of chairs there were. Eighteen big leather easy chairs that swivel with headrests, every one of them with a mike. This inlaid table, this beautiful place! Right in the middle of this horseshoe in the open end was this little wooden table, about 3' × 3' with a little wooden folding chair, for the hearee.
>
> When we found out that was where we were going to meet we went down there thirty minutes early, and we all took our places in the leather chairs. Here comes Gliedman and his aides in; first thing when he enters the door of the room, he says, "What is this? Am I under indictment here?"

He wasn't smiling either. One of his aides, who happened to be a Black guy who was obviously a front man, just blew up. He felt that he had been betrayed. He had set up this meeting with us and Gliedman, I guess, out of courtesy to some of the Black leaders in EBC. He felt that we had done a job on him. He just went berserk. Gliedman had to publicly shut him up. And so it was a very embarrassing moment for the guy. And that's the way the meeting took place. Gliedman took his seat at the little wooden table, and it was our agenda, and we were the people in the leather chairs.[1]

An occupational hazard for employees at HPD is that they personify the city and the myriad disappointments of its housing policy. Hapless staffers are often offered up as sacrificial lambs when a community group wants to have a city representative at an evening meeting where residents can vent their anger at the city's failings. Gliedman's humiliation at the hands of an insurgent neighborhood group was of a piece with indignities lower-level HPD officials suffer as a matter of course.

Here, again, the IAF maxim: no permanent enemies; no permanent allies. The groups' almost cavalier attitude (we may publicly question your integrity one day, but, if you come through for us the next, we'll praise you to the sky) is at times a little hard to swallow for some public officials. Into this category of those who are not so willing to let bygones be bygones put Fernando Ferrer. Then worry lurked that perhaps not all HPD staffers would be so stoically accommodating to SBC's overtures to new leadership at HPD. If the new commissioner came from within the agency, there would be the poisoned history of bad blood to contend with.

When Dinkins took office in January 1990, he delayed for months the appointment of a housing commissioner. Published speculation had it that Kathy Wylde of The New York City Housing Partnership, touted strongly by David Rockefeller, was the leading outside candidate. But, in the end, the new mayor appointed Felice Michetti, a 41-year-old Italian American who had spent her whole career in municipal housing agencies and was one of the architects of the Koch's Ten-Year Building Plan.[2]

This appointment plunged SBC into despair. They knew Felice Michetti as an implacable foe, as a faithful agent of the uncooperative former Commissioner Abe Biderman. On 18 March 1990 during an evaluation after an *action* at Methodist Tremont that brought out

one thousand activists, John Heinemeier candidly told the leaders
who assembled in the bare-bones auditoriumlike church lit from
above by tiny, modern art, stained-glass windows:

> We are a small organization. I don't know of any other organi-
> zation around the whole country that IAF works with that has
> got as much flak as this one. . . . I mean this city is *down* on us.
> All you have to do is remember who was appointed HPD Com-
> missioner yesterday. Felice Michetti! The worst news we ever
> got! This city is down on us. And we are standing tall. We will
> not be broken![3]

Michetti came up through the ranks at HPD holding various
jobs, but significantly she spent the early years of her career in the
Bronx, first with the Bronx office of the City Planning Commission
in 1973 and later shifting to the Tremont Avenue office of HPD in
1979. Of the new commissioner the *Times* questioned whether she
could "play the role of advocate for housing in areas that go beyond
the disposition of city-owned land and buildings," but it did concede
that "admirers consider her exceptional at both conceiving housing
production programs and making them work."[4] Unlike the more
landlord/real-estate policy-oriented types who are usually tapped for
this kind of position, it would seem that Michetti had the right pedi-
gree to appreciate SBC's agenda. Indeed, even the *Village Voice*, an
utterly consistent and stalwart enemy of landlords and developers,
anointed her debut by planting a big wet kiss across its pages titled,
"A Hands-On Commissioner: New Housing Chief Is a Bronx Native
Who Knows Her Stuff,"[5] About her Bronx roots the *Voice* gushed:

> It's where the 41-year-old commissioner grew up, where she be-
> gan her career in housing, and the place for which there will al-
> ways be a soft spot in her heart. . . . Throughout the previous
> administration, she took a back seat to Ivy League men whom
> she had to teach about housing. Her straightforwardness, with
> all its rough edges, meant she probably would never have be-
> come a commissioner under Ed Koch.

Despite SBC's initially low expectations for Michetti's tenure,
there was a dramatic change in the city's willingness to meet SBC
halfway. Ferrer, whose own political position was bolstered by his
shrewd, relatively early backing of Dinkins, was still defiant and
not so readily placated. He remained an inert roadblock to the ex-

pansion of Nehemiah to Site 404 and, thus, to the South Bronx. But Michetti's early career-building success hinged on her collaboration with the Northwest Bronx Community and Clergy Coalition, an early attempt to forge a power organization rooted in parishes. Indeed, the parallels between this organization and SBC run so deeply that it is no coincidence that the principal founders of the Northwest Bronx Community and Clergy Coalition had all gone through IAF Training.[6]

SBC's antipathy to Michetti was based on her uncooperativeness when Biderman delegated to her responsibility for negotiation with SBC over Site 404. Yet, once she was in power, fences were quickly mended, so much so that by IAF's gala fiftieth anniversary celebration in a faded, but elegant restaurant on the old World's Fair grounds in Queens a few months later (on 31 May 1990) she was hailed by Jim Drake as a woman who was willing to join with SBC in rebuilding the South Bronx. Indeed, Michetti even attended the IAF fund raiser as a guest of honor, a startling development in itself. It is impossible to imagine a Koch administration figure lauding the tradition embodied in IAF agitating. Moreover, she did follow through; and, although she never budged on Site 404, she paved the way for the compromise that the IAF leaders had gathered to consider in April 1990.

Despite this unexpected armistice with HPD the Battle for 404 went forward on other fronts. The new tactic surprisingly relied, not on mobilizing masses of the working poor and bitter confrontations with the power elite, but on the muffled swordplay of dueling lawyers.

This legal skirmish on Site 404 was inadvertently launched by the Koch administration during the heat of his reelection campaign. By late summer, it was clear to Koch's handlers that Dinkins was pulling ahead, and, in the time-honored tradition of all desperate incumbents, Koch began to use his control of the municipal purse strings to curry favor. With Koch's back against the wall, SBC confidently glided in and tried to strike a deal with Commissioner Abe Biderman that would allow ground to finally be broken on Nehemiah. Pitilessly pragmatic as always, SBC leaders said they had no problem publicly giving Koch credit for any breakthrough that would allow them to start building.

Stoutly sticking to his guns Biderman was still unable to cut the strings to Site 404, but, in late August 1989, he considerably enhanced the deal already on the table. He temptingly dangled additional cleared South Bronx acreage in front of SBC. Proffering a smile and a pen, he unveiled a legally-binding five-page *Memorandum of Understanding* dated 25 August 1989:

> In recognition of the substantial commitment of resources by SBC, HPD agrees to recommend to the Board of Estimate [or its successor] that the City-owned sites listed in Attachment B be sold to SBC for $1 per home. In addition, HPD agrees to recommend that $15,000 a unit of City subsidy be made available to make the homes affordable to the target income group.[7]

Specifically Biderman offered city-owned sites for 450 homes during a Phase One portion of the plan and another 250 or so sites in a Phase Two arrangement, which included parcels that were privately owned and which HPD promised to acquire through condemnation, demolition, and relocation.

What did Koch and HPD want in return? The *Memorandum of Understanding* was explicit:

> As one part of the effort to provide affordable housing in the South Bronx, SBC and HPD agree to work together to develop approximately 700 units of owner-occupied housing for moderate-income households on City-owned sites in the South Bronx ["the Program"] modeled on the successful Nehemiah project in Brooklyn. Another element of the effort to provide affordable housing in the South Bronx is the development of Site 404 [by the NYC Partnership]. HPD's agreement to participate in the Program is based on the overall provision of affordable housing in the South Bronx, and so relies on SBC's agreement to support the development of 404 as Partnership housing. Should SBC fail to comply with its agreement to support Site 404 as Partnership housing, this *Memorandum of Understanding* will terminate.[8]

It was certainly a straightforward trade-off: Promise to relinquish 404 and also not disrupt The Partnership's plans for the site, and we'll give you plenty of other land. Robbins was outraged by the offer. He was adamant that SBC needed the cleared contiguous blocks of Site 404 as the linchpin for a successful transplant of Nehemiah to the South Bronx. What doubts others had about passing up this tantalizing proposition were suppressed both in deference to Robbins and with the hope that Koch would be expelled from office by the voters in November and a new alignment of political power might prove more hospitable.

However, instead of passively rejecting the offer, Robbins lashed out and personally bankrolled a lawsuit against Koch, Biderman, and HPD, alleging that linking the offer of land to a promise to give up his citizen's rights to protest a development decision on adjacent acres was unprecedented and illegal.

Bringing suit was blasphemous IAF heresy. Earlier that summer, as part of standard IAF training, activists in Los Angeles were bluntly admonished by Larry McNeil:

> Avoid lawyers at all costs. They do things *for* people; they don't teach people. Getting mixed up in the courts freezes action. Everyone has to stop and wait to see what the judge will do.

> What's more, lawyers are walking slot machines. They just suck money right up. They eat money![9]

In offering the deal, was HPD being unreasonable? Kathleen Dunn, a technical and erudite assistant commissioner of HPD, candidly said of this contract a few months later:

> The *Memorandum of Understanding* asks them to support the Partnership's development of 404. Look it, it was a *quid pro quo.* I mean we weren't going to go ahead with South Bronx Churches on one thing and then have them fight us at the same time. It would do us no good for either [The Partnership on 404 and the adjacent Nehemiah project] to have us start with a developer and then have a lawsuit in the middle of it. We are either partners in this, or we aren't partners in it.

> We have had *Memorandums of Understanding* with other groups we have been involved with, particularly one that I have been involved with on the Lower East Side.

> All we are saying is that we want to build affordable housing. We want to build affordable housing with you, but we want to build more of it; therefore, we don't want to build single-family [dwellings] on 404. We've worked with Mr. Robbins in Brooklyn. We've had our moments, but it has resulted in housing being built. We did move along. I don't know why 404 has to be the stumbling block here.[10]

True to McNeil's warning about the deflection of energy that lawsuits bring, years later the case meanders through the courts. And not only has the pall it cast over the development of Site 404 contributed to the delay in building, but it also has stymied SBC's efforts to move forward in cooperation with HPD.

So by April 1990 when the leaders gathered at St. Jerome's, they were weighed down with the realization that 404 was slipping further away, and its centrality to both them and the city was blocking any Nehemiah construction in the South Bronx.

At the St. Jerome's summit of SBC leaders the opening prayer called on God's "blessing and enlightenment to permit wise decisions . . . and to help us make a new beginning."[11]. Jim Drake began optimistically with a report to the group about a break-through meeting he and a few other SBC leaders had had with Felice Michetti two days earlier.

The persistently bad news was that the city's position on 404 was unchanged, and Michetti didn't foresee any likelihood of change. She acknowledged that Borough President Ferrer remained unshakable: "he is your biggest opposition." However, she was willing to offer a dusted-off two-stage strategy that would permit the building of hundreds of Nehemiah homes in areas adjacent to 404.

She proposed a Phase One arrangement that called for the immediate erection of 210 single-family Nehemiah homes and seventy-eight of the more compact Nehemiah garden apartments[12] which would allow for a slightly higher density. Once this construction was completed, she envisioned a Phase Two program with a mixture of another 157 single-family Nehemiah homes and 140 Nehemiah garden apartments. Phase Two would be contingent on the completion of the first wave of homes and the successful relocation of some 104 families who now live in buildings that would have to be demolished in order to clear land for the second stage.

Father John Grange of St. Jerome's reported that Michetti had sweetened the pot further by also identifying a number of other sites that would be suitable for Nehemiah homes. Ten blocks south of Site 404 is St. Mary's Park, a twenty-square block expanse of worn greenery. Grange said that below the park is an area planners call St. Mary's South, and there Michetti offered two sites.[13] Grange also reported that nearer to 404, at Prospect Avenue and 161st to 163rd Streets, is another site that is ripe for development, although Planning Board Three officials (who control decisions on land use in this part of the South Bronx) strongly advocate higher density. Michetti told the SBC leaders that she would be willing to push these officials for Nehemiah. On the Planning Board Three site, 208 homes could be built.

As the SBC leaders were trying to absorb this new information and visualize the disbursement of homes, Jim Drake stepped up to a large white pad propped up on a stand and summarized the Michetti proposal: "Right now," he said, "we have fourteen acres for certain. On this we can build 170 single family Nehemiah homes and 230 garden apartments, or a total of 400 homes. Michetti has complete control of this site, and she and [Mayor David] Dinkins are solidly behind giving it to us." This fourteen-acre site lies to the east of Site 404 and doglegs south beneath it. The Phase Two parcel, in an area even further east near Prospect Avenue, encompasses five acres but could hold up to 576 homes if most of them were Nehemiah garden apartments. Building this phase would involve relocation, and that makes the enterprise much more problematic. Finally, there is the possibility of another eight acres in St. Mary's South.

Michetti's major concession, Drake explained, was that "there is no linkage between 404 and all the rest." In other words, SBC would not have to renounce its intention of eventually building on Site 404. Drake speculated, "We show that we can build at half the cost of the Partnership, and then we will have a better shot at 404."

When everyone had thoroughly digested Michetti's proposal, Drake revealed that he and I. D. Robbins, Ed Chambers and Mike Gecan, the Lead Organizer during the Brooklyn Nehemiah construction, had hammered out a counterproposal that he asked the group to now consider.

Drake suggested, "We agree to Phase One, and ask for the Prospect area to be included also. On this first site, instead of mixing the traditional single-family Nehemiah house with the Nehemiah garden apartment, we create a modified higher density Nehemiah condo." This would be a slightly smaller version of the Brooklyn prototype. Each two-story duplex apartment would have a private entrance, one bath, and two bedrooms but would not have a basement or a private backyard. Each individual building would contain eight condos, all with separate entrances and no public halls. The only common areas would be the roof of the buildings and the gardens. Maintenance of common areas is always a vexing problem in multi-family dwellings so that an escrow account would have to be set up in perpetuity to provide for care of the common areas. The present 1,250 square feet of the classic Nehemiah home would be diminished significantly, to 1,000 square feet.

Drake claimed the reason for this altered version of the original Nehemiah home was that the new site presented unique topology challenges: "Here we will be playing roulette with the land. It is filled with rocks and is not level. Site 404 is a smooth sandy plot. We need to downsize to guarantee the $45,000 price to our people. Also there are obvious advantages in just sticking to one mode of house during Phase One." This version of Nehemiah would permit forty homes per acre on Phase One's fourteen acres for a total of 560 homes for this phase. Built into the selling price would be a $15,000 second mortgage subsidy. Provision would have to be made for the expense of maintenance of the common areas. This cost could be front-loaded or taken care of from an endowment.

Further, Drake advocated that they keep the lawsuit alive and in the meantime demonstrate that The Partnership's "$100,000 apartments at higher density are not appropriate for this part of the South Bronx. Also we think we should take St. Mary's South under advisement and also take the rehabs under advisement."

Complicating the issue, this counterproposal had to be signed within severe time constraints. Formal city approval for this project would have to come through the Board of Estimate which, as a result of an autumn referendum, was going out of existence in a few weeks. All new zoning issues henceforth would be adjudicated by a reinvigorated City Council, and their startup times and political alignment were highly speculative. At a minimum it was believed that ground-breaking would be delayed at least six months. Also, Drake reported, SBC's "financing is under pressure." The money to begin construction would come from a fund set up by church hierarchies and be re-paid when local residents bought the completed homes. With other demands on the church funds, it could not be guaranteed that the money would always be available if the dispute dragged on endlessly and no actual construction was imminent.[14]

At this point Ed Chambers, who was sagely sitting off to the side, joined the discussion by cautioning the leaders that they were about to venture into dangerous territory. "We need a critical mass to sustain this new community. We can't do less than five hundred homes, and, even then, if we can't do more than the present 560, we could have problems." It has always been an article of faith for Chambers and I. D. Robbins that unless a certain critical mass of homeowners was rooted in a defensible area, the momentum of de-struction that has claimed large parts of the South Bronx would over-whelm the pioneer homeowners. Chambers also revealed that I. D. Robbins at first "started out saying no to the South Bronx. He did not want to set up a construction team in the South Bronx and not have enough work. Now that Michetti has given us fourteen acres, we can get I. D. up here working, and then once he gets established other pos-sibilities are in the offing."

For SBC the stakes were high and the problems daunting: hold-ing together the coalition of member churches who desperately needed a clear victory, something concrete to point to; securing approval and cooperation from the city; retaining the good will and support of the funding sources; and keeping I. D. Robbins happy all had to be balanced against the hazards of launching and sustaining an ambitious, perhaps risky, building project. Timing was pivotal.

Once the revised proposal was fully laid out, Drake went around the room asking for everyone's personal assessment. John Heinemeier voiced "a serious concern about the smaller square footage" in the downscaled Nehemiah home. This theme was picked up by most of the other leaders who worried about storage space and the possibility that some homeowners would have extended families living with them and be squeezed by the modest dimensions of the floor plan.

But, in the end, the logic of the proposal was overwhelming. The eagerness in the room was palpable—everyone wanted to finally get something going. Since SBC had made the building of Nehemiah homes the cornerstone of its organizing efforts, it was imperative not to let the opportunity to begin construction slip away just because the conditions were not ideal. Despite some qualms about the small size of the apartments and the worry that the apparent abandonment of Site 404 would demoralize some members who had been told for a solid year that there would be no compromise (that indeed, there could be no compromise on 404, and no Nehemiah without 404), it was unanimously decided to bite the bullet and back the revised proposal to Michetti and begin building 560 Nehemiah condos adjacent to Site 404.

The next stage, once the proposal was approved by the Board of Estimate, was not going to be smooth sailing. As Chambers bluntly told the Bronx leaders, working with I. D. Robbins was "like guerrilla warfare; he's a difficult guy to work with. Eighty percent of the time he's creative, and twenty percent of the time he goes off." Chambers, given his own surly outspokenness, ironically fretted about the "problems he causes us with his opinions. When he called [HPD Commissioner] Biderman a liar that got us into a lot of trouble. But he is the only guy that can bring in Nehemiah at these prices."

John Heinemeier magnified the momentousness of the vote:

We have now made a qualitative leap. We have to be more involved now with demanding details like screening potential buyers, etc. Let us know what we are getting into. The selling price of $45,000 will cause a war [among developers and politicians]. Gigante who proudly boasts that he sells a two-family house for $150,000 will bring every pressure.

Although the vote backed away from making a stand on 404 and represented a profound shift in strategy, everyone was eager to put the best face on this retreat. Drake, with never-say-die IAF optimism, insisted, "We've still got a good lawsuit on 404, and we will be fighting The Partnership not with just words but with deeds."

At the end of the meeting just before the closing prayer, Drake went even further, claiming "We won on 404. They have got nothing, and we are building."

However, despite this breakthrough, progress was glacial: by early 1991 there was still nothing in the ground.

The *New York Times* summarized the situation as of the summer of 1990:

> Ms. Michetti said that an understanding had been reached with South Bronx Churches, a nonprofit housing organization, to develop 400 to 500 housing units on sites in the vicinity of East 163rd Street and Jackson Avenue in the Bronx. Trying to establish in the Bronx a low-income, for-sale housing program similar to the one mounted in Brooklyn as the Nehemiah Plan by East Brooklyn Churches, the organization staged a protest when the Koch administration decided to award a more centrally located urban-renewal tract known as Site 404 to a different developer.
>
> . . . South Bronx Churches is expected to develop one-family units in the town house and back-to-back styles on sites it was offered by the Koch administration. The houses will probably be sold at average prices lower than the builder will get for condominium units on Site 404 land—4.35 acres in the Melrose section near the commercial district at Third Avenue and East 149th Street. There the Procida Construction Corporation plans to build 275 units in three- and four-story walkups, to be sold through the New York Housing Partnership.[15]

Five months later, at the end of 1990, another article took a long look at the development prospects for the South Bronx. It began on an upbeat note:

> Over a vast, half-desolate swath of the South Bronx, a place of lonely businesses, empty lots and storefront evangelists, planners are drawing the core of a new city.

Their proposal seeks to transform the appearance and economic potential of one of the country's most resilient symbols
of urban blight by creating a synergy among a wide range of development projects, some already under construction, others
merely proposed.

Little more than a decade after some city officials and planners were declaring the South Bronx to be beyond renewal, the
huge plan's ambition is itself a powerful sign of progress in the
borough.[16]

Abruptly the rose-colored glasses came off, and the grim reality
of the South Bronx reasserted itself:

Yet as New York's financial outlook has darkened, the questions that the plan faces have sharpened, and its support at City
Hall has waned.

Of course one of the key components of this new "Camelot" in
the South Bronx is the ambitious Melrose Commons plan of which
Site 404 is either the crown jewel or, depending on which way the
wind is blowing, the most vital bordering component. The article
unsentimentally surveys the obstacles blocking the path:

To build an entire neighborhood where there are now mostly
vacant lots and abandoned buildings would cost more than
$400 million over 12 years. City housing subsidies alone are es-
timated at $100 million, and some officials are skeptical about
developers' chances of drawing better-off home buyers into an
area ringed by housing projects.

The plan faces other questions about the borough's poor public transportation links and the difficulty of drawing investment to an area that counts its high concentration of empty,
city-owned land and the underemployment of its labor force as
chief attractions.

Mr. Ferrer and his aides do not deny the drawbacks. Their plan,
they argue, is merely the best option to integrate some of the
city's youngest, poorest and least-employed residents into the
economic mainstream, while wresting the South Bronx from
the grip of poverty.[17]

The governmental wheels ground sluggishly. Yet, one by one,
obstacles were cleared. The City Council approved the plan, a dubi-
ous I. D. Robbins convinced himself that the city was serious, nu-

merous zoning clearances and permits were approved, and finally, by February 1991, the bulldozers were ready to scrape through the rocky terrain of the South Bronx.

It seemed the long, bitter struggle was almost over.

On 7 February 1991, the Nehemiah groundbreaking was celebrated in the historic Thessalonia Baptist Church, near the first cleared site, some half-dozen blocks east of Site 404. Over five hundred people crammed into the church pews to hear Mayor David Dinkins, I. D. Robbins, John Heinemeier, Felice Michetti, and even Fernando Ferrer hail the beginning of the first phase of Nehemiah building in the South Bronx.

The initial effort, due to be completed in 1992, would consist of 540 homes on city-owned lots in the St. Mary's Park section of the South Bronx. The final compromise is a hybrid of Nehemiah types: there will be a mix of the traditional Brooklyn one-family, two-story rowhouses, and, on the larger sites, three-family structures with two duplexes over a single-family unit. According to City Hall:

> The condominium-style stacked housing model increases the number of units per acre, satisfying both the city's and the community's concern that higher density housing be built on these sites to make the best use of limited resources.[18]

South Bronx Churches, even without the fat wallet of the Roman Catholic Archdiocese, managed to raise $4 million to be used as an interest-free revolving construction fund. The city claims that the $65,000 cost per unit will be reduced to $50,000 when city subsidies of $15,000 per unit are factored in. All this public money will be recouped "from profits realized by the resale of the unit; the owner must return to the city all profits up to $15,000 that are gained from such a resale."[19]

Dinkins dedicated this first phase of construction to the working people of the Bronx:

> In 1992, when this project is to be completed, nurses' aides and paralegals, transit workers, young teachers, secretaries and postal workers will finally have the opportunity to become homeowners, to stake their hard-earned claim in the American Dream.[20]

Just before the umbrella-wielding crowd straggled outside in a driving rain to anoint the bulldozer with holy water and offer prayers before the giant yellow machine dug into the muddy rubble, they presented I. D. Robbins with "the key to the South Bronx."

After a standing ovation, an emotional Robbins told the crowd:

This is certainly a high moment in my life. Although it's been five years since we have tried to come here, we are here now. I want to pay tribute to Jim Drake. . . . It has taken us quite a while to get here, but nothing comes easy when you are trying to do God's work.

This is a small job we are starting, only 540 houses. But I can only promise you that with your help we will stay here until we complete the reconstruction of the South Bronx.[21]

IV

✳

Analysis

12

Was It a Just War?

By 1993, the battle sputtered to a halt. The foundations of the first housing to be built on Site 404, ending a generation of festering neglect, began to be sunk in the debris-encrusted ground. These relatively low-density condos were built by The New York City Partnership. It was The Partnership's home-building program that finally extinguished twenty-five years of blighted emptiness on 404. Rising in the summer of 1993 were multistory condos that were projected to sell for $75,000 per apartment which, according to city formulas, should be affordable to people with incomes of $32,000 per year.

Although Nehemiah homes were not ever built on site 404, the Nehemiah concept was successfully imported to the South Bronx. While the 404 housing was still a shell, some two hundred families moved into Nehemiah homes a few blocks east of 404. After the anticipated foot-dragging by municipal agencies, Nehemiah building progressed steadily. By 1995 plans call for 550 more homes and condominiums in the neighborhoods around 404. The prices of the Nehemiah houses inched up to $55,000 in 1993 but are still $20,000 cheaper than the competing city-sponsored housing.

Proud homeowners of the first Nehemiah houses fall into two categories: those who were active members of South Bronx Churches, and others who recognized a good housing bargain when they saw it.

Carlos Gordon, a retired window washer, earned the right to his home by fighting in every battle that SBC waged with the city. Long before the 1989 Site 404 rally, Gordon's parish priest sent Jim Drake to visit Gordon, who was an influential parishioner. Gordon participated in an early SBC confidence-building confrontation with the local police captain which eventually resulted in improved police patrols targeting street addicts. After that, the Panamanian-born Gordon was dispatched to the Ten-Day training in Houston where he was steeped in IAF ideology.

The Nehemiah struggle was not Gordon's first involvement in the housing crisis of the South Bronx. In the 1950s when Gordon first arrived from Central America, he settled in Harlem but aspired to an apartment in the Bronx, which were hard to come by in those days. He was offered a burnt-out apartment in the Bronx by the landlord on the condition that he fix it up, which he did. This was a decade before the fires raged out of control in the South Bronx. He settled in comfortably, and his building managed to hold on much longer than most. But by 1981, "The landlord just abandoned us. He said to the tenants, 'You take the building yourself.' The tenants picked up the pieces. We suffered a lot of cold weather there. We got together, but a lot of the tenants didn't want to contribute for oil for the boiler. The little bit of rent we get we use for oil. We formed a tenant association and tried to make the city take over."[1]

The city eventually assumed ownership and filled the boiler's oil tanks, "But we were fighting with the tenants who weren't giving anything. The city trained a few of us, I was one of them; and two years afterwards they sold us the building at $250 a apartment. So it was a coop."

Losing the landlord and gaining ownership was not the salvation that some anticipated. The residents were forced to deal with the considerable pragmatic problems of running a South Bronx building. The building leaders had to take recalcitrant tenants to court to get them to pay. But, according to Gordon, "The court is inclined more to the tenants. They don't consider that it is a cooperative. I was victimized because I was the one who was working to get one of the [nonpaying] tenants evicted. I come to find out that they burnt my car. The thing that hurt was that they could pay the rent, but they didn't want to. We went to court so many times."

After the successful conclusion of the SBC wars with the city, Gordon submitted through his parish an application to enter the lottery for the new Nehemiah homes. Unlike Brooklyn, where most of the homeowners were not EBC activists, a seeming majority of Bronx Nehemiah residents were involved in the struggle. As Gordon admits, "The way I see it, most of the ones who fought the city, I notice they got themselves a little house."

One of Gordon's neighbors is Edwin Forty, a 32-year-old doorman who has lived in the South Bronx his whole life. Forty, and his wife Naomi who teaches public school in the city, were not as involved in the SBC struggle, although they rallied with the other protesters at the 1989 demonstration on Site 404. Forty, an expansive and friendly man, is delighted with his new home, although he is not oblivious to the risk of sinking his life savings in a house in a neighborhood that is still marginal. Safety is a perennial concern. On the walk home from the subway, he stays alert. "When I get to my block, I know I'm safe." He carries a personal alarm which is a small electronic noise maker."My wife has one, and I'm getting them for my kids."[2] He is hopeful for the stability of the area because, as Nehemiah expands, more residents will own their homes. "Anything that you *buy* will be sound housing," he reasons. "Some people are bad; it doesn't matter. You might be a bad person, but when you buy something, and it's yours, you protect it." Pointing across the street from his front yard, he says,

> "If that was a city-owned building, there would be four families in it. They would dirty it up; they wouldn't even care. It's not theirs, someone else would come and clean it up for them. But when it's yours, you have to clean it up yourself. It's like when it's you car. If you rent a car and get a little scratch on it, hey, no problem. If it's your car, and you get a little scratch on it, you get out and start screaming.

Asked about the lack of density, the imposition of a suburban grid on a formerly bustling inner city neighborhood, he was not nostalgic for the old cluttered Bronx where he was raised, after his parents arrived from Puerto Rico.

> "If it's too crowded you are back to where you really started. That's how people end up killing each other. When everything is so tight, anything bothers you; you are upset all the time. Like where I was, I was upset all the time. I didn't show it, but I was, always. You know, you go in and, "I'm back to this place." "You hear your neighbors problems. And one day you walk out, and you're mad, and he's mad, and before you know it. . . . "

How should we think about the problem of imposing single family housing in the South Bronx? Who is right? Is small scale suburban development a solution for the seemingly intractable problems of the Bronx as the new Nehemiah residents fervently believe, or is it just a quick fix that ultimately betrays the poor by displacement? At this point, it is appropriate to step back from the fray and try to untangle the questions that this type of development raises.

Many questions remain. Were the planners at HPD, politicians like Mayor Koch and Borough President Ferrer, local officials like the majority of Planning Board Three and successful South Bronx builder Father Gigante right in opposing this version of owner-occupied housing? Does the extremely low density of the Nehemiah homes squander valuable, centrally-located land that historically served numerous low-income families? Or was I. D. Robbins right? Are low-density homes where the resident has a unequivocal stake in his dwelling and his neighborhood the most promising solution for an area that for decades has been swamped by social problems of overwhelming magnitude? Is the Bronx, as Jim Drake maintains, "occupied territory like South Africa," and, therefore, should its fate rightly rest in the hands of those who seize it in the people's name from the city which has, until recently, idly acquiesced in its neglect?

Besides density, there are also the hotly disputed issues of cost and the related question of determining who is to live in any new housing in this ruined part of the South Bronx. Is it most productive to try to attract more affluent middle-income people in order to stabilize the area by cultivating income diversity or should any new construction benefit those low-income residents who have valiantly held on during the firestorm of the last two decades doggedly fighting for neighborhood improvement?

In addition to density and income level, a third bone of contention is the issue of demolishing abandoned but still sound multifamily rental buildings which, if properly rehabbed, might house many more families than single-family dwellings. Or, even more poignantly, is it socially defensible at this stage of Bronx history to level wounded buildings that still shelter people, thus forcing them to move somewhere else? The Bronx historically has been a borough of renters; will SBC's insistence on using the limited land of the South Bronx to build houses only for people who have the money to buy their homes paradoxically squeeze out the majority of the very people they are organizing to protect?

These are all complicated questions that do not yield crisp, unambiguous conclusions. The public debate essentially turns on these problems. But peel away these complications, and there is another layer to the dispute. Much of it turns on ego and the more parochial concerns of both sides. SBC charges that Koch and Ferrer were more concerned about pleasing real-estate developers by keeping business as usual than they were motivated by any scrupulous concern about density and appropriate development. Who can doubt that Koch's seething long-term enmity to IAF tactics or Ferrer's wounded pride did not play a major part in the struggle over Site 404? And, on the other side, it is clear that the IAF has bigger fish to fry in the South Bronx. It is blunt about wanting to build a power organization that will advance a hugely ambitious agenda, and the building of Nehemiah homes will, as it has in Brooklyn, put the group decisively on the map. If the type of housing it had expertise in building were five-story elevator buildings, would it not fervently deride transplanting an inappropriate suburban model of low-density owner-occupied rowhouses to a once-crowded urban setting originally designed on the more inclusive model of rental apartments?

Density, because it intersects with almost all of these other factors, is a key to this dispute. What really is at stake?

As we have seen in previous chapter, the housing situation in the South Bronx has been grim. The meager funds which were expended over the last generation for housing were largely wasted. During the Reagan boom years of the 1980s, virtually no government housing resources found their way to the South Bronx.

Towards the end of the decade, New York City belatedly began to digest the fact that no aid could be expected from Washington. Relatively flush with huge tax revenues fueled by Wall Street-driven economic prosperity, the municipal government began to channel some serious money into rebuilding Harlem, the Lower East Side of Manhattan, various parts of Brooklyn, and the bellwether symbol of housing despair, the South Bronx.

Mayor Koch committed the city to a huge assault on the housing crisis. In his 1989 book, he boasts:

New York City has now made the largest commitment to housing of any city or state in the country. In 1986, I made a ten-year commitment to spend $4.2 billion to build and rehabilitate a quarter of a million housing units. In 1988, I went even further. The Ten-Year Plan, as we call it, now totals $5.1 billion, most of which, $4.4 billion, is City funds. That might seem like a lot of abstract numbers. But when you consider that we used to spend $25 million (not billion) a year on housing production, $5 billion is astronomical—probably the size of the budget of some entire cities, states and even countries.[3]

Koch's ambitious plan had three major components: the rehabilitation of abandoned buildings, the reconstruction of inhabited city-owned structures, and the building of new homes on city land.

Of first priority, according to Koch, was the rehabilitation of abandoned

blighted buildings that are owned by the City and which are structurally sound. That's 5,000 buildings that will be turned into affordable housing for people making $32,000 a year or less. In total, we expect to create 47,000 units out of vacant buildings from what is referred to as our *in rem* stock: buildings taken over by the City because the owners didn't pay their taxes.[4]

In Koch's original plan, one-third of these apartments would go to the homeless, one-third to people making below $19,000 a year, and the last third to moderate-income families making between $19,000 and $32,000 a year.

The second arm of the Ten-Year Plan called for rehabilitation of buildings presently occupied. Koch states:

"Through the Department of Housing Preservation and Development, we are the second-largest landlord in the United States. The first is in New York City Housing Authority (which manages all the public housing projects). We did not plan it that way; but, as landlords abandoned their buildings in neighborhood after neighborhood, we became the owner of 4,000 occupied buildings. . . .The people who live in these buildings generally are the poorest people in the City, and if this housing disappears as a result of our failure to invest in it, there will be no choice for these people but the City's shelter system, and that's unacceptable.[5]

These city-owned occupied buildings are the kind that have been turned over to Father Gigante's South East Bronx Community Organization (SEBCO) to manage. Koch hails Gigante and claims rightly that "Father Louis Gigante has been able to succeed where so few others have. These formerly *in rem* occupied buildings are not only attractive houses now, but they are graffiti-free, too, in sharp contrast to their surroundings." Camilo Jose Vergara writing in *The Nation* describes this section of Hunts Point:

A dozen or so years ago this was one of the poorest and most-crime-ridden sections of the Bronx. Today it is a showcase community, where people of modest means live near parks, a plaza,

churches, libraries, shops, health centers and transportation facilities. . . . [I]n 1977 SEBCO began to rebuild the mostly Latino
neighborhood around St. Athanasius [Father Gigante's parish].
Unlike other such projects that concentrate efforts on a few
projects, SEBCO embraced many, among them the rehabilitation and construction of 1,500 handsome dwellings and a Span-
ish-style plaza in front of the church. SEBCO also has sponsored
a city park and collaborated in an impressive public arts program. No part of the population has been ignored: SEBCO built
for the elderly and for families, for homeowners and renters, for
working people and for those on public assistance.[6]

The third major part of the Ten-Year Plan was a commitment
to building new housing on city land. Koch pointed out, "Our biggest
new construction program is the one that we have developed in conjunction with the New York City Housing Partnership, a group of
leading businesses committed to improving New York City. All together we expect to create 23,000 housing units over the next decade
through this middle-income program . . . "[7]

It is perhaps surprising that Koch shamelessly included the
Brooklyn Nehemiah houses as part of the new housing component
of his triumphal Ten-Year Plan, given that he only grudgingly supported Nehemiah, often trying to block its expansion. The *New York
Times*, for example, reported:

One of the most successful housing efforts of the 1980s, the
Nehemiah plan in the East New York and Brownsville sections
of Brooklyn, is threatening to stop working in New York unless
it is awarded more land on which to build inexpensive, two-
story brick row houses for middle-income families. The Koch
administration denied Nehemiah several sites in Brooklyn,
Queens, and the Bronx.[8]

Assessing his involvement differently, Koch warmly remi-
nisces about his cordial relations with Nehemiah dating back to its
inception:[9]

[Nehemiah] came about when the Bishop of Brooklyn, Rev-
erend Francis J. Mugavero, approached me on behalf of the
East Brooklyn Churches group. Bishop Mugavero said: "Mayor,
we've managed to raise eight million dollars from local churches
and parishioners to build homes for families in Brownsville. If

you can arrange for the City to donate enough land and con-
demned property, we can build them well and sell them cheap.
Just help us cut through the red tape." How could I refuse?
From that exchange a unique model of Church-State cooperation was born, one that is reviving a dying community and
helping shore up beleaguered families.[10]

Koch crowed,

"Run by a coalition of religious groups known as East Brooklyn
Churches, the Nehemiah Project has already produced over
1,000 new homes sold "at cost" to moderate-income people at
a price of only $50,000. This low price is made possible by a
City subsidy of $20,000 a unit. [Half of the cost is for site prepa-
ration.] In total, more than 5,000 units are slated for construction under the City's Ten-Year Plan over the next decade.[11]

The accuracy of the size of the subsidy is a item that IAF groups
dispute. The city contends that $20,000 is the cost of site prepara-
tion, which essentially means clearing and leveling a building lot,
and so the true cost of Nehemiah is really closer to $70,000 a unit.

Not everyone expected that the city's ambitious building and
rehabilitation program would deliver on its promise. By the spring of
1990, 3,500 new subsidized apartments in formerly abandoned buildings were opened to low-income tenants, although the recession
which began in August 1990 began taking its toll and funds for housing began to dry up quickly.

Density

But the problem of appropriate density remains at the core of
the dispute. According to the *New York Times*, "The principal leaders of non-profit assisted-housing development in the South Bronx
over the last decade feel that the Nehemiah approach uses too much
land to accommodate too few people of a low-income level. Their
preference is for mixed-income, higher-density development."[12] At
the same time, and presumably as a result of its clashes with SBC,
The Partnership's plans for Site 404 were scaled down significantly
from the April 1989 announcement. Originally HPD Commissioner
Abraham Biderman promised 350 units on the 4.35 acres of 404, or
roughly eighty units to the acre. A few months later, when specifi-
cations were published for bidding by developers, plans called for

251 units or roughly fifty-seven to the acre. Nehemiah's density in Brooklyn is about twenty units to the acre, but the new Nehemiah condos proposed by SBC in late April 1990 allow for some forty homes per acre, significantly reducing the spread between The Partnership and SBC. By way of comparison, it will be remembered that the density of the Charlotte Street development, with its expansive lawns, is six homes to the acre.

As the *Times* notes:

> The basic problem is density and housing mix. Extended too broadly, the densities that the Nehemiah plan espouses are too low to satisfy local leaders' interests in gradually rebuilding, at least partly, the areas's decimated population. The South Bronx may never become the crowded metropolis it was in 1950, but neither it is going to shrink away to a suburb of one-family homes.[13]

Ironically, even The Partnership's fifty-seven units to the acre, according to the *Times*, "would have been derided by community officials as exemplary of the 'planned shrinkage' doctrine that housing officials once put forth as the policy that should guide new development planning."[14]

Planned shrinkage was an unofficial city policy that tried to cope with the loss of hundreds of thousands of New York residents during the 1970s and the fiscal crisis of the late 1970s. According to Harold Derienzo writing in *City Limits:*

> Areas such as the South Bronx were the hardest hit, with Community Boards 2 and 3 [cheek by jowl with Site 404 which falls into Community Board 1 limits], for example, losing about 70 percent of their population. Mounting public doubt of Mayor Beame's administration's ability to balance the city budget led various officials and civic leaders to debate the city's options.

> Roger Starr, the head of the city's Housing and Development Administration [the precursor to the Department of Housing Preservation and Development], urged the consideration of an official policy of planned shrinkage. Its purpose: to "accelerate " the already-occurring population decreases in certain "slum areas," including the South Bronx.[15]

Derienzo also recalls that civic leaders like Felix Rohatyn, the celebrated Wall Street financier who headed the corporation that dealt with the city's near-bankruptcy in the 1970s, advocated taking "a 30-block area, clear it, blacktop it, and develop an industrial park." In fact, suggestions like these were followed, and the once vibrant Bathgate Street neighborhood, lovingly invoked in Doctorow's best-selling novel *Billy Bathgate*,[16] was leveled, blacktopped, and now has acres of heavily fortified one-story buildings that serve as warehouses but employ only a handful of residents as security guards.

How did HPD determine that single-family homes are inappropriate for Site 404? According to Kathleen Dunn, HPD's assistant commissioner, the analysis is essentially apolitical:

The issue is a planning issue, not a political issue. I know from SBC's point of view, it is politics. But from the point of view of development, we go about looking for sites for development of housing in pretty much the same way, regardless of the borough and regardless of the existence of a community group. That's not to say that we do not respond to community groups.

Our mandate is to build housing, to build single-family housing, where single-family housing makes the most sense because of topography or some other consideration, or because in the surrounding area there are single-family homes, or to build high-rise low-income developments, if that's the type of housing that's needed or if the funding is available.

In the sixties, that is certainly what people did. In the seventies, there was a backlash against high-rise developments because there were problems in Housing Authority projects.

So, in the eighties, we looked at developing housing based on what we learned in the sixties and the seventies and based on the kind of resources that are available to us both in land and in money. And, in the case of Site 404 and in all of the land we are looking at for SBC, both of those criteria were very big in the decision making. Much larger from my point of view than any political considerations.[17]

So, if there was general agreement that high-rise density was inappropriate, why not replicate SBC's universally-acknowledged success in Brooklyn and plant Nehemiah homes on this vast stretch of land? Dunn replies:

On Site 404 under the present zoning you can build six hundred units. We had thought, and we still think, six hundred is inappropriate for the site, because even if we had had the financing we were interested in building moderate- to low-middle income housing on the site because we didn't think it was a good idea to put six hundred units there in the midst of all this other vacant land. Nobody would move there: if you lived there what kind of environment would you have? So we were looking for something that was in between.

What Nehemiah was proposing was fifty-six units of single-family homes. The site does not really lend itself to single-family development. We just didn't think in terms of land resources that this was a good idea, to take a site that could easily hold six hundred units of housing and use it for fifty-six when we had other sites there not too far away from it that would be able to satisfy Nehemiah's needs.

So, in the end, politics was driving it from SBC's point of view; I still don't know why, but from our point of view it was really a land resource thing. And why put fifty-six units, I still don't understand it, on that land when you could accommodate Nehemiah in the rest of the area?

What was so fundamentally central to SBC about Site 404? Early on the city offered hundreds of other sites nearby. Why not compromise, conclude the bickering, and roll up their sleeves and commence construction? For SBC, this large expanse of contiguous land was deemed absolutely pivotal. Chambers does not mince words:

Nehemiah won't work on the scattered sites because we need cleared, vacant land. And a lot of those other sites [initially offered by HPD] have buildings on them.

When you approach five hundred units, we have really created a new city. A new environment and that drives out the bad. If you just put a few in, knowing these communities, there is not enough of a critical mass to carry it into the year 1990, 1995, into the year 2000.

We are building community; we are not just building housing. The city's approach is an abstract, theoretical kind of thing that you can build single-family housing anywhere. We know what the city does. It goes in and rehabs certain buildings. Come back four years later and it's torn up. Millions of dollars have been poured into programs that do this infill sort of thing.

We are not going to that because it will not last. The 404 site is barely a critical mass from our point of view. Because in that immediate area, across the street and down a little bit we can probably get two hundred [homes]. We think we can pull it off particularly if the city will demolish the other vacant buildings. Take down the [abandoned] brewery; take down the vacant school. Instead of saying you can have the land by the vacant school, but we are leaving the vacant school.

If we can get a stake of two hundred we can do another two hundred, three hundred on noncontiguous land. But we can't start on a noncontiguous basis. We can't build on a noncontiguous basis and build enough of a critical mass to sustain itself. It will be folded in with the bad buildings. We'll have Nehemiah homes, and we'll have shooting up with drugs in the abandoned school. What kind of sense is that? That is not building community.

That is the issue in a nutshell. SBC is not just building housing; it wants to create a community where newly politicized citizens band together to defend their turf from neighborhood predators, hold their children's schools accountable, and resist an insensitive city bureaucracy.

Once SBC has put all its rhetorical chips on Site 404, how can it back away gracefully and build east of the site? One answer was Drake's: SBC is not backing off, but digging in with hundreds of Nehemiah homes nearby and biding its time until The Partnership proves incapable of building at a higher density on 404. But will the critical mass be there without 404? Kathleen Dunn contends that 404 did not always occupy such a pivotal role in SBC's thinking:

In the last six months there have been certain statements made by I. D. Robbins and by SBC to the effect that this project can't work without 404. They need that critical mass of 404 to kick it off. That is a fairly recent way of looking at Nehemiah housing. It certainly was never the point of view taken back in '86, '87, and '88 when we were first working with [SBC].

We thought we were working with SBC, a community organization that wanted to go in to sponsor development and raise funds to build this housing. And we were all too willing to do it, which is why [HPD's initial] survey was done. We generally don't work with community agencies that think: this site belongs to us.

All our sites are selected competitively, either by the city or the state through RFPs.[18] We told Nehemiah they were very welcome to respond to the RFP for development. But they weren't interested in building anything other than single family homes.[19]

Income Level

Who should this new housing be for? Chambers leaves no doubts:

There is no substitute for home ownership. And single-family row houses is the historical process, like brownstones, that the ethnics have always had like the Irish, the Italians, the Slavs, the Jews.

It was an opportunity for those with two incomes to get into some equity. Now, why, when Blacks and Hispanics come along, locked into areas like Brownsville, East New York, the South Bronx, why is the city so resistant to a different kind of immigrant having the same opportunity? Particularly those who are city employees and are locked into jobs that will never pay that much money. People who are making $22,000, 26 are never going to make 50, 56. And yet these are the civil services employees who make New York work. And three subway stops away from the job.

Why did they waste all that valuable land for the Bathgate development? Why did they do this obscene Ed Logue thing [the Charlotte Street development] with a ranch-style house two to an acre? This is only a few years ago. They wiped out acres and acres. One for warehousing; no jobs. If there are thirty jobs in all of goddamned Bathgate you're lucky. And then the Ed Logue thing! Where were all the high-density people then? Where was Borough President Ferrer, Biderman; where was Koch when that was happening? The truth is the business of NYC officials is greed.[20]

In order to make The Partnership's proposed housing on 404 more available to lower-middle-income families, the city has pumped enormous subsidies into each unit. According to Kathleen Dunn, "The city and the state together committed a subsidy of $35,000 and the borough president committed money on top of that. It will be affordable to families earning approximately $31,000."

Nehemiah, on the other hand, is targeting families with more modest income, although they too have been criticized as pampering the more affluent members of their church-based organization. Rev. Johnny Ray Youngblood, chairman of East Brooklyn Churches, quarrels with this interpretation:

> Since there are people in public housing who could purchase their own Nehemiah homes if we are able to build them, we free up their public-housing apartment, and persons of lower income can go into those apartments. In Brownsville, 40 to 60 percent of our present-day Nehemiah homeowners have come out of public housing. While it has been said that we do not consider low-income persons, that is not totally true. Low-income people are the beneficiaries of our being able to build affordable housing for persons who were in public housing.[21]

Who will get houses on this land really goes back to the basic problem of the finite amount of land that is available in the South Bronx. According to Sam Kramer, the Director of Bronx Planning for HPD:

> The Regional Plan Association working under contract with the borough president's office to chart the future of Bronx estimates a 77,000 unit housing deficit. They are certainly not thinking that that can be solved by single-unit housing. They are into this density concept. They want to see Melrose Commons with three thousand condos. This is a little bit anachronistic for SBC to come now with a plan for single-family units.
>
> The South Bronx, once you've played around in it for quite a while, like I have, [you realize], unlike Brooklyn with its wide tracts, it is a very compact and diverse neighborhood. Things happen there like in Manhattan—you drive down one block, and you are seeing things that are totally different. There is not a prairie out here, except for Melrose Commons. Land is a very scarce resource. There are no options really.[22]

In the final analysis, it is clear that the Nehemiah homes will be more affordable than houses built by other contractors, even in the unlikely event that all the promised government subsidies materialize. The prospect that the Ten-Year Plan would be fulfilled grew more remote in 1991 as the city and the state we're stricken by a looming financial crisis that prompted talk of huge layoffs and major cutbacks in social services and public works.

The director of economic studies at the Brookings Institution, a research organization based in Washington, said at the end of 1990:

> The fiscal plight seems to be worse than at any time during my memory. I think you would have to go back to the Great Depression to find similar anguish, in terms of the number of states that are facing an unprecedented cutback in service or significant increases in taxes.[23]

Given this severe revenue shortfall and the voracious demands on the city and state budget from mandated spending on prisons, education, Medicaid, and welfare, one wonders whether it is realistic to think that the hugely generous subsidies The Partnership is banking on for 404 will be available to construct new apartments in the middle of the South Bronx—subsidies to lure middle-income condo buyers to a wounded neighborhood gripped by problems of drugs, crime, poverty, homelessness, and AIDS.

In the teeth of this reality, SBC's virtually subsidy-free Nehemiah homes have to look more and more attractive.

Demolition or Rehabilitation

Inextricably connected to the problem of density is the related knot of how to deal with derelict buildings. Can they, should they, be rehabilitated or wiped out in the interest of creating a new community? The city's Ten-Year Plan comes down decisively on the side of rehabilitation of sound housing stock.

I. D. Robbins is not a believer in wholesale rehabilitation. What about all the occupied housing that is routinely foreclosed by the city? Can it be rehabilitated? An unsentimental Robbins asserts:

> Not at a reasonable cost. You can build two Nehemiah houses for every one you can rehabilitate. You have to build enough to have a critical mass to create a healthy neighborhood. If there are huge areas of the city which have no value, then why not assemble those no-value parcels and use them? There are in New York maybe 35,000 acres of vacant land. They're not all big tracts. Relocate three or four hundred people in order to build housing for a few thousand.[24]

In the early eighties, the solution in the East New York section of Brooklyn, albeit a very different neighborhood from the South Bronx, was ruthlessly to level the delinquent buildings and start fresh. The advisability of demolition, relocation, and new construction, long a thorny problem in planning circles, may be solving itself. Even in neighborhoods which are virtually defined by vacant lots and derelict buildings, the city "is running out of abandoned buildings to renovate," according to the *New York Times*.[25] In the spring of 1990 the *Times* estimated that the city would "deplete its portfolio of 5,000 vacant, burned-out buildings—probably by 1992 or 1993."

Then the only possibility will be to build new housing. Since there never was a shortage of lucrative high-income housing, what remains to be solved is how profit-driven developers can be induced to build housing for the lower-middle-class and the poor and the working poor. The *Times* estimated, based on recent studies, that the city needs no less than a staggering 231,000 apartments and houses. In this context, the *Times* noted:

> Mr. Biderman, who is now working for an investment firm, said taller structures should be built, so that the city's last remaining housing resource—land—could be used most efficiently. He argued that low-rise construction would not produce enough apartments. While he was commissioner, Mr. Biderman refused several times to grant more land for Nehemiah housing.[26]

Others argue that this is a false way of framing the problem. It is not so much a question of higher density to solve the housing shortage as a problem of getting the right mix for a particular neighborhood. Along with Ed Chambers, Ron Shiffman, the respected planner and director of the Pratt Institute Center for Community and Environmental Development in Brooklyn argues:

> The issue is to rebuild viable neighborhoods so the housing is maintained and the families are weaved back into the fabric of life. What we need to do now is community planning with housing, day care, health centers, and other community affairs planned in a coordinated way. The overall policy should be to encourage diversity.[27]

Three years later in 1993, after Nehemiah's toehold in the South Bronx and the relatively low-density Partnership condos were under construction, Shiffman sees the pendulum swinging. The *Times* reported that in an interview with him, "that while [Shiffman] applauded the effort of the Housing Partnership and South Bronx Churches, future housing developments should be modified. 'We need to strike a balance between what we had in the past, when density was too high, and single-family homes, which can make a community auto-dependent,' "[28]

Ego and Power

To what extent is the city's obstinacy over Site 404 a result of more than sober planning decisions? What roles do politics and personality and bruised pride play? How, for instance, does a veteran professional planner like Sam Kramer react to SBC's provocative confrontational style? With surprising tolerance he says:

Frankly there's a lot to be admired about it. I'm told they come out of the same organizing school as Alinsky of Chicago. The Northwest Community and Clergy Coalition worked the same way, essentially beating [up] bureaucrats, and gradually we worked together in a very productive relationship. Housing gets built; communities get organized.[29]

Kramer went on to express admiration for SBC's confrontational style in the campaign against Lincoln Hospital; however, about 404, he demurred:

But here they employ that heavy-handedness to a problem where a little bit more of a velvet glove is necessary. We do have things we can do with them. We can't work on a "Do it my way, or else, basis."

We don't consider ourselves as criminals in our housing program who need to be corrected. We think we do a pretty good job basically. We are pretty adaptable within programmatic and financial and planning limitations.

Let me say that not far from here the major cry of another community board is different. The major issue in Community Board 3, practically as strident as anything we are talking about with SBC, is take your single-family and your two-family houses and stop.

Because in 1950 they had a population of 200,000. They have no sympathy for [The Partnership's] single-family houses. We get hit on the head if we so much as mention anything like that.

We are now down to 58,000 from 200,000. We have a political problem. We have churches that need a congregation. We have politicians, we have people who need jobs to run this community board. [They say] we might be merged into some other community boards by city rules. If you build anything, make sure it is four stories or more.

Ed Chambers, with his take-no-prisoners style, disdains any talk about a neutral apolitical planning process being responsible for the city's position on 404:

The city, Gigante, Ferrer want the site because arrangements have been historically made, probably payoffs. They want the site at all costs. Basically this isn't even a battle over land. It's a battle over power. It's a battle over who is going to control the South Bronx—Borough President Ferrer and Koch or these groups of Catholics and Protestants, called South Bronx Churches.

And that's why former housing commissioner Tony Gliedman, who is now working for Donald Trump, told my associate when he's relaxed and talking about the old days: "We made a mistake once," we being the city. "We will never make it again. There will be no more Nehemiah in the city, ever." Because the more Nehemiah you build the more it is a total embarrassment to all the other city programs which are heavily loaded with free subsidies to developers, including the Partnership with all their subsidies going anywhere from $30,000 to $70,000. Just pure takeoff. The genius of Nehemiah, the reason it works, is that we don't take those profits.

HPD is a give-away program to developers. Millions and millions of dollars. It's all a setup.

So what you are fighting here is a tremendous culture. You say we didn't do them any harm? Yeah, it did them a lot of harm. When foreign dignitaries come to this country, they want to see Nehemiah. The city used to host them, you know, and bullshit them around. Now they say no, we want to go see Nehemiah.

I'm telling you about the hate and the fear of mobilized citizenry who aren't playing the electoral politics game against the machine. What we have in New York is the machine is dying.

It's about much more than land or any technicalities. There are no technicalities about 404. They are using The Partnership to intervene so that they don't have to take the hit directly. The Partnership is supposed to develop poor land that other communities don't want. Here's a community that wants some land, and has wanted it for two years. It's a battle for power.

Robbins agrees that at its root this a brawl that is fueled by politicians who are threatened:

The politicians see people [like East Brooklyn Churches and South Bronx Churches] as representatives of a different power base, a different approach. These ministers genuflect only in the church. People in higher city administrative jobs have been quite wonderful, but people in the housing bureaucracy are defending what they have done wrong.[30]

What about someone like Fernando Ferrer? Here is a representative of a new generation of minority politicians coming into power in the Bronx. Given that leaders of SBC like Jim Drake, Ed Chambers, and John Heinemeier are white and relative newcomers to the South Bronx, is it not a little presumptuous for them to be claiming possession of the South Bronx in the name of its residents? Chambers is dismissive of the notion that Ferrer is any kind of political novelty in the Bronx who might portend a progressive new direction:

It is not in his self-interest to have this fight. But we don't know what all the prevailing forces are. This man is part of the Stanley Friedman era.[31] He was trained by Stanley Friedman, which is a concept of zero-sum power.

If you got the power and position, the way you keep it is never give anybody else anything. It is a philosophical misunderstanding of true power. True power is relational. You cut people into it, you know what I mean? Their share, *quo pro quo*, and as they are cut in you have more power. But as a kid [Ferrer] was part of one of Louie Gigante's clubs. Gigante had clubs for kids. So he's had that influence. And he's had Stanley Friedman.

You don't build organizations around issues; you build them around relationships.[32]

Who Is Right?

Weighing arguments on both sides of the issue, what are the dictates of plausibility? In this historical moment, are the Nehemiah homes the right policy direction for Site 404 and the surrounding neighborhood?

As compellingly persuasive as SBC activists are, in my view the planners at HPD are essentially right: the low density of the Nehemiah concept is inappropriate for 404 but is defensible, on an infill basis, for much of the surrounding blocks. A large, contiguous, flat expanse like 404 cries out for more ambitious, more inclusive, development. Hilly areas on the periphery would better accommodate the small-scale rowhouses of Nehemiah and still allow viable, inhabited buildings to be reintegrated into a new neighborhood fabric.

Given the permanence of architecture, the decisions made today may have to be lived with for a number of generations; so the stakes are high.

I believe the most perceptive reading of the situation is from Roberta Brandes Gratz, a reporter who has chronicled in a classic book similar battles for inner-city turf across the country. She writes:

> The controversy over the new South Bronx housing, which pits the Nehemiah Housing Program against The New York City Partnership, oversimplifies the choices available for community rebuilding. The best solutions are not even part of this debate.
>
> The Nehemiah formula may be appropriate for some vacant sites, but it is reminiscent of the long discredited "bulldoze and rebuild" approach of Robert Moses and should be contained, not enlarged and replicated. To its credit, Nehemiah is the only privately developed new construction program addressing the needs of lower-income potential homeowners—households making as little as $20,000 a year. But it is a suburban formula, with front lawns, driveways (car use by rich or poor should be discouraged), and sterile design. It is the Levittown of the urban landscape.[33]

Gratz rightly faults The Partnership for catering to higher-income families, those making from $32,000 to $53,000 a year, but praises their attempt to harmonize their structures with surrounding neighborhoods. I part company with her when she takes the absolutist view that "We need not lose one more standing building in this city, occupies or vacant" because I believe Robbins and Chambers are right—blighted buildings preserved, with the hope of future rehabilitation, in the middle of new housing are a recipe for disaster.

Yet the justice of this War on 404 does not stand or fall on some esoteric urban-planning dispute over the fate of this emblematic tract of empty land. This is a battle about empowering citizens and putting to the test the restorative powers of democracy and citizen participation. Who can doubt the validity of Chambers' insight?

> You fail to realize the deliveries that have gone on already. Hundreds of thousands of small victories. We are interested in what happens to people's lives who take a stand or get up in front of a group and talk, or reach out and get a relationship with people they don't know.

> Those victories are going on all the time. Substantive victories can't be expected right away. SBC wasn't set up for substantive victories in year one, two, three. Those come in year five, or like Nehemiah for EBC in year seven.

It would be better ultimately if the city were able to build affordable, higher-density housing on a prime stretch like 404. Five-story rental elevator buildings with stores on the ground floor mixed with a variety of smaller owner-occupied walk-ups would probably serve this neighborhood better, but this is not an available choice. Chambers, with his eye on bigger issues than just housing, contends that, in the long run, it is better to have to struggle against the city on these policy questions. In fact, having an official like Fernando Ferrer on his side is a detriment:

> You don't understand that your enemies, those that go against you, are generally your most effective organizers. If Ferrer had fallen down, and if Koch had fallen down, "Yeah I'm all for you, we'll give you the land"—that's nothing [he adds with relish] like a fight to have to get the land.

> So the ownership would stay with them, the benevolent patrons, helping the poor people in the South Bronx. Kind of like the cardinal's position, "I'll do whatever I can to help you so that the more they deliver stuff, the more dependent you are on them."

> The people have to fight, to struggle, mobilize, organize, reach out, leaflet, talk to, defend, negotiate. That's how they grow. People can't grow when you give them stuff. That's called pa-

ternalism, colonialism. So a skirmish like this, organization-
ally, is healthy, therapeutic. If you've got to win or lose this
month, then you have lost. You got a time frame to win over.

Is it foreordained that newly empowered citizens will always
have to bitterly fight a paternalistic government distorted by its own
self-indulgent priorities? Is there a learning curve for government officials; or, more specifically, can the Bronx Borough's office profit
from a brawl like this with an enraged citizens group?

In a precedent-shattering development, it looks as if Bronx government may be digesting some of the lessons of this years-long contentious battle with South Bronx Churches. In a rather startling
reversal, the Borough President's office has begun to invite grass-
roots participation of residents in planning the next incarnation of
Melrose Commons. Invariably, past practice has been to present a
fait accompli to the citizens for review while demolition crews
gunned bulldozer engines.

Condo construction has already begun on the eastern edge of
Melrose Commons, on Site 404, but the original Melrose project
calls for many more blocks of new construction. Beyond that, Melrose Commons, at least on paper, has now been incorporated into a
mammoth new project, one deemed Bronx Center, that will stretch
all the way across the lower central part of the South Bronx to Yankee Stadium on the western boundary of the borough.

This new three hundred-block plan is almost breath taking in
its ambition or, perhaps more cynically, its wishful hubris. In June
1993 a few months before a City Hall election, Mayor David
Dinkins joined Fernando Ferrer and Governor Mario Cuomo to her-
ald a new blueprint for resuscitation of the heart of the South Bronx.
According to an account in the *Times*, "The total cost would be as
much as $3 billion and the overall plan would evolve as it is devel-
oped to include small parks, high schools, shopping areas, health care
units, access to the Harlem River and improved transportation."[34]

The plan is anchored in four major public projects which are already on the books: Melrose Commons which eventually is scheduled to balloon to 2,600 housing units, a new Police Academy, a new
courthouse and a Juvenile Detention Center. Apart from the fraction
of Melrose Commons that includes Site 404, nothing else has actually begun except for the Detention Center, a municipal facility that
all neighborhoods shun like the plague. Ironically, the only other
planned Juvenile Detention facility, which incarcerates the city's
most violent offenders under the age of fifteen, is slated for EBC's

bailiwick of East New York in Brooklyn. Even Ferrer in 1992 was caught asleep at the switch with the placement of this juvenile jail. An oblivious City Hall wedged it in on the edge of the Hub, the still enterprising shopping area that is the economic lifeblood of the South Bronx. Ferrer was left sputtering to the press: "You are taking prime, income-producing land and turning it into nothing. Besides sending a message to the community that any old place will do, you're also sending a message to the business community that we have no vision, and are throwing away potential sources of revenue for the future."[35]

Whether the Bronx Center eventually achieves its grandiose aims or not, something genuinely novel is occurring in the planning process. Perhaps it was Ferrer's experience of being on the other end of a high-handed municipal decision and getting publicly burned by the city that influenced him to rethink the a priori planning mechanism of government. In any case, the Borough President's office disgorged a remarkable one hundred page document in May 1993 that belatedly reversed gears and blessed a new policy of grass-roots inclusion from the *beginning* of the planning process. In "A Report to the Bronx Borough President Fernando Ferrer from the Bronx Center Steering Committee" the message is clear: "Effective and meaningful planning must be the product of a 'bottom up' community-based process." Ostensibly the report merely sketches a particular vision for this large section of the South Bronx and calls for new initiatives for economic development, health and human services, education and culture, "housing, open space and urban design," and transportation. Given that the funding for this prophecy is not in place and includes no guarantees for financing, a first impulse might to be file it on the long shelf of dust-gathering dreamy reports that called for a Bronx Renassiance. However, there is something authentically intriguing, something that perhaps cannot be undone once the dikes are thrown open. A group of residents who were initially outraged at being excluded from the planning process of this major fraction of the South Bronx, and who, in some cases, stood to lose their homes or businesses because early versions of the plan blithely swept away all in its path, have now organized. What is unique is not that they have come together as a group, named "We're Staying Committee," but they have coalesced with the help and encouragement of Ferrer's Office. Ferrer has lent them the services of a professional organizer and according to the *Times*, "Borough officials also helped to halt the plan's certification while the group canvasses residents and met regularly to redraw the plan."[36] The Bronx Center plans are being reshaped to accommodate the views of the residents, an unprecedented novelty in the Bronx. For instance, the original blueprints called for a four-acre park in the center of the complex, a rather predictable feature for high steroid ambitious, bull-dozer-driven redevelopment schemes. However, the park was scrapped after world-weary residents included in the planning process pointed out that it would quickly degenerate into a lure for addicts and would not be defensible. Instead, the community residents called for a series of smaller parks and plazas that would ground a more modest-scale conception of neighborhood. As one savvy participant pointed out: "We have mom-and-pop stores, extended families and there's a certain manner the community has established, a way of life we have that's not commonplace everywhere. Those are ideas that have served this community well. "[37] This is a local gritty reality that the traditional, more cerebral planning process can easily miss.

One has to guard against overoptimism. It is true that the borough president's report even holds out an olive branch to SBC and encourages its participation by trumpeting—"And a proposed new high school sponsored by South Bronx Churches would be a highly welcome and valued addition to Bronx Center facilities."[38]—and it pays more than lip service to citizen involvement, but is this because so much of it has such remote chance of being funded? Naturally government officials are claiming it represents a decisive break with the past. South Bronx residents remain prudently wary. Aware that preelection posturing has a way of losing its urgency after November, participants in this new style planning process have taken the unsentimental precaution of organizing a voter registration drive while simultaneously pursuing the planning goals. As one of the leaders of the We're Staying Committee put it in words that echo Ed Chambers, "The government is cooperating but by no means are they our savior. We want to make sure all the promises are kept. If the project takes 10 years to complete, we'll be around 20."[39]

13

Learning from South Bronx Churches

Disregard for a moment the particular merits of SBC's battle to wrestle a dozen or so derelict South Bronx acres from the City of New York. Stripped of the tactical particularities, a consideration of this campaign to empower citizens yields generic information that is both cautionary and inspiring.

Every situation has its unique fingerprints, and, in the difficult work of revitalizing battered areas, there are no templates. Yet the hope is that there are some universals, some clues and bits of advice that can be recommended to people of good will who strive to improve opportunities for inner-city citizens.

Of the dozens of factors that come into play in such an ambitious endeavor, we can isolate nine that seem to be of decisive importance: They are intended to highlight major strategic considerations. For a step-by-step guide to organizing a community like the South Bronx there are useful handbooks[1] that take the aspiring organizer by the shoulders and shepherd him through the details. Here we will attend to more general ideas that advance or hinder the process.

This analysis focuses on how senior leaders of the IAF see themselves and their work. The best place to begin probing their thinking is at the IAF's Ten-Day Training seminars for community activists that are held three times a year. I attended a session in July 1989 in Los Angeles and sat in on training sessions conducted by all five of the senior leaders.[2] Each of these leaders heads a regional operation consisting of a number of autonomous organizations that are equivalent in size and scope to South Bronx Churches.

What follows is a discussion of nine ideas that need to be grappled with if the intention is to make a difference in a wounded community like the South Bronx.

1. Build on a Broad Base

Larry McNeil, an IAF Cabinet Member, is the supervisor of four community organizations in California, each approximately the size of SBC. He appears to be in his early forties, making him roughly a decade younger than the other four senior leaders. Like many of the other supervising IAF organizers, he came from a rural background and, like John Heinemeier, set off early from the backwaters of Texas to the seminary. Like Chambers, he grew disillusioned and chose not to pursue a clerical career. His has been organizing for two decades. In common with his fellow IAF Cabinet members, he is a notable raconteur, spicing his generalizations with specific, fine-grained, and frequently humorous anecdotes. His detailed comparison of how broad-based groups like the organizations spawned by the IAF differ from movements and civic groups provides an orienting, wide-angle view of how the IAF sees itself.

For purposes of comparison, the IAF divides all citizen action groups into three distinct, overarching categories: broad-based, civic, and movement groups. By analyzing these groups across a range of variables, it is possible to distinguish among them and assess the strengths and weaknesses of each; and therein lie clues to IAF's remarkable string of successes. Two relevant categories are membership considerations and degree of organization.

In this definitional scheme, groups like the PTA and Rotary are considered civic, and organizations that advocate for women, peace, abortion, civil rights, the environment, and the like are defined as movements. The IAF considers itself a fundamentally different kind of collective—a broad-based organization which attempts to knit together diverse constituencies of many races and religions to agitate for a wide range of continually evolving issues.

A crucial variable in distinguishing among broad-based, civic, and movement groups, according to McNeil, is the composition, numbers, and devotion of the membership. Both civic and movement groups allow anyone who agrees with them to join, McNeil points out disdainfully. As a result, movements often splinter into warring factions, and membership in civic groups tends to be small. By contrast broad-based groups are "organizations of organizations." He rejects the designation of such groups as being grass-roots efforts: "Grass has shallow roots; you can just pull 'em up! Our organizations are based in churches and unions—institutions with deep roots. We work with people who are already organized and have abiding relationships."

Broad-based groups seek diversity. Groups like South Bronx Churches encompass an impressive span of races, age groups, denominations, and geographical reach. An IAF tenet: *You can't have too much diversity.* Another axiom they subscribe to is: *The broader the base, the more the power.* "It's just not *engaging* when all people think alike," McNeil ruefully concludes.

What about the problem of too many chiefs and not enough Indians? Or the chaos that erupts from many diverse interest groups struggling to squeeze under one umbrella? "Don't worry about losing control. What can you lose? Control of your powerlessness?" In this context, McNeil counterintuitively compliments the Catholic Church for its admirable tolerance of theological diversity and holds that this tolerance is one of the reasons for its power and longevity. He implies, in this respect, that Protestants are hopeless: "They start a new denomination at the drop of a hat!"

On the other hand, "You don't just want everyone. Don't take on dead weight. Everyone must pay dues, and deliver quotas [of members for actions]," McNeil warns.

What is the nature of the relationships within these three categories of citizen groups? Civic groups are often loosely organized, and members tend to be friends. It is rare for them to cultivate people they don't like, an unappetizing task that is nonetheless essential in broad-based groups. In movements, relationships tend to be thin, with *The Cause* being the only real glue. For an IAF group to function, it needs to be built around "relationships with a purpose." Discipline and mutual reliability are important. So, for instance, when an action is called, every leader—and each group needs dozens of leaders—is responsible for a fraction of the quota of participants. A citizen's organization that calls for an action with two hundred angrily protesting citizens and fails to muster a respectable turnout shoots itself in the foot.

What are the motivational lures that impel people to volunteer their time and energy for these organizations? For movements, it is clearly *The Cause,* and, for civic groups, it usually springs from particular needs in a community. Often there is a strong aftertaste of obligation involved in tackling such problems, according to McNeil.

Broad-based groups, like the IAF organizations, trumpet an unadorned reliance on self-interest as the motivational engine. McNeil explains: "Liberals [fueled by airy idealism] talk great but leave when the real conflict comes." This is so, he says, because they are confused about their real self-interest. IAF groups "have to keep asking themselves, is what we are doing in the interest of our members, our volunteer leaders, our member churches? This keeps our organizations honest," according to McNeil.

Although symbolism is a useful tool, actions can't be taken for purely symbolic reasons; the goal must connect to a genuinely felt need.

This insistence on broad-based "organization of organizations" must be seen in its context to appreciate its novelty. With the possible exception of South Bronx People For Change, other South Bronx improvement groups are positively parochial in the reach of their membership. People For Change strives to be more inclusive, yet it has not cemented any non-Catholic parishes in its mosaic. Although, as we'll see below, SBC is vulnerable to criticism for its cranky approach to building alliances, the fact endures that in the South Bronx there are no other groups that have such diverse and sweeping backing.

2. Organize For Power, Not Issues

Power, and how to attain it, is the proposition that really lights up the IAF leaders and, judging by the relish with which they talk about it, seems closest to their hearts. They disparage civic groups which tend to be issue-oriented rather than power-oriented. Movements are found wanting because of a similar single-minded devotion to an individual issue. IAF leaders also condemn movements as relatively ineffectual at acquiring staying power. The fact that it is still possible to hear debates about whether the anti-Vietnam War movement hastened or hindered the disengagement of American troops bears this out.

IAF leaders are brazenly explicit about their appetite for power. They pride themselves on evaluating each decision by carefully weighing, in McNeil's words, "Is this action going to give us more or less power?"[3] They would never take on a struggle like the decade-long battle in Manhattan to transfer hundreds of millions of dollars from a proposed superhighway along the West Side to a fund for mass transit, despite the struggle's importance to the poor or the high-stakes allure of locking horns with immensely powerful real-estate developers. That particular battle was won essentially by one lone woman, Marcy Benstock, who improvised what temporary coalitions she could along the way but felt no compulsion to create a power organization. "Never get in freeway fights," McNeil urges; "they never end. And they dissipate power."[4]

IAF teaches that you can't operate in public life without power: "the only way to get in doors is to knock them down." But it's wise to be methodical and cautious: "Don't overreach; only do what you have the power to do," advises McNeil.

3. Build On Institutions With Deep Roots

Civic groups focus on their neighborhoods and are turf-oriented Movements fixate on the blurry New World that is to come. But why do broad-based organizations root themselves in churches? Certainly on a "power pattern," congregations are largely irrelevant. In fact, they can be disparaged as merely glorified service-oriented agencies. From the IAF point of view, it is true that churches are not plugged into power arrangements. In places like the South Bronx, however, they are the only entities that have a genuine claim on people. It is the Lead Organizer's job to refocus churches outwardly, to wean them from fulfilling traditional expectations. The controversial Catholic Bishop's Letter on the Economy is a good example of how some churches have dipped one foot into public life and have started to flex their muscles.

Ask Jim Drake, SBC Lead Organizer, why he started with conservative, apolitical churches:

> In this neighborhood? The only other organization that is viable is the drug one. I would say that the only set of values that is as strong as the Judeo-Christian set of values are the ones around drugs. There is no Kiwanis; there is no Elks. There are no PTA's. There are only two mediating institutions that can work here. You know what I mean by mediating?[5]

Mediating institutions, Drake explains, are a rippling outward set of concentric circles that help an individual contend with the world. In this scheme, the family is the primary mediating institution, and the neighborhood is next, and then perhaps the schools or the churches. All are institutions that allow the individual to cope with the outside world.

> In a place like the South Bronx, it used to be that—you talk to people about [times] thirty years ago—they will tell you that you could sit on the front porch. They didn't have air conditioning. The windows were open so they could hear if somebody was breaking into a car. They didn't have television so

they weren't mesmerized. Air conditioning and television pretty much destroyed all mediating institutions at the most basic level. Everybody is hermetically sealed against the rest of the world.

So what comes along is the subsidized church. The bishops keep putting in the money in hopes that the neighborhood will change some day, hoping it will come back so they will make some money off this place, to pay for all the heat. Those buildings have been kept up, and those pastors have been paid and kept there. That is an incredible investment. Can't say that about the [public] schools. More schools are torn down than churches. And the investment is not the same. So I guess that if I couldn't build it around the church then I couldn't build it.

Another reason to rely on institutions with deep roots like neighborhood churches is their permanence. Drake observes:

Alinsky used to come to a place like this and try to organize it, try to develop neighborhood organizations. And it didn't work because people move. There was no institutional base there, like the church that survives when somebody moves away. So the leader moved, or the leader would die, and the neighborhood group would disintegrate. The organizer would have to come in and start all over again. So they never really had the strength.

4. Alliances Work Only If You Are Willing To Share Power

Despite their emphasis on broad-based coalition building, the IAF, at least in the South Bronx, has managed to alienate other local activist groups who would have seemed to have been plausible allies. Before John Heinemeir and Jim Drake arrived in the South Bronx, there were at least a half dozen local groups that were organizing residents in the battle to restore housing stock in the local neighborhoods. Some like the Mid-Bronx Desperadoes and Father Gigante's SEBCO were successfully working with the city housing department to manage rehabilitated apartments. Others, like the Catholic parish-based South Bronx People For Change were in implacable opposition to the city government. Although South Bronx Churches officials had discussions with many of the leaders of these groups, no genuine alliances were forged. Only a few of their activist members were lured into SBC. Many of these groups have vocally opposed SBC initiatives, and, when speaking off the record, neither the established groups nor SBC evinces much mutual respect.

Their inability to enter into genuine collaborations on any terms but their own, to share power and build geometrically in membership with other groups, saps power and constitutes SBC's single must debilitating flaw.

5. Organize Relationally

The foundation of South Bronx Churches is built on what IAF director Ed Chambers calls "the radical tool of the IAF, the art of getting relationships."[6] A central tenet of the IAF is that time must be taken to build relationships skillfully with allies, power brokers, and with ordinary citizens.

This process is triggered by thirty-minute relational conversations, the "one-on-one's" that the SBC leaders had proposed with Morris parents, students, and staffers. Chambers told a class of activists at the July 1989 training in Los Angeles, "What you are looking for in these sessions is to discover a person's real self-interest. Where do they put their energy, and why? And, importantly, do they sound like they have talent?"

To accomplish anything in these meetings, it is necessary to "totally focus on another person's life. Do they have a vision?" Chambers warns that it is important to keep the conversation all in the public realm. "Politely disassociate if they get into private stuff." Additional cautionary advice is nested within a broad generalization: "People with personal problems are not good in public life."

To crack open a conversation, Chambers advises, "credential yourself. Tell them right off the bat who you are and how it is that you've come to their house to talk. And no chitchat," Chambers chides. Also, "Don't be a sponge; don't just ask questions; share some of yourself." Don't waste time with someone who is not a potential leader. This exercise is "not for followers. They just de-energize you." Pivotally, there is no *task* associated with these meetings. The purpose is simply to get, or at least begin, a relationship.

At the Ten-Day National Training, a full morning-to-evening session was spent in practicing one-on-one meetings. Two strangers are summoned to the front of the classroom, seated at tiny student desks and then instructed to plunge in and get to know each other. Chambers is a harshly impatient teacher, and after each one-on-one drill he gives almost everyone low marks. He says that a breakthrough in becoming skilled at this assignment comes only after doing seventy-five to one hundred such meetings.

There's an unavoidable artificiality in these fish-bowl encounters "performed" in front of an audience. Yet it is clear that this technique, time-consuming and chancy though it is, resides at the heart of the success the IAF has had in building large membership organizations. This also underscores the insight that there is no easy way to construct a broad-based organization. It is built piece by piece, person by person. Therein lies its strength.

6. Confrontation Is a Tool But Beware of the Point of Diminishing Returns

The opposite side of relational interaction is confrontation, and that, perhaps paradoxically, is no less important to the IAF. Ernesto Cortez, arguably the most successful IAF organizer, is the Cabinet Member who heads their extensive Texas regional operations. Over many years Cortez has built a series of tough organizations in the parched, hard-scrabble Latin American communities of Texas. His message, liberally sprinkled with literary and philosophical references to the organizers-in-training, is to grasp power, to evaluate self-interest unsentimentally, and to confront authority.

Cortez contends, "There is no nice way to bring about change. All change comes through pressure and threats."[7] He approvingly quotes an aphorism that was one of New York power-broker Robert Moses' favorites, "You can't make an omelet without breaking some eggs."[8] "For change to occur," Cortez goes on to say without qualification, "there has to be conflict and confrontation."

Confrontation, and the natural (and it was implied, cowardly) inclination to avoid it, was a constant theme at the Ten-Day Training. "Sure, once you have power you can afford to be nice, and, let's face it, most of us try to avoid confrontation." Cortez deplored this lack of stiff-backed courage because, "Without confronting people you can't have accountability. And accountability is the only way to achieve justice." The idea here is that people in power will be alert to the larger equity issues only when they have to contend with frequent, pitiless confrontation.

IAF teaches that confrontation promotes change. "Isn't the success of Alcoholics Anonymous based on the act of confronting yourself?" Cortez asserts, "In *"The World As It Should Be,"* there is unity, but in the real world diversity is what we find. If in the real world you were actually able to achieve unity, what would you get? You'd get fascism."

He draws an example from America's revolutionary past, explaining, "Madison recognized this. He saw that people tended to form factions right away. He wrote in the *Federalist Papers* that there were two ways to deal with this problem. On one hand, you could strive to eliminate all factions, but that cure is worse than the problem. Or, you could encourage many factions, and let them compete for recognition, for power."

Madison's view prevailed, and Cortez celebrates its legacy: "We embrace tension, compromise, and the pluralism of divided loyalties. We look for heterogeneity because we want power."

The centrality of confrontation was a note frequently sounded during the ten days of instruction. "You know what I mean by confrontation?" Chambers rhetorically asked his class at one point. "Eyeball to eyeball," he declares with almost mean-spirited relish. There are two types of confrontation, Chambers maintains: "You confront people and institutions that are important to you, like your family, friends and children. And, you confront those that have power, the leaders of institutions."

In his world view, confrontation is a persistent, desirable necessity. "If you can get a meeting with the mayor without confrontation, fine; do it. Then confront him!"

The actions, are, says Chambers, "the mechanisms of confrontation." He asserts, "Confrontations cause a change in the relationship, as when you confront your child." But, if possible, Chambers counsels, "Avoid showdowns. The threat of a strike is better than striking."

IAF groups are action-oriented. As California Cabinet Member Larry McNeil proclaims, "Action is to the organization what oxygen is to the body. Ours are action organizations, not bureaucracies." Constant self-feeding action is the life blood because it binds people to the group by "building the collective egos in the action." It transforms "spectators into citizens." It is important to stir up the troops because angry public confrontations, in McNeil's words, "put drama into people's lives; they create opportunities for people which are more interesting than they get from television."

But, in order to have a galvanizing action, you need a target. Here is where things get sticky. The target needs to have powerful symbolic value. The dynamic is unvarying in IAF's view: a group needs action, the action (or display of power) needs a lightning rod to

focus it, and the action, in turn, will provoke a reaction that can pro-
pel events forward. Chambers also preaches that it is absolutely essential to select a ripe target and build animosity towards him or her.
"If you are not targeting, confrontations won't build a broad-based
organization," he says flatly.

Urban blight is too diffuse and abstract to provoke wrenching,
galvanizing action. The pervasive problem, banal in its familiarity,
has to be humanized, personalized; a target has to be selected and
mercilessly zeroed in on. The enemy in SBC's housing campaign was
originally New York Mayor Edward I. Koch, who made the final decision not to turn over Site 404 to SBC. Koch, a reliable foil for the
IAF ever since the Queens group first wrestled with him in 1977, had
become too shopworn to continue to light up anyone's emotional
switchboard. So IAF activists targeted HPD Commissioner Abraham
Biderman, The Partnership's James Robinson and Kathy Wylde, and
Bronx Borough President Fernando Ferrer as action lightning rods.

IAF believes the need for enemies is as necessary as the need for
allies. Evoking the Birmingham sheriff who unleashed dogs and fire
hoses against civil-rights marchers, McNeil contends, "Bull O'Connor was as important to the civil-rights movement as Martin Luther
King. That's why they chose to march in his town! Let your enemies
help you do your organizing. You can always count on them doing
something stupid. Inevitably they overreact when you put them under pressure."

The absolutist view of "targeting" an opponent and provoking
him into overreaction has certain limitations and costs. The South
Bronx is not Birmingham of a generation ago. The Bronx Borough
President is a young, ambitious minority politician, not a cartoon opponent of housing justice. Rather than cultivating him, "get[ting] a
relationship" with him, he was targeted as a stock villain, a lackey
of the corrupt political establishment of the Bronx, and his enmity
proved to be a massive stumbling block on Site 404.

It is indisputable, as Chambers contends, that Ferrer came out
of the corrupt Friedman machine politics of the Bronx, but is it of
no import at all that he is from a new untested generation of minority officials?

7. Cultivate and Train Local Leaders

Leadership is, of course, crucial. Central to the task of turning
around the South Bronx is developing a cadre of committed, re-

sourceful local leaders who can focus the energy and despair of the local residents. How is such latent talent uncovered?

SBC is working with generally older, churchgoing families, many with a traditionally pious devotion to *The World As It Should Be*. How do you crack their conventionality and energize them? Often these devout folks have modest jobs and are not self-assertive political sophisticates; neither are they used to (or sometimes, even interested in) wielding power.

Civic community groups usually have at the top three or four people who are already, almost by definition, effective leaders. Movements, or at least successful movements, generally have a single charismatic leader. One thinks of Martin Luther King. The built-in liability is that effective leaders are often already spread thin and do not have time to teach and train others. When such leaders are gone, movements can collapse. One thinks of Ralph Abernathy failing, valiantly, at the daunting task of filling Dr. King's shoes and inadvertently contributing to the subsequent disarray in the civil-rights movement.

IAF claims to develop collective leadership with no one dominant person. There is instead, in McNeil's words, "a deliberate creation and expansion of collective leadership." The public leadership of an IAF group like South Bronx Churches seems to shift, leapfrogging among three or four spokespeople during a typical action.

More importantly, there is a continuous and conscious effort to groom new leaders. However, whether there is widely dispersed group *decision making* on key issues remains an open question. Leaders like Jim Drake claim they already know how to redirect the energies of a community like the South Bronx. Although they are content to let the local residents select the issues, like the improvement of Lincoln Hospital's emergency room, they have a map in their heads that sees individual issues more as interchangeable tools rather than ends in themselves. Making a tiny improvement is not the point. Extracting leaders and building power from the accumulation of small inconsequential victories, no matter what the issue, is their prime focus. Getting the snowball rolling at the top of the hill matters most. It does not matter whether the task is traffic lights at school crossings or eradication of junkie infestation in abandoned buildings. What counts is the magnitude of the forward momentum of the snowball at the bottom of the hill. As manipulative as this may be, the fact remains that, in the South Bronx, there is no group that is as serious and successful in cultivating new leaders as South Bronx Churches.

The real aim is to spark creative tension in the local pastors. The church leaders will be in the South Bronx long after various SBC organizers are rotated out, and to them the traffic lights and reclamation of turf from the junkies weigh heavily. In the 404 conflict, what matters most to the pastors is actually getting housing planted, allowing their parishioners to live in decent quarters, whereas the SBC staffers are fixated more on the Big Picture. Schools, hospitals, housing: it doesn't really make a difference. For them what counts in *real politic* terms is power and teaching people, getting people to *own* the idea that in a democracy, they can count.

Like all successful organizations with staying power, the IAF has had its share of outstanding leaders. In fact, it would be hard to imagine a more impressive roster of skilled organizers than the present IAF Cabinet of Ed Chambers, Ernie Cortez, Mike Gecan, Larry McNeil, Arnie Graf, and Jim Drake. Once effective leaders are in place, the real challenge is to get the charismatic veterans to loosen their grip, share authority, and plunge into the time-consuming effort of cultivating new leaders, new potential rivals. As IAF Cabinet Member Larry McNeil confesses, there needs to be a realization that "the only way I can get more power as a leader is to teach others everything I know about power."

Alinsky was not generous about sharing the spotlight, as Ed Chambers' bitter criticism of Alinsky for having claimed credit for his work in Rochester attests. It is surprising that this is the case. Alinsky, in his perceptive biography of the autocratic labor leader John L. Lewis,[9] was well aware of the suffocating limitations of a dominant figure brushing others aside and hogging the limelight. Yet, translating insights into practice is always tricky.

What are the mechanics of this process of leadership development? How does one take an idealistic and pious church activist and test her under fire, bolster her confidence, and cultivate her leadership skills?

The IAF thinks of its leadership development efforts as yielding three levels of evolving management. All three categories of volunteers are directed by a paid Lead Organizer, who is himself hired and fired by the assembled collective leadership.

At the top of the hierarchy is the small collective of Primary Leaders, who ultimately are responsible for the whole organization. They worry about the budget, recruit new members and congregations, and train and maintain. These four to twelve people are metaphorically the generals of the operation. They spend a year or two in this position before being gently rotated out.

On the next rung are the Secondary Leaders, who typically head up a piece of a particular campaign. These members, who, in a healthy local, number anywhere from fifty to one hundred and fifty, organize at the congregational level and meet with parishioners in one-on-one meetings. In a military analogy, these people are the captains; or, in a baseball analogy, these are the minor leagues where talented players are given room to grow and are carefully groomed by seasoned managers.

Beneath them are the more narrowly focused sergeants, the Tertiary Leaders, a category that encompasses one hundred and fifty to five hundred in a mature group like SBC. Primarily concerned with their own congregation, they must genuinely feel they have a piece of the larger organization. The more talented leaders emerging here are rotated into the second tier.

All others are referred to as followers, the necessary prerequisite for any leaders. In fact, the IAF defines a leader, circularly, as someone who has a following and, crucially, can deliver it. As McNeil says, "There is no mystique to leadership. It boils down to whether or not you can deliver. A leader has to be able to inspire confidence in others, and has to be tested. We don't need any 'mouth leaders' who can talk a good fight but have no following."

There is nothing static or permanent about leadership. "Leaders have to be continually critiqued and agitated," McNeil contends. "It's part of the culture of our organizations. It is like a university where people can learn about public life, not in the classroom, but by doing things."

The IAF holds that it is healthy when a secondary leader's ego begins to swell, and he itches to move up to the primary stage. "We want leaders who go berserk when the governor does something without checking with him first," McNeil boasts.

8. Diverse Sources of Income Guarantee Independence

Having a reliable, independent income stream is also crucial to the success of the Lead Organizer. Virtually all other South Bronx community development groups get their funding through government sources or, in the case of People For Change, rely on the archdiocese. The IAF avoids this dependency like a plague or perhaps more appropriately, like an addiction. Who, then, bankrolls them? Jim Drake asserts:

> If you are going to bring together power, you have to have your own money, and there has to absolutely be no question of how

you spend that money. If there is question, then you give it back. For that you need diverse sources of funds, so that if you want to pull out our money, fine, we still have Episcopal money; if they want to pull out, then we've got Lutheran money. Plus, the fact that over three years we have put over $150,000 of our own money in the bank. So they can all take a big flying fuck, I don't care. They can all go because we have $150,000 and that's enough to go two years if we had to. What I'm saying is that organized money is power. What SBC has is organized money. Its congregations pay dues.

9. Make Organizing a Professional Career

The three tiers of leaders are presided over by a staff of professional organizers. This is where almost all of the budget is spent. At the top of the pyramid are Lead Organizers like SBC's Jim Drake. He is not an executive director of the organization, and he is not the spokesperson. He is someone the leadership hires and fires, someone meant to agitate people. "The Lead Organizer's job," McNeil says with perverse delight, "is to make your life more complicated and more miserable." He is guided by IAF's Iron Rule: *Never do anything for people they can do for themselves.*

Ordinarily a Lead Organizer endures seven or eight years of detailed mentoring. He has to have a steady hand on the tiller and a clear overview of the community. "He is like a surgeon; he has to be able to figure out where to cut." McNeil explains that communities like the South Bronx where IAF wants to set up shop are already organized, but "they are organized for powerlessness. You have to come in and disorganize, and come up with new configurations. This calls for the finesse of a scalpel."

Lead Organizers do not come cheap; the IAF believes in paying a generous wage so that talented people can make a solid career out of organizing.[10] They do, however, economize by dispensing with fancy offices, because "you can't organize in an office. You have to be out teaching and stirring things up all the time."[11] And beyond that, according to McNeil, "All growth happens in the unfamiliar. There is no growth without pain and anxiety."

That highlights another salient aspect of cultivating leaders—giving people the opportunity to fail. "You have to get people to move outside their comfort zone. The organization should get you to try to do things you never tried before." Failure is no disgrace. In fact, according to McNeil, another definition of an organizer is "someone who has failed more than anyone else, but who has reflected on these failures."

The IAF takes the position that their organizations are vehicles for adult education. In their terms, in the organization people learn how to be adults in *The World As It Is* rather than floundering in *The World As We Wish It Were.*

The most eloquent statement of what animates these men is the response of Mike Gecan, who reacted to Ed Chambers' challenge to put in words why he does what he does:

> There's no one answer to the question, Why do I organize? The composite answer includes scores of memories and incidents, actions and inactions, desires and fears, hostilities and hopes that more or less make up the "me" of 1990.
>
> I do know that it was easier to answer this question in 1975, when I began with IAF, than it is today. Easier, because there were fewer memories. Easier, because the drive to organize was rooted geographically in Chicago and rooted relationally in my parents and the people of a single neighborhood and a single city. Easier, because organizing was fresh and new and spinning off the excitement of the civil-rights and peace movements and because racial tensions were high but so were the hopes for racial relations of dignity and depth.
>
> All of this has changed. Metaphorically, I've moved from the Plains, where the views are long and there is less for the eye to absorb, to the more crowded, more cluttered, more complicated place where it is harder to see and where there are more distractions. It's the nature of the middle—of a career, a project, an effort, a life—to be less clear, more muddled, more demanding; there's more opportunity and more risk; more tension and more meaning.
>
> I organize more for my children and myself now and less for my parents and for people in general. I organize more for the love of the daily activity of organizing—the individual meetings, the relationship with people like Johnny Ray Youngblood and Pat Oettinger and Tom Sinnott and Stephen Robertson, and thinking and rethinking and re-rethinking, the imagining and positing and implementing, than for some single identifiable victory or goal. (In the same way, I run for the love of running more than for the need to win a race.) I organize more out of a usu-

ally controlled fury (more controlled than at the start, much more) than out of disappointment about the betrayal of a single person or a single place. I organize because I've learned that people pray in different ways, and organizing, I believe, is the best way some of us know how—however crudely—to pray.[12]

Afterword

If the previous analysis is correct, if attending to some of the cardinal rules described above allows an organizer to mobilize a community, what then? If, as in SBC's case, a battered community can marshal large numbers of people and pry land from the city and, in addition, politicize church hierarchies so they shake loose enough capital to bankroll the rebuilding of the neighborhood, where will that lead? Won't the new buildings ultimately fall prey to the overwhelming centrifugal forces in the community and be engulfed by the surrounding decay? What end does all of SBC's brilliant work serve?

The real theme of this study, as my friend Donald Oliver notes, is the search for the appropriate engine of reform to reconstitute and restructure urban life into genuine communities. Should citizens look to the mayor's office, the school board, private enterprise, civic organizations, special interest groups, or movements for support in the effort to reestablish viable neighborhoods? Clearly, in the case of the South Bronx, relying on municipal agencies is futile.

Jim Drake put is succinctly:

Nehemiah is the flip side of what the city did. [Our vision of community] is the counterpart of everything that Roger Starr [the theoretician of "planned shrinkage"] said you have to take out. You have to put back firehouses, you got to put back schools, you got to put back subways. The housing is a great symbol of the struggle. Nehemiah is the exact opposite of what the city did.

The better story is why did the South Bronx get the way it is? Why hasn't anybody really caught the story that the people who made it the way it is. Friedman, Biaggi, Simon, Garcia, [all government officials] are now in prison?

What a kind of miraculous people's movement was generated here around resolute old priests and ministers and leaders of congregations! How tenacious they were! There's this whole other story about New York politics and the greed of the Rockefellers, of the downtown people who have no intention of living here, but who need places to put people who run their service industries, their computers.

It's like Iraq. We bomb the shit out of it in order that our industrialists can go and rebuild it. It is *exactly* what happened in the South Bronx. We bombed the shit out of it. We pulled out the infrastructure and let is collapse in order that the same people who promoted the idea of letting it collapse could go back and rebuild it. That's capitalism run amok.[13]

It seems clear that the organizing of the South Bronx must lead to more than new dwellings: it must somehow build a new community, one with restructured schools, revitalized civil institutions, and remade relations among neighbors.

This is a tall order. Can SBC and the forthcoming South Bronx Nehemiah neighborhood make these fundamental transformations? How do you begin to organize the Nehemiah residents for such a daunting task? I. D. Robbins sketches out a vision:

The value and the strength of the community organization will depend on the continuing leadership of SBC.

These families tend not to be very dependent people. These are people who had enough energy to save money, to get jobs, to raise families. And they are pretty confident.

I felt, and I have felt right along, that you have to first organize around a service function for homeowners. You can't organize around an agitational function. There's nothing wrong with an agitational function. The church does that. Monsignor Spengler has posters about don't kill the Nicaraguans, and all the rest of the stuff that goes on in the Spanish churches. But I think if you talk about homeowners: you organize them around service combinations. You can organize, not social things because that's another step, and the churches do that, but you can organize services for them. They need somebody to go up on the roof once in awhile, or they are going to buy refrigerators, or any other thing they want to do. Somebody has to administer this association.

Now the organization has lots of money; we saw to that. All of these [Nehemiah resident] associations are well-financed. They get five dollars a month from everyone who buys a house. You get sixty dollars a year per family, times two thousand families. With that you can run one wonderful association.[14]

Once the leader wins the confidence of the residents by building working alliances that deliver services, where do you go from there? On this firm foundation much can be built. According to Robbins:

From there, why there is no limit. These are the kind of people who send their kids to school. They are active people, people who will really go to work when you give them the chance. I suppose I could think of a hundred different things they could do, and so could anybody who gave some time to it. If you have the people trained and harnessed you can move in any direction you need to move.[15]

The prime reason significant educational reform has floundered in inner city areas is that, no matter how wonderful the school becomes, the homes and neighborhoods where the children live are dysfunctional. Government has been unwilling or unable to create jobs and so small school improvements often get buried alive in neighborhoods dominated by the out-of-work underclass. Now in the South Bronx there is a more ambitious effort to rebuild an entire community. After finishing my account of the early struggles of SBC, Jim Drake objected:

I think [our] housing is important, but the real case study should be more around the lives of the some of the people. Somebody whose life has radically changed; that would be kind of a stream through all this organizing. It's a modern *Billy Bathgate* of color. What happens to a character who participates in this stuggle of a community to be reborn?

Referring to the 1986 book about the Bronx that chronicled its decline and then picked through the debris of the devastated borough looking for faint signs of renewal and found precious little cause for optimism, Drake said, "To me it's as if you take *We're Still Here;* that book that is kind of a preliminary introduction to your book, which should be called *Fuckin' A, We're Still Here!*

Notes

Introduction: The Design and Purpose of the Study

1. Jill Jonnes (1986) is a notable exception. The last third of her book, now sadly out of print, offers the most comprehensive account currently available of the precipitous decline of the borough beginning in the middle 1960s.

2. Other important collections are at New York Public Library's Bronx Reference Center at the Fordham branch and the Bronx Archives at Herbert H. Lehman College of the City University of New York.

3. Hermalyn is about to publish the definitive account on the origin and early years of Morris: *Morris High School and the Creation of the New York City Public High School System.*

4. "Of Patronage and Profit: Tale of School Board 12," *New York Times* 16 Dec 88. The *Times* charged that members of the school board systematically turned "the district into an enterprise for patronage and profit by trading jobs for political favors, seeking payoffs, putting relatives on the payroll and allowing school supplies to be looted."

5. In a revealing detail, the *Times* reported that the addicted woman "said she had been involved with drugs and as a result was homeless. But she contended that using heroin should not necessarily be a bar to serving on a school board."

6. Fourteen months later Wilfredo Abreu was indicted and charged with soliciting a bribe, attempted grand larceny, and official misconduct. Reported in the *New York Times,* 1 Feb 90.

7. The subsequent reporting about how he presided over his South Bronx school was chilling. According to a long report in the 27 Dec 88 *New York Times,* the principal had during his sixteen years at the helm "a history of drinking, absenteeism, lateness, and serious lapses in professional performance, yet the mammoth educational system never acted to remove him. . . . Parents and colleagues reported he was often drunk, would doze at meetings and frequently appeared slovenly. He would spend much of the day watching television game shows."

8. "A Bronx 13-Year Old Is Shot While Going To Buy Cereal," (*New York Times,* 23 Feb 90) is a typical routine spot news story in local news-

papers. The mother of the boy caught in a drug dispute crossfire was quoted: "I heard the shots, but I always hear shots."

9. The taped interviews took place at St. Thomas Aquinas rectory on 23 October and 14 December 1988.

10. The taped interview with Blanca Ramirez took place at the offices of South Bronx People for Change on Morris Ave. 5 January 1989.

11. An account of this branch of the research will be included in the next chapter.

12. According to an article in *Catholic New York* (2 Jan 88) South Bronx Churches alleged "that Lincoln Hospital administrators were selling illegal drugs to patients, that medical foul-ups have included one woman whose baby died after she was left to deliver it unattended, that patients were recently double billed to the tune of $100,000, and that a woman, scheduled for a mastectomy, nearly had her leg amputated when her chart was confused with another patient's." A few months later a New York State Health Department report charged that Lincoln Hospital suffered from mismanagement, overcrowding, and crucial staff shortages. The *New York Times* reported 28 Oct 88): "The emergency ward was found to keep patients for as long as six days in crowded holding rooms and hallways before beginning treatment or admitting them."

13. This interview with staff organizer Tony Aguilar was taped on 5 Jan 89 at the offices of SBC in St. Jerome's.

14. This taped interview was conducted on 26 Jan 89.

15. This second taped interview with Jim Drake occurred on 30 Jan 89.

16. This quote is from an evening training session for volunteers conducted by Jim Drake in the basement of St. Augustine's church on 29 September 1989.

17. The charter to establish South Bronx Churches was signed in October 1985, and the first major action was launched at St. Jerome's in February of 1987.

18. Long, formal taped interviews with John Heinemeier occurred on 27 Jan, 7 Feb, 10 Mar, 2 Apr, 5 Apr, 2 Jun, and 30 Aug during 1989. Also, we had many conversations during 1990.

19. This letter is dated 18 Jun 89.

20. I am aware that my friendship with John Heinemeier and others presents some delicate problems. Nonetheless, I believe this does not distort my findings because it is in their self-interest to help me get a clear and accurate view of their side of the story, and they are aware that I strive not to

be openly partisan. An essay by Stephen Levy (1987) helped me clarify my thinking on this. Writing about qualitative research, he concludes: "The search cannot be conducted without the help of others. It is a participatory project. Those giving me information are, in effect, my partners in the search." Of course a balance must be struck. Bogdan and Biklen (1982) offer the sensible caution that: "Over-participation can lead to 'going native,' a phrase used in anthropology to refer to researchers getting so involved and active with subjects that their original intentions get lost."

21. Taped on 26 Jun 89.

22. I first interviewed them at HPD headquarters 4 Jan 90.

23. This interview took place on 1 May 89.

24. The taped interview took place 7 Jun 89 in a Nehemiah home that serves as Robbins' administrative office.

25. Byrne, David. *True Stories.* New York: Penguin Books, 1986.

Chapter One: The Bronx: "The City Without a Slum"

1. Wolfe, Tom. *Bonfire of the Vanities,* Farrer, Strauss, & Giroux, 1987. The publication and the filming of this lurid, cynical book has raised tempers in the Bronx, entangling Borough President Ferrer in reams of bad publicity for his ham-handed defense of the honor of the Bronx. See, for instance, "Bonfire in Bronx!!! Wolfe Catches Flak!!!" *New York Times* (11 Mar 88) and "Filming Puts Bronx Vanities Out of Joint" (8 Sep 90). Perhaps the best comment on the book is from Irving Howe who deplored the "impulse toward pseudo-aristocratic snottiness" that he says Wolfe exemplifies.

2. When a forty-year-old, white male researcher wearing student clothes entered one of the courtrooms, he was conspicuous because of his unwitting violation of the dress code. To the habituates, it was a glaring *faux pas,* like showing up to a wedding in Bermuda shorts. The judge immediately dispatched a clerk to ask the intruder to identify himself. Later the clerk revealed that the observer was not assumed to be a tenant battling a dispossess order, presumably because of his race, but was initially suspected of being an incorrectly attired housing advocate.

3. Interviewed January 1989.

4. The report is called *Five-Minute Justice.*

5. According to tenant advocates the West Bronx "is one of the few neighborhoods left in New York where there is a decent supply of affordable housing." *New York Newsday,* 27 January 1989. And yet, even here, two-

thirds of all the apartments in the West Bronx neighborhoods of the High-bridge and South Concourse sections rent for over $300 a month, according to figures calculated in 1987. (The West Bronx is actually the western por-tion of the South Bronx.)

6. Landlords who make improvements to their rent-stabilized build-ings can legally raise the rent by evoking Major Capital Improvement (MCI) increases. Such capital improvements increase the value of the apartments and are ultimately financed by the tenants. In addition, there is also some-thing called J-SI's which are laws that substantially reduce property taxes for landlords who upgrade their buildings.

7. Interviewed 7 Feb 1989.

8. *New York Times,* "Mini-Courtrooms Aid Crowded Dockets," 5 Apr 90.

9. *New York Post,* "The Housing Courts and the Homeless," 26 Mar 89.

10. *New York Newsday,* "Justice in the Real `People's Court," 27 Jan 89.

11. *New York Newsday,* "New Weapons in an Old Fight," 27 Jan 89.

12. Ultan, Lloyd, "The Story of the South Bronx 1776–1940," *Devas-tation/Resurrection: The South Bronx,* The Bronx Museum of the Arts, 1979.

13. Jonnes, Jill, *We're Still Here: The Rise, Fall, and Resurrection of the South Bronx, Boston:* Atlantic Monthly Press, 1986.

14. Ultan, Lloyd, "Jonas Bronck and the First Settlement of The Bronx," *The Bronx County Historical Society Journal,* XXVI, no. 2 (Fall 1989).

15. Price, Mark, *A History of the Bronx Schools 1898–1944: From Con-solidation to the Present* ("compiled at the suggestion of Hon. Anthony Cam-pagna, Bronx Member of the Board of Education"), unpublished report, 1945.

16. Ibid. Price, 1945.

17. Cited in Dominic Massaro's "Gouverneur Morris: The Constitu-tional Penman Revisited," *The Bronx County Historical Society Journal,* XXIV, no. 2 (Fall 1987). Roosevelt's biography of Morris was published in 1888.

18. According to Dominic Massaro, "[Morris] gave the document sym-metry, strength and grace. He boldly coined the Preamble, designating 'We the People of the United States,' a wholly new phrase at the time, as the ul-timate authority, thereby elevating the sights of government and couching its purpose in eloquent language."

19. Ibid. Jonnes, 1986.

20. Ibid. Jonnes, 1986.

21. The travails of this police precinct were also the subject of a 1976 best-selling book by former officer Thomas Walker and a 1981 Hollywood movie starring Paul Newman.

22. Bradshaw, Jon, "Savage Skulls," *Esquire* (June, 1977).

23. *New York Times*, "Pulling Out of Fort Apache, the Bronx," 23 Jun 93.

24. See Robert Olmsted, "A History of Transportation in The Bronx," *The Bronx County Historical Society Journal*, XXVI, no. 2 (Fall 1989).

25. Ibid. Price, 1945.

26. Ibid. Jonnes, 1987.

27. Hermalyn, Gary, "The Bronx at the Turn of the Century," *The Bronx County Historical Society Journal*, XXVI, no. 2 (Fall 1989).

28. Ibid. Price, 1945.

29. Ibid. Jonnes, 1987, p. 23.

30. Ibid. Ultan, 1979.

31. *New York Post*, 30 Mar 1988.

32. Ibid. Ultan, 1979.

33. Sullivan, Donald, "1940–1965: Population Mobility in the South Bronx," *Devastation/Resurrection: The South Bronx*, New York, Bronx Museum of the Arts, 1979.

34. Lemann, Nicholas, *The Promised Land: The Great Black Migration and How It Changed America*, New York, Alfred A. Knopf, 1991.

35. Another good source is the anthology, *Up South: Stories, Studies and Letters of This Country's African-American Migrations*, Edited by Malaika Adero, New York, New Press, 1993. The classic book on the Puerto Rican immigration to New York City has yet to be written.

36. *New York Times*, 21 Oct 77.

37. Ibid. *New York Times*.

38. Ibid. *New York Times*.

39. The building's name, carved over the entrance, ironically is "Last Hope." It is still inhabited but is now called "New Hope."

40. *New York Daily News*, 27 Feb 77.

41. Ibid. Jonnes, 1986, p. 208.

42. Ibid. Jonnes, 1986.

43. *New York Times,* 13 Jun 77.

44. Ibid. *New York Times.*

45. *Sunday New York Daily News Magazine,* 27 Feb 77.

46. Ibid. *Daily News.*

47. Ibid. *Daily News.*

48. *New York Times,* "Renovations Set for Area Near Yankee Stadium," 14 Aug 93.

49. Ibid. Jonnes, 1986.

50. *New Directions for The Bronx: A Program of the Regional Plan Association in cooperation with Bronx Borough President Fernando Ferrer,* 1990. Background research prepared by N. David Milder.

51. *New York Times,* 13 December 1986.

52. *New York Times,* 11 Jul 90.

53. These statistics were quoted to me by Bronx historian Gary Hermalyn, and, although they fit with other local health numbers, I have not been able to independently verify their accuracy.

54. *Time Magazine,* 9 May 1988.

55. *New Directions for the Bronx: A Program of the Regional Plan Association in Cooperation with Bronx Borough President Fernando Ferrer,* Task Force on Health Education, and Human Services, 1990.

Chapter Two: Why Did the South Bronx Collapse?

1. See, for instance, Jenson, Robert, "Introduction: South Bronx Devastation," *Devastation/Resurrection: The South Bronx,* New York, Bronx Museum of the Arts, 1979.

2. Ibid. Jenson, 1979.

3. Wilson, William Julius, *The Truly Disadvantaged: The Inner City, the Underclass, and Public Policy,* Chicago, The University of Chicago Press, 1987.

4. Kasarda, J.D., "The Regional and Urban Redistribution of People and Jobs in the U.S.," paper prepared for the national Research Council Committee on National Urban Policy, National Academy of Sciences, 1986.

5. Ibid. Kasarda.

6. Glazer, Nathan, "The South Bronx Story: An Extreme Case of Neighborhood Decline," *Policy Studies Journal*, 16, no. 2 (Winter 1987).

7. *New York Times*, 1 November 1977.

8. *New York Times*, 13 November 1977.

9. Ibid. *New York Times*.

10. *New York Times*, 14 January 1978.

11. Ibid. *New York Times*.

12. Op. cit. Sullivan, 1979.

13. Jackson, Kenneth, *Crabgrass Frontier: The Suburbanization of the United States*, New York, Oxford University Press, 1985.

14. Ibid. Jackson, 1985.

15. Alinsky, Saul, *Rules for Radicals: A Pragmatic Primer for Realistic Radicals*, New York, Vintage Books, 1971.

16. Op. cit. Wilson.

17. Sleeper, Jim, "Days of Developers: Boom and Bust with Ed Koch," *Dissent*, New York, Fall, 1987.

18. *New York Times*, 12 May 1988, op ed article.

19. Lemann, Nicholas, *The Promised Land: The Great Black Migration and How It Changed America*, New York, Alfred A. Knopf, 1991.

20. Op cit. Jackson, 1985.

21. Cited in Jackson, 1985.

22. Ibid. Jackson, 1985.

23. Tabb, William K., *The Long Default: New York City and the Urban Fiscal Crisis*, New York, Monthly Review Press, 1982.

24. Ibid. Tabb, 1982. The study Tabb cites is *Rental Housing in the City of New York: Supply and Condition 1975–1978*, New York: The City of New York, Division of Rent Control, 1979, by Peter Marcuse with Harvey Goldstein and Moon Wha Lee.

25. Ibid. Tabb, 1982.

26. Salins' argument is found in his 1980 study *The Ecology of Housing Destruction: Economic Effects of Public Intervention in the Housing*

Market, New York, New York University Press. Here I rely on Nathan Glazer's 1987 summary of Salins' hypothesis.

27. Ibid. Glazer, 1987.

28. Newfield, Jack and Barrett, Wayne, *City For Sale: Ed Koch and the Betrayal of New York,* New York, Harper & Row, 1988. Ed Chambers, the director of the Industrial Areas Foundation, first urged me to read this book to understand the context in which his New York groups were functioning.

29. Ibid. Newfield & Barrett, 1988.

30. Ibid. Newfield & Barrett, 1988.

31. *New York Times,* "The Crimes and Punishments of Wedtech," 22 Oct 89. An exceedingly well-written and scrupulously researched book on the scandal is James Traub's *Too Good To Be True: The Outlandish Story of Wedtech,* New York, Doubleday, 1990.

32. *New York Times,* "Power Built on Poverty: One Man's Odyssey," 24 May 93.

33. Ibid. *New York Times.*

34. Op. cit. Wilson.

35. Ibid. Wilson.

36. Sleeper, Jim, "Looking at Our City," *Dissent,* New York, Fall 1987.

37. Op. cit. Jenson.

38. Smith, Dennis, *Report from Engine Co. 82,* New York, Saturday Review Press, 1972.

39. Op. cit. Tabb, 1982.

40. Ibid. Jenson.

41. Ibid. Glazer, 1987.

42. *New York Times,* 12 November 1976.

43. Ibid. *New York Times.*

44. Caro, Robert, *The Power Broker: Robert Moses and the Fall of New York,* New York, Vintage Books, 1975.

45. Ibid. Caro, 1975.

46. Ibid. Caro, 1975.

47. Ibid. Caro, 1975.

48. Ibid. Caro, 1975.

49. Ibid. Caro, 1975.

50. Ibid. Caro.

51. *New York Times*, 7 November 1983.

52. Ibid. *New York Times*.

53. Op. cit. Wilson.

54. Moynihan, Daniel Patrick, *The Negro Family: The Case for National Action*, Washington, DC: Office of Policy Planning and Research, U.S. Department of Labor, 1965.

55. Op. cit. Wilson.

56. These statistics come from Wilson.

57. *New York Times*, 23 Jun 90.

58. This statistical roundup comes from the August 1990, issue of *Spy* magazine which sneered that Borough President Ferrer's objection to the Bronx-bashing movie *Bonfire of the Vanities* was, in light of these appalling statistics, "feel-good cheerleading of the most implausible kind."

59. Katz, Michael, *The Undeserving Poor: From the War on Poverty to the War on Welfare*, New York, Pantheon Books, 1989.

60. Ibid. Katz, 1989.

61. Ibid. Katz, 1989.

62. West, Cornel, *Race Matters*, Boston, Beacon Press, 1993.

Chapter Three: Alinsky, Chambers, and Citizen Movements

1. IAF claims that its twenty-eight organizations in New York, New Jersey, Maryland, Texas, Tennessee, Arizona, and California "reprsent more than 1.5 million families." *IAF 50 Years of Organizing For Change: Industrial Areas Foundation*, Franklin Square, New York, 1990.

2. Howell, Leon, "The Legacy of the IAF" in *New Conversations* March 1982.

3. This quote comes from notes taken during a training session for IAF leaders on 14 July 1989, in Los Angeles.

4. Unless otherwise attributed, all the quotes from Chambers are from interviews with him on 1 May and 9 June 1989. The taped interviews took place in his office on Long Island, NY.

5. An evocative biography of the remarkable Dorothy Day is Robert Coles, *Dorothy Day: A Radical Devotion*, Reading, MA, Addison-Wesley Publishing Co., 1987.

6. Ibid. *New Conversations*, 1982.

7. IAF's characterization of the company at the time was—"Kodak's only contribution to race relations was the invention of color film."

8. Alinsky's books are a biography, *John L. Lewis* (1940), *Reveille For Radicals* (1947), and *Rules For Radicals* (1971).

9. Horwitt, Sanford D, *Let Them Call Me Rebel: Saul Alinsky—His Life and Legacy.* New York, Alfred A. Knopf, 1989.

10. Ibid. Horwitt, p. 6.

11. A researcher who has spent a lot of time pounding the streets of the South Bronx was fascinated to learn that Alinsky's doctoral thesis was a first-hand, inside study of the Al Capone gang. Relying on his ingratiating skills as a good listener, Alinsky shadowed the gangsters for two years, taking copious notes. One has to admire his success in negotiating what must have been a rather dicey problem of access. Less happily, he never did finish the dissertation.

12. Alinsky, Saul, *Rules For Radicals*, New York Vintage Books, Random House, 1971.

13. Ibid. Horwitt, p. 108.

14. Ibid. Horwitt.

15. Alinsky, Saul, *Rules For Radicals: A Primer for Realistic Radicals*, New York, Vintage Books, 1971.

16. Ibid. Alinsky, 1971.

17. Cited in Horwitt, p. 105.

18. Cited in the 1968 edition of *Current Biographies*.

19. Op. cit. *New Conversations*.

20. A masterful synthesis of the literature of neighborhood organizing is Robert Fisher's *Let the People Decide: Neighborhood Organizing in America*, Boston, Twayne Publishers, 1984. In a comprehensive bibliographic essay, Fisher notes that "The only book-length surveys of the history of neighborhood organization are Sidney Dillick, *Community Organization for Neighborhood Development: Past and Present*, New York, William Morrow, 1953, which traces the history of community organization

for social welfare from the late nineteenth century through the early 1950s and *Community Organization for Urban Social Change: A Historical Perspective*, ed., Fisher, Robert and Peter Romanofsky, Westport, Greenwood Press, 1981."

21. Two classics of that time, written by pioneering neighborhood organizers are Jane Addams, *Twenty Years at Hull House With Autobiographical Notes*, New York, Macmillan, 1910 and Lillian Ward, *The House on Henry Street*, New York, Henry Holt and Co., 1915.

22. Burghardt, Steve, "Community-Based Social Action," *Encyclopedia of Social Work*, 18th Edition, 1987.

23. This quote is from a remarkable fifty-page booklet IAF published in 1990 to mark its fiftieth anniversary. *IAF 50 Years of Organizing For Change: Industrial Areas Foundation*, Franklin Square, New York, 1990. Surprisingly, and disappointingly, the IAF has, since Alinsky's death in 1972, relied wholly on an oral tradition to transmit its insights and values. However, in its anniversary year there seem to be the beginnings of a shift. Ed Chambers has initiated, *IAF Reflects*, an experimental program of intense two-week seminars for veteran leaders, and one hopes that this will, in turn, generate some more documentation about strategy, tactics, philosophy, and history.

24. Op. cit. Fisher, 1984.

25. Present-day IAF organizers tell stories about Alinsky's outrageous sense of improvisation with obvious relish. A particular favorite is the time that Alinsky threatened to shut down O'Hare Airport by having his supporters monopolize all the bathrooms; Alinsky grandly referred to it as the first "shit-in."

26. See Kramer, R., *Participation of the Poor*, New York, Prentice Hall, 1969, and Piven & Coward, *Poor People's Movements: How They Succeed, Why They Fail*, New York, Pantheon Books, 1977.

27. There are a number of books which chronicle the short history of these New Left groups. The two best are James Miller, *Democracy in the Streets: From Port Huron to the Siege of Chicago*, New York, Simon and Schuster, 1987, and Todd Gitlin, *The Sixties: Years of Hope, Days of Rage*, New York, Bantam Books, 1988.

28. Katz, Michael, *The Undeserving Poor: From the War on Poverty to the War on Welfare*, New York, Pantheon Books, 1989.

29. Ibid. Katz, 1989 quoting from Piven's *The Great Society*.

30. Alinsky quoted in Horwitt, 1989, p. 481.

31. In a representative comment, Horwitt quotes a social activist's memory of a droll Alinsky address to a convention of social workers: "He got up and said—here's a thousand social workers at a meeting, and at the

same time the Packinghouse Workers Union is meeting in Chicago—and he said, 'You can bomb this social workers' meeting and nobody would know the difference, but if it were the Packinghouse workers, that would be a big difference.' " (Horwitt, p. 291)

32. Two important books by Harry Boyte deal with these issues: *Commonwealth: A Return to Citizen Politics*, New York, Free Press, 1989, and *The Backyard Revolution: Understanding the New Citizen Movement*, Philadelphia, Temple University Press, 1980.

33. Op. cit. Fisher, 1984.

34. Ibid. Burghardt, 1987.

35. See Karen Paget, "Citizen Organizing: Many Movements, No Majority," *The American Prospect*, Summer, 1990, no. 2, Princeton, NJ: Gary Delgado, *Organizing the Movement: The Roots and Growth of Acorn*, Temple University Press, 1986; S. Kahn, *Organizing*, New York, McGraw-Hill Book Co., 1982, and J. Fisher, *Let The People Decide*, Boston, Twayne Publishing, 1984. This issue will be returned to in Chapter 14.

36. This recounting of IAF history took place during a taped interview on 1 May 1989.

37. Taped interview on 1 May, 1989.

Chapter Four: The IAF in Queens and Brooklyn

1. This quote is from "Faces of Faith: John Heinemeier: Hope Blooming in the Urban Desert," an interview conducted by William O'Brien in a religious magazine called *The Other Side* and published in May 1988.

2. Ibid. Horwitt, p. 292.

3. Ibid. Horwitt, p. 301.

4. Ibid. Horwitt, p. 302.

5. *The Wall Street Journal* article was cited in Leon Howell's *New Conversations* piece.

6. This account of QCO's initial encounter with Koch was told with much drama and humor to a group of IAF trainees at a seminar in Los Angeles in August 1989.

7. Koch, Edward I., *Mayor: An Autobiography*, New York, Simon and Schuster, 1984, p. 76. This scene of mayoral confrontation is also fictionalized and recreated in Tom Wolfe's novel about the South Bronx, *Bonfire of the Vanities*.

8. Ibid. Koch, 1984, p. 77.

9. Most of these remarks come from an interview conducted 24 April 1989 and supplemented by material in interviews on 27 January 1989 and 10 March 1989.

10. Eccklein, Joan Levin & Lauffer, Armand *Community Organizers and Social Planners: A Volume of Case Studies and Illustrative Materials* New York: John Wiley & Sons, 1972.

11. This is the number of completed Nehemiah homes as of March 1991. Cited in "Groundbreaking," *The New Yorker*, 25 March 1991.

12. In the Old Testament, in the Book of Nehemiah, the prophet said: "You see our wretched plight. Jerusalem lies in ruins, its gates destroyed by fire. Come let us rebuild the wall of Jerusalem and be rid of the reproach."

13. Jones, Arthur, "Brooklyn People-Power Spreads to South Bronx," *National Catholic Reporter*, 13 February 1987.

14. Ibid. Jones, 1987.

15. Gittings, Jim, "Churches in Communities: A Place To Stand," *Christianity and Crisis*, 2 January 1987, p. 5–11.

Chapter Five: Old Testament Builders Nehemiah and Robbins

1. Unless otherwise indicated all of Robbins' quotes from a two-hour interview at his Nehemiah office on 7 Jul 89.

2. Robbins, I. D., "Blueprint for a One-Family House," *New York Daily News Sunday Magazine*, 1978.

3. Unless otherwise noted all quotes from Mike Gecan come from remarks he made at IAF's Ten-Day Training in Los Angeles on 18 Jul 89.

4. Freedman, Samuel G., *Upon This Rock: The Miracles of a Black Church*, New York, Harper Collins, 1993.

5. The Lutherans, according to John Heinemeier, had already committed substantial funds at an earlier stage.

6. This is Mike Gecan's account of the events.

7. This is Mike Gecan's characterization.

8. Ibid. Freedman, 1993.

9. The $10,000 subsidy is comparatively quite low. Its purpose is to reduce the cost to the buyer so that families with working-class salaries can

more easily afford the homes. The Brooklyn Nehemiah homes which cost the owners $45,000 are now worth $110,000 on the open market, according to Gecan, so that repaying the $10,000 grant to the city is not a burden to the seller. Other costs to the city include clearing the land which sometimes involves extensive demolition and relocation.

10. Robbins quotes come from a taped planning session at SBC headquarters.

11. Robbins, I. D., "How To Save Money Building the City's Housing," *Crain's New York Business,* 17 April 1989.

12. In point of fact, the stark reality is that even at the bargain price of $45,000 Mike Gecan estimates that two-thirds of EBC leaders can't manage the cost of these homes which are affordable only to those with an annual salary of $20,000. Gecan maintains that EBC rank and file are still loyally behind the concept because changes in the neighborhood are so profound. Stores have opened, addicts have been driven out, and many hope that perhaps their children will someday be prosperous enough to afford a Nehemiah home. This does, however, raise many other questions. We will return to this problem in Chapter 13.

13. *New York Times,* 16 April 1989.

14. Ibid. *New York Times.*

15. The architect also receives another $50 per house, according to Robbins in a March 1991 interview. The architect gets $25 for testing the soil conditions and another $25 for a "punch list" that is a checklist for defects after the house is built.

16. Ibid. Robbins, 1989.

17. Op. cit. *New York Times.*

18. Op. cit. Robbins, 1989.

Chapter Six:
Relational Organizing: The Launching of South Bronx Churches

1. Quotes from John Heinemeier, unless otherwise noted are from taped interviews with him on 27 Jan 89 and 10 Mar 89.

2. Morrisania, in the heart of the South Bronx, comes close to leading the league in depressing statistics. For instance, the Community Service Society reports that of the births in 1985 in Morrisania, 11.7 percent of the infants were born with severely low birth weights, 37.7 percent of the mothers received little or no prenatal care, and 21.3 percent of the births were to

teenage mothers. Overall, infant mortality rates are double the city's average. (*New York Times*, 2 Apr 89).

3. O'Brien, William, "Faces of Faith: Hope Blooming in the Urban Desert," *The Other Side*, May 1988.

4. This taped interview dealing with his family situation took place on 24 April 1989. A few years later at the urging of his wife and family, he moved from the parsonage to City Island in the northeast Bronx.

5. Community School Districts 7, 9, and 12 take in most of the South Bronx and the percentage of low-income students there is staggering. According to the Community Service Society in these districts anywhere from 62 percent to 72 percent of the students are impoverished. New York City's Human Resources Administrator estimates that "one-third of the nearly half-million children on pubic assistance are living in isolated pockets of such intense poverty that they are cut off from the world of work and independence." He specifically cited the South Bronx neighborhoods of Morrisania, Mott Haven (to its south), and Tremont (to its north). (*New York Times*, 2 Apr 89).

6. From a taped interview 7 February 1989.

7. From a taped interview 9 June 1989.

8. On salty language: Ed Chambers is reflexively blunt. I agreed to his request to exercise discretion in transcribing the taped transcripts and he insisted: "And make sure you take out all the swear words. I don't want no swear words!" By and large, I have honored his request to excise the salty language, but I have not sanitized the text when doing so would have distorted the tone of his remarks. The IAF organizers do not talk like ministers and priests (indeed, sometimes the ministers and priests do not talk like ordinary clergymen), and blue-penciling all their rude language adds propriety but subtracts flavor.

9. Remarks are from a taped interview in Chambers' office on 1 May 89. Unless otherwise cited, quotes from Chambers in this chapter are from this interview.

10. Father John Flynn also spent a number of years Venzuala.

11. Jim Drake's quotes in this chapter come from taped interviews conducted on 26 Jan 89, 30 Jan 89, and 10 Mar 89.

12. Chambers, Ed, "Organizing for Family and Congregation," published by Industrial Areas Foundation, 36 New Hyde Park Road, Franklin Square, NY 11010, 1978.

13. Eccklein, Joan Levin and Armand Lauffer, *Community Organizers and Social Planners: A Volume of Case Studies and Illustrative Materials*, New York, John Wiley & Sons, 1972.

14. In contrast, People for Change didn't have a critical mass: they had only nine Catholic churches out of twenty-four and only six of them were really invested, according to Drake. In March 1991 South Bronx Churches includes Lutherans, Methodists, Disciples of Christ, Baptists, Episcopalians, Pentecostals, Catholics, Muslims, and Presbyterians.

Chapter Seven: South Bronx Civics: Morris High School

1. *New York Times*, 11 June 1904.

2. From a *New York Times* Op-ed essay "New York's Next Crisis: Worse than 1975," 30 September 1989.

3. The entire Bronx is divided into six school districts. District 8 straddles the South Bronx and also takes in the relatively more prosperous eastern end of the borough. Districts 7, 9, and 12 made up the rest of the South Bronx.

4. For example, a December 1989, State Education Department listing of the worst schools in the state included forty-three academically troubled public schools. All but four were in New York City, and the South Bronx, with seventeen schools cited, topped the list. (The criterion used to rank the schools included student performance on standardized tests, attendance statistics, lack of school resources, and continued decline in testing results, according to the 19 December 1989 *New York Times*.)

5. *New York Times*, 13 November 1989. The union activists are able to seize control of the districts in a number of ways. The *Times* points out: "While teachers, along with principals, could not run in the districts where they worked, they could become [school board] members in other districts, often trading favors among themselves. Board of Education employees, mostly principals, accounted for nearly a third of the local board members until a recent law prohibited them from serving. Teachers accounted for about 10 percent of the seats." Also: "The U.F.T. [United Federation of Teachers] found it could easily influence the makeup of school boards through endorsements and campaign contributions. Until a recent change in policy, the union could also challenge nominating petitions of candidates it opposed. Such candidates were usually overmatched by the union's formidable legal and financial resources."

6. This account is based on notes I made during the negotiation session at Morris. All quotes, unless otherwise attributed, come from this meeting.

7. Most particularly in the last half-dozen years, there has been increased awareness by business leaders that schools are inadequately educating minority youth, and, consequently, corporations are having serious difficulty in finding skilled young people to fill entry-level positions. For in-

stance, Chemical Bank's director of employee relations points out that in the New York City only one in six applicants passes the bank's eighth-grade level teller test. (Cited in *New York Times*, 5 Oct 89). As David Kearns, chairman of the Xerox Corporation, acknowledges, "More than a third of tomorrow's work force will be minorities, and half of those are kids growing up poor. A fourth drop out and another fourth don't come close to having the skills to survive in an advanced economy. (quoted in the *New York Times*, 2 Oct 89) Felix G. Rohatyn, the corporate figure brought into city service during the fiscal crisis of the 1970s, flatly asserts, "New York City's economy will rapidly deteriorate without a supply of skilled employees for tomorrow's predominately service economy. Furthermore, the cost of unemployment and crime resulting from the high dropout rate will drive more people and business out of the city." (*New York Times* 1 Sept 89) As a result of this perception, business and education are increasingly linking their worlds. According to the *New York Times* 3 Sep 89), "Seven years ago, the American Express Company confronted hiring pools of high school graduates whose abilities were mediocre and who often did not understand the need for courtesy and punctuality in the workplace. It decided to develop a special program to prepare students for careers in finance and helped set up academies at seven New York City high schools." The future is likely to see more corporate efforts in New York City schools.

8. Among the special programs presently available at Morris High School are ASPIRA, a project designed for Hispanic youngsters that offers leadership training, improvement of basic skills, counseling, family assistance, networking, etc.; S.P.A.R.K., a substance abuse and teenage pregnancy counseling service; a "house" system for all ninth graders that allows them to select from six different curricular foci, including Business Academy, Music Academy, Honors Academy, Bilingual Academy, Project Vista, and Discovery Academy; there is also an After School Occupational Skills Program; Shared Instruction with local vocational schools; Volunteer Internship Programs; and a myriad of other programs and special staff.

9. These figures reflect 1986–87 statistics and come from a Morris High Chapter 1 project proposal.

10. *New York Times*, 24 March 1989.

11. It is worth noting that an arms-length attitude towards community involvement in the school is not a consistent feature of the history of Morris. Bronx historian Gary Hermalyn in his soon-to-be-published *The Creation of New York City's First Public High School: Morris High School in the Bronx* recounts that, at the turn of the century, the first principal of Morris, Edward J. Goodwin, "wanted parents to be intimately involved with the school. Goodwin felt that it was the duty of the principal to be open to the parents from whom he 'may get much needed and valuable information about his own school.' " Goodwin made it a point to set aside time each

week for conferences with parents and reported that, "As an outcome of these conferences, which increased in number and length from year to year, perplexing cases of discipline were amicably settled, misunderstandings were cleared up, elective studies were adopted, and, best of all, the school thereby obtained a stronger hold upon the community's confidence and co-operation."

12. Incidentally, the Chancellor of the New York City's schools at that time, Joseph A. Fernandez, made his reputation in Dade County, Florida, and secured the New York job by pledging to institute "school-based management," a concept that explicitly involves parents, teachers, and administrators in school governance.

13. This account is based on attendance at a preliminary planning session for the meeting with Fitzgerald held at Pastor Heinemeier's parsonage, the meeting in the principals's office on 6 September 1989, and three evening training sessions for the Morris volunteers at St. Augustine's a few blocks from Morris on 28 September, 5 and 12 October 1989.

14. During that academic year, city schools were invited by the new Chancellor to submit school redesign proposals that would advance shared decision making. Many faltering South Bronx schools did. Morris was conspicuous by its absence.

15. This quote came from a telephone interview on 26 February 1990.

16. This line of inquiry was suggested first by Nathan Glazer.

17. Raywid, Mary Anne, "The Evolving Effort to Improve Schools: Pseudo-Reform, Incremental Reform, Restructuring," *Phi Delta Kappan*, October 1990.

18. Here Raywid cites H. Dean Evans, 1983, and Theodore Sizer, 1983.

19. Ibid. Raywid.

20. In the same article, she points to success in similar nearby schools in Manhattan's "District 4—Spanish Harlem—where virtually all of the students are minority and 80 percent come from families poor enough to make them eligible for free or reduced cost school lunches. Here, all junior high schools, a number of elementary schools, and two senior high schools operate on a choice basis. Since the adoption of choice, student achievement levels have risen remarkably, along with attendance, attitudes towards school, and post-school plans." Raywid cites documentation backing up these claims in Raymond Domanico's *Model for Choice: A Report on Manhattan's District 4*. New York: Manhattan Institute for Policy Research, 1989. Also see, Fliegal, Seymour and James MacQuire, *Miracle in East Harlem*. New York: Times Books, 1993.

21. In addition, there were other ripe targets. A potent weapon available to SBC for rallying community support against the status quo at Morris is the school's drastic under representation of minority leadership. In 1990, the New York City school system, whose student population is 80 percent non-White has a staff of teachers and principals which is 70 percent White. the statistics for the three school districts that are wholly in the South Bronx, Districts 9, 7, and 12, are startling. According to the 16 February 1990, *New York Times*, students in District 7 are 99.6 percent non-White and the percentages of non-White teachers and principals respectively is 53.7 and 48.6. In District 9, 99.7 percent of the students are non-White and 56.6 percent of the teachers and 44.3 percent of the of the principles are non-White. In District 12, 99.3 percent of the students are non-White, and 50.5 percent of the teachers and 60.7 percent of the principles are non-White. But, as the *New York Times* noted two weeks later, (27 February 1990), "Urban school systems around the country are fiercely competing for the same shrinking pool of black college graduates, and they are increasingly loosing not to each other but to higher paying careers that are also seeking to increase minority representation." The numbers are distressing: "Between 1977 and 1985, there was a 58 percent decrease in the numbers of black students and a 17 percent decrease in the number of Hispanic students receiving baccalaureate degrees in education."

22. *New York Times*, "Harlem's Witness for the Chancellor," 10 Aug 92.

Chapter Eight: Here We Will Build!

1. An el is an above-ground elevated subway.

2. Willensky, Elliot, and Norval White, *The AIA Guide to New York City*. New York, Harcourt Brace Jovanovich, Third Edition, 1988.

3. During the arson-plagued years of the 1970s, "People were setting fire to buildings so they could rip out the copper plumbing after the firemen had hosed down the place, and a cottage industry [to fence the stolen metal] sprang up to accommodate them," according to Edward McCarthy, a spokesman for the Bronx District Attorney. Now that the number of buildings left to burn is radically diminished, enterprising South Bronx thieves, according to the *New York Times* (21 Sept 89), have begun to look to another source for scrap metal: They have begun severing copper cables that supply power to the signals that regulate the railroads which slice through the Bronx. This, of course, disables the trains, on one recent occasion bringing 149 trains to a grinding halt and delaying 100,000 commuters for hours.

4. Details of this plan are found in Chapter 13.

5. *New York Times*, 3 April 1989.

6. Interviewed 5 April 1989. Incidentally, Father Connally's of Sts. Peter and Paul Church is not an official member of South Bronx Churches.

7. *The Federal Writers' Project Guide to the 1930's New York*, New York, Pantheon Books, 1982 (first published in 1939). "The population [of this neighborhood] is predominately Jewish, mixed with Irish, Italian, and German." p.529

8. *New York Times*, 15 February 1989.

9. These quotes are from a tape I made of the service.

10. Claremont Village, which, despite its problems, has tens of thousands of people on its waiting lists, 4,100 apartments, and anywhere form 16,000 to 20,000 people, is responsible for one-third of all the reported criminal activity in all public housing projects in the Bronx. These statistics come from an interview with Rev. Heinimeier on 18 January 1989. He also pointed out that all four victims of Bernard Goetz, the celebrated subway gunman/vigilante, were from Claremont.

11. The New York Housing Partnership is a key player in this story, and Chapter 10 provides an account of the dispute on 404 and commentary about the tactics of South Bronx Churches from Partnership president, Kathy Wylde.

12. *New York Times* , 3 April 1989.

13. From transcript of the rally, 2 April 1989. Samuel Freedman's *Upon This Rock*, New York: Harper Collins, 1993, is a powerful biography of Johnny Ray Youngblood.

14. Unless otherwise attributed all quotes in this chapter are from a transcript of the 2 April, 1989 rally.

15. These quotes are from a tape of Guiliani's remarks.

16. This quote is taken from remarks McNeil made during training of IAF leaders during the Ten-Day Training in Los Angeles in July 1989.

17. The next day's *New York Times* put the number at five thousand but the *New York Post*, which sighted slighted the story by giving it only ten paragraphs, pegged the number at 3,500. *New York Newsday*, which initially went with the five thousand figure, upped it to eight thousand in subsequent articles.

Chapter Nine: War on 404! The Reaction to the Action

1. Letter is dated 30 March 1989.

2. *New York Newsday*, 6 April 1989.

3. Quote from *His Eminence And Hizzonor*, by Edward Koch and John Cardinal O'Connor. Also cited in column by Sidney Schanberg in *Newsday*, 11 April 1989.

4. There are twenty-four Catholic parishes in the South Bronx, and, of that number, thirteen are dues paying members of South Bronx Churches.

5. Bastone, William, "The Priest and the Mob," *Village Voice*, 7 March 1989. The *Voice* lauded Gigante for his achievement in building two-thousand low-income housing units, but said: "A four-month *Voice* investigation reveals that Gigante has used his housing operation not only to line his own pockets, but to create a $50 million 'opportunity' for the mafia. The homes of the father's flock were built largely by firms owned by or tied to the Genovese family, a syndicate ruled by a man quite close to the priest: Vincent "The Chin" Gigante—his older brother."

6. A neutral and largely uncritical account of Velez's career appears in Jill Jonnes' *We Are Still Here*, (1986), although she does describe him as "a short, corpulent man with a sensual baby face and radiant smile [who at first] . . . was underestimated because his style rendered him a bit ridiculous, a caricature of the macho Latin male." In the late sixties, as a general in the federally-funded War on Poverty, Velez "had constructed the largest antipoverty empire in the City. He controlled one thousand jobs and $12 million in poverty funds" (p. 168). By the late 1980s, Velez was still a power to be reckoned with, and SBC had clashed with him the year earlier when it tried to have his political appointees removed from the governing board of Lincoln Hospital.

7. Williams' telegram said in part: "As I sat on the dais on Sunday April 2 and listened to remarks being made to local South Bronx residents and their supporters I was embarrassed to hear that the Mayor has given Jim Robinson [President of American Express] and David Rockefeller of the Partnership the land known as 404. The Nehemiah's South Bronx Churches, with one church adjacent to the site, want this land with great passion and I strongly believe we at The Partnership should not get in the way of this happening. I strongly request that we withdraw. . . . There are many other sites we could use. The Partnership has much more flexibility in the type of sites it can work with than Nehemiah."

8. All quotes in this section, unless otherwise attributed, are from notes made on 6 April, 1989.

9. See especially Martin Anderson's devastating *The Federal Bulldozer: A Critical Analysis of Urban Renewal 1942–62*, Cambridge, MA, MIT Press, 1964. It is worth noting in this context that the Nehemiah homes in Brooklyn also displaced residents who had been living in substandard

dwellings that were leveled. According to Kathy Wylde of The Partnership, there was vehement and unrelenting criticism of East Brooklyn Churches for having uprooted poor people living in rental apartments in order to build dwellings for more affluent homeowners.

10. Koch said in a press release on 9 April 1989: "With an enhanced subsidy for development of Site 404, we are now doubly sure these units will be affordable to members of the community. At the same time we will still be achieving the maximum density—and the highest number of home ownership opportunities—on this property. We welcome Borough President's Ferrer's contribution to this important project." In the same release, Ferrer was quoted as proclaiming, "I have always maintained that there is room and need for both Nehemiah housing and the Melrose Commons development to alleviate the critical shortage of housing in the South Bronx." Press Release 134–89 Office of the Mayor, Edward I. Koch. For release Sunday, 9 April 1989.

11. *New York Times*, 3 April 1989.

12. From meeting at SBC on 10 April, 1989.

13. The account of this meeting is from notes made on 10 April, 1989.

14. *New York Times*, "A Bronx Rehabilitation Is Now a Ruined Dream," 12 Feb 78.

Chapter Ten: Digging in for the Long Haul

1. Kahn, Si, *Organizing: A Guide for Grassroots Leaders*, New York, McGraw-Hill, 1982, p. 157.

2. Serrano in his letter to Robinson wrote: "There are two reasons for my support of South Bronx Churches' low-density home ownership and tenant rehabilitation plan. One, SBC is a grassroots coalition which advances a people-driven agenda. They have articulated a plan which addresses the housing needs of the low-income working people of the South Bronx. SBC reminds us that low-income people also aspire to home ownership. I happen to believe that those aspirations are legitimate and have to be fulfilled. Two, the SBC plan better addresses the housing needs of the Bronx families who are doubled up or homeless. Unlike Mayor Koch's condominium plan. The SBC plan will more realistically involve those South Bronx residents who presevered despite the area's twenty-year decline."

3. From text of letter from Jose Serrano to James Robinson dated 9 June 1989.

4. Interview conducted on steps of American Express corporate headquarters on 14 June 1989.

5. John Heinemeier interview at St. John's on 2 June 1989.

6. This wide swath of land with Site 404 sitting in the dead center includes roughly five blocks to the east and six blocks to the west of 404.

7. The quotes from the rally are from a taped transcript.

8. The rally occurred at the time the old-guard leaders in China brutally suppressed the burgeoning movement for democracy.

9. Kathy Wylde interview 27 June 1989 at The Partnership office.

10. Two classic headlines spring to mind. During the city's fiscal crisis in the late 1970s the *News* characterized the federal government's reluctance to help bail out NYC from impending bankruptcy with the blaring headline: "Ford to City: Drop Dead." Another that captures the flavor is the 1969 breaking news story about a riot at the Stonewall bar which sparked the gay rights movement in America: "Homo Nest Raided, Queen Bees Stinging Mad."

11. *New York Daily News*, "South Bronx Fight: The Locals Are Right," 28 April 1989.

12. From a taped interview with Ed Chambers in his IAF office on Long Island on 9 June 1989.

Chapter Eleven: Armistice in the War on 404

1. From an interview with John Heinemeier on 30 Aug 89.

2. The ambitious Ten-Year Plan, which calls for up to $5.1 billion to be spent on New York City housing, is discussed in detail in the next chapter.

3. From taped remarks by John Heinemeier at a rally at Tremont Methodist Church 18 Mar 90.

4. *New York Times*, "Putting a Dinkins Imprint on a Koch Plan," 8 Jul 90.

5. *Village Voice*, 1 May 90.

6. A thorough treatment of the largely successful history of this group is found in Jonnes, 1986.

7. Quoted from *Memorandum of Understanding* from HPD to SBC dated 25 August 1990.

8. Ibid. *Memorandum of Understanding*, 25 Aug 89.

9. From remarks made by Larry McNeil at IAF's Ten-Day Training in Los Angeles, July 1989.

10. From a taped interview with Kathleen Dunn at her office at HPD on 4 Jan 90.

11. The account of this meeting is based on notes I made that day.

12. This version of the single-family Nehemiah homes is described in Chapter 10.

13. Specifically, one patch, which needs at least eighteen months for "urban renewal, is behind [SBC member Church] St. Luke's. Planners are receptive to low density there," Grange told the group. The St. Jerome's pastor said presently there were two homeless shelters nearby, "And we could build either 139 simple-family Nehemiah homes or if we mix in some garden apartments we could have housing for 270 families." Slightly to the west, also in St. Mary's South, is another area that could accommodate seventy-two units of rehabbed apartments.

14. The critical initial seed monies to fund SBC's Nehemiah Plan came from the Parish of Trinity Church and the Evangelical Lutheran Church in America. According to the dinner program of IAF's 50th Anniversary Celebration (31 May 90): "Support and participation are expected from Roman Catholic sources, bank supporters and other denominations."

15. *New York Times*, "Putting a Dinkins Imprint on a Koch Plan," 8 Jul 90.

16. *New York Times*, "In the Ravaged South Bronx, a Camelot Is Envisioned," 17 Dec 90.

17. Ibid. *New York Times*, 17 Dec 90.

18. From a City of New York press release No. 57–91 7 Feb 91.

19. Ibid. Press Release 7 Feb 91.

20. Ibid. Press Release 7 Feb 91.

21. Quote is from taped remarks at the groundbreaking ceremony at Thessalonia Baptist Church 7 Feb 91.

Chapter Twelve: Was It a Just War?

1. Carlos Gordon was interviewed in his Nehemiah home on 29 May 1993.

2. Edwin Forty was interviewed in his Nehemiah home on 29 May 1993.

3. Koch, Edward and O'Connor, John Cardinal, *His Eminence and Hizzonor: A Candid Exchange*, New York, William Morrow and Company,

1989. It is worth noting in this context that, despite the huge proportions of the housing crisis throughout his twelve-year administration, Koch mentions housing only once in his 1984 political autobiography. There he refers to his role in the Charlotte Street renovation that originally has conceived as an ambitious 26,500-unit project. He candidly mentions that he favored the plan for purely political reasons even though his own housing experts were unanimous in the opinion that it was an ill-conceived project. When it finally collapsed, leaving only the handful of suburban ranches in its wake, the self-absorbed Koch's only response was vindictive rejoicing because its failure injured a political rival of his.

4. Ibid. Koch, 1989, p. 193.

5. Ibid. Koch, 1989, p. 195.

6. Vergara, Camilo Jose, "Ruins and Revivals: A South Bronx Landscape," *The Nation*, 6 March 1989, pp. 302–306.

7. Op. cit. Koch, 1989, p. 197.

8. *New York Times*, "Should the Poor Get the Housing That Koch Built?" 18 Mar 90.

9. EBC's Lead Organizer Mike Gecan's version of this negotiation is in Chapter 5.

10. Ibid. Koch, 1989, p. 198. I. D. Robbins also independently corroborates Mike Gecan's version of Koch's reluctant participation. Robbins told *New York Newsday* on 25 May 88: "We met with Koch and brought Bishop Francis Mugavero, the bishop of Brooklyn. He's the hero of this thing. Koch was very noncommittal. We waited a few days and got no commitment. The bishop decided we would announce we were going ahead. It was all over the papers the next day. Koch called up the bishop and screamed at him for 10 minutes. He said, Robbins put you up to that. The bishop let him yell and then said, `When shall we see you again?' Koch said, `Come in tomorrow morning.' He knew when he lost."

11. Ibid. Koch, 1989, p. 197.

12. *New York Times*, "A Struggle over Sites in the South Bronx: Churches as Builders," 22 Oct 89.

13. Ibid. *New York Times*, 22 Oct 89.

14. Ibid. *New York Times*, 22 Oct 89.

15. Derienzo, Harold, "Planned Shrinkage—The Final Phase," *City Limits*, April 1989, p. 10. Kathy Wylde of The Housing Partnership called my attention to this article because it was critical of even the Partnership's relatively low-density projects. Derienzo opens his article by recalling that

his first impression of the South Bronx was one of teeming street life that he encountered on his way to volunteer tutoring at Casita Maria Settlement House in Hunts Point in 1972. Coincidentally, I also spent time volunteering at Casita Maria in the late sixties, and, although I was already familiar with the area, it was impossible not to be struck by the colorful jostling intensity of this Latino neighborhood.

16. Doctorow, E. L., *Billy Bathgate*, New York, Random House, 1989.

17. From a taped interview with Kathleen Dunn at HPD on 4 Jan 90.

18. RFP is bureaucratese for Request For Proposals.

19. Ibid. Kathleen Dunn, 4 Jan 90.

20. From a taped interview with Ed Chambers at IAF's headquarters on 9 Jun 89.

21. From an interview with Johnny Ray Youngblood in *New York Newsday,* "He Turns Parishes into Power Centers," 4 Jan 89. I. D. Robbins calls this freeing up of public housing apartments "trickle-up."

22. From a taped interview with Sam Kramer at HPD headquarters, 4 Jan 90.

23. Quoted in the *New York Times*, "80's Leave States and Cities in Need," 30 Dec 90.

24. From an interview with I. D. Robbins in *New York Newsday*, "People's Developer," 25 May 88.

25. *New York Times*, Renovators Running Out of Abandoned Buildings," 16 Apr 90.

26. Ibid. *New York Times*, 16 Apr 90.

27. Ibid. *New York Times*, 16 Apr 90.

28. *New York Times*, "Moderate-Income Families Staking Claim to the South Bronx," 29 Jun 93.

29. Ibid. Sam Kramer, 4 Jan 90.

30. From an interview with I. D. Robbins in *New York Newsday*, 25 May 88.

31. Stanley Friedman, the legendary Democratic County Chairman, is now in jail for his role in a number of political scams.

32. Op. cit. Chambers interview, 9 Jun 89.

33. From an article in *New York Newsday* 21 Apr 89 adapted from her 1989 book *The Living City*.

34. *New York Times*, "Plan Seeks to Rebuild Downtown of the Bronx," 11 Jun 93.

35. *New York Times*, "Bronx Group Opposes Site of New Juvenile Center," 2 Aug 92.

36. *New York Times*, "Revolution of People Power Wells Up in the Bronx: Residents Who Survived Bad Times Alter Development Plans for Their Neighborhood," 8 Jul 93.

37. Ibid. *New York Times*.

38. "The Bronx: A Report to the Bronx Borough President Fernando Ferrer from the Bronx Center Steering Committee," May 1993. Indeed, SBC activists have not been slow in capitalizing on this foot-in-the-door opportunity. They participate in all the plan's subcommittees and dominate in at least one task force.

39. Ibid. *New York Times*.

Chapter Thirteen: Learning from South Bronx Churches

1. Especially useful are Si Kahn's two books that essentially cover identical territory but are separated by a dozen years. They are *Organizing: A Guide for Grassroots Leaders*, New York McGraw-Hill Book Co., 1982, and *How People Get Power: Organizing Oppressed Communities for Action*, New York, McGraw Hill Book Co., 1970. For a more lofty, philosophical consideration of these issues, see Harry Boyte's *Commonwealth: A Return to Citizen's Politics*, New York, Free Press, 1989.

2. The senior organizers comprise the IAF Cabinet, with Ed Chambers serving as the director. The leaders are Larry McNeil (Southern California), Mike Gecan (New York City and New Jersey), Ernesto Cortez (Texas, Arizona), and Arnie Graf (Mid-Atlantic).

3. The quotes from McNeil are based on notes taken 13 July 1989 during an all-day training session for IAF leaders presided over by McNeil in L.A.

4. In point of fact, Benstock's group, The Clean Air Campaign, which is basically a one-woman operation, prevailed in the end after a dozen years of struggle. However, partly bearing out McNeil's cautionary advice, Benstock, who left no organization behind her, has been forced into another David-and-Goliath battle years after the transfer of funds to mass transit was supposed to begin to flow. In order to secure the victory from encroachment from real-estate developers and politicians who want the money for other uses, including rechanneling it to a bloated highway scheme, she had to begin practically from scratch and recruit fresh ad hoc allies. She left no organization in place to preserve the victory.

5. The quotes in this chapter from Jim Drake are taken from a number of taped interviews with him on 30 Jan 89, 26 Jan 89, and 10 Mar 89.

6. Chambers' remarks are from notes taken during an all-day training session he conducted on 14 July 1989 in L.A.

7. These remarks are taken from notes made on 12 July 1989 during an all-day training session conducted by Cortez in L.A.

8. For Bronxites in the class, this was a particularly unfortunate, even offensive, allusion because this was Robert Moses's standard, dismissive reply when deflecting criticism of his disruptive Cross Bronx Expressway. This highway built in the 1950s and early 1960s sliced through the heart of the Bronx and shattered viable working-class neighborhoods. Bronxites almost always cite it as one of the principal causes of the destruction of the South Bronx.

9. Alinsky, Saul, *John L. Lewis: An Authorized Biography*, New York, Vintage Books, 1970 (first published in 1949).

10. The Lead Organizers are paid from $35,000 to $55,000 a year. Their deputies, the Associate Organizers, earn from $25,000 to $35,000 per annum. In 1989, IAF Cabinet members pulled down salaries of $60,000 to $80,000 a year. The IAF Cabinet is all White and all male. Overall, according to IAF officials, the IAF employs forty organizers, and seventeen are women, nine are Black, eight Hispanic, and one is Asian.

11. SBC's office is in what was an unused room above the chapel in St. Jerome's Roman Catholic Church near the southern tip of the South Bronx.

12. Quoted in *IAF 50 Years: Organizing for Change*, Industrial Areas Foundation, Franklin Square, NY, 1990.

13. This is from a taped interview with Jim Drake on 22 March 1991. Drake had read a draft of this book and was reacting to issues raised in the manuscript.

14. These remarks were made during a taped interview with I. D. Robbins at his South Bronx headquarters in the basement of the rectory at Sts. Peter and Paul's across the street from Site 404 on 26 March 1991.

15. Ibid. Robbins, March 26, 1991.

Bibliography

Books

Addams, Jane. *Twenty Years at Hull House with Autobiographical Notes.* New York: Macmillan, 1910.

Adero, Malaika, ed. *Up South: Stories, Studies and Letters of This Century's African-American Migration.* New York, New Press, 1993.

Alinsky, Saul D. *John L. Lewis: An Authorized Biography.* New York: Vintage Books, 1970 (first published in 1949).

———. *Reveille for Radicals.* New York: Vintage Books, first published in 1947.

———. *Rules for Radicals.* New York: Vintage Books, 1971.

Anderson, Elijah. *Streetwise: Race, Class, and Change in an Urban Community.* Chicago: The University of Chicago Press, 1990.

Anderson, Martin. *The Federal Bulldozer: A Critical Analysis of Urban Renewal, 1949–1962.* Cambridge, MA: MIT Press, 1964.

Barth, Roland. *Improving Schools from Within: Teachers, Parents, and Principals Can Make the Difference.* San Francisco: Jossey-Bass Publishers, 1990.

Bellah, Robert, et al. *Habits of the Heart: Individualism and Commitment in the American Experience.* Berkeley: University of California Press, 1985.

Berman, Marshal. *All That Is Solid Melts into Air: The Experience of Modernity.* New York: Simon and Schuster, 1982.

Bobbio, Norberto. *The Future of Democracy.* Minneapolis: University of Minneapolis Press, 1987.

Bogdan, Robert C., and Biklen, Sari Knopp. *Qualitative Research for Education: An Introduction to Theory and Methods.* Boston: Allyn and Bacon, Inc., 1982.

Boggs, Carl. *Social Movements and Political Power: Emerging Forms of Radicalism in the West.* Philadelphia: Temple University Press, 1986.

Boyer, Ernest L. *High School: A Report on Secondary Education in America.* New York: Harper & Row, 1983.

Boyte, Harry. *Commonwealth: A Return to Citizen Politics.* New York: Free Press, 1989.

————. *The Backyard Revolution: Understanding the New Citizen Movement,* Philadelphia: Temple University Press, 1980.

Byrne, David. *True Stories.* New York: Penguin Books, 1986.

Caro, Robert. *The Power Broker: Robert Moses and the Fall of New York.* New York: Vintage Books, 1975.

Coles, Robert. *Dorothy Day: A Radical Devotion.* Reading, MA: Addison-Wesley Pub. Co., 1987.

Comfort, Randall. *History of the Bronx Borough, City of New York.* New York: North Side News Press, 1906.

Cook, Harry T. *The Borough of the Bronx 1639–1913: Its Marvelous Development and Historical Surroundings.* New York: Harry T. Cook, 1913.

Delgado, Gary. *Organizing the Movement: The Roots and Growth of ACORN.* Philadelphia: Temple University Press, 1986.

Dewey, John. *The Public and Its Problems.* Athens, OH: Swallow Press, 1954.

Dillick, Sidney. *Community Organization for Neighborhood Development: Past and Present.* New York: William Morrow, 1953.

Doctorow, E. L. *Billy Bathgate.* New York: Random House, 1989.

Domanico, Raymond. *Model for Choice: A Report on Manhattan's District 4.* New York: Manhattan Institute for Policy Research, 1989.

Dunham, Arthur. *The New Community Organization.* New York: Thomas Y. Crowell Company, 1970.

Durso, Joseph. *Yankee Stadium: Fifty Years of Drama.* Boston: Houghton Mifflin Co., 1972.

Eccklein, Joan Levin, & Armand Lauffer. *Community Organizers and Social Planners: A Volume of Case Studies and Illustrative Materials.* New York: John Wiley & Sons, 1972.

The Federal Writer's Project Guide to 1930's New York. New York: Pantheon Books, 1982 (first published in 1939).

Fisher, J. *Let The People Decide: Neighborhood Organizing in America.* Boston: Twayne Publishing, 1984.

Fisher, Robert and Peter Romanofsky, eds. *Community Organization for Urban Social Change: A Historical Prospective.* Westport: Greenwood Press, 1981.

Fliegel, Seymour and James MacGuire *Miracle in East Harlem* New York, Times Books 1993.

Fluhr, George J. *The Bronx Through the Years: A Geography and History.* Bronx, NY: Aidan Press, 1964.

Freedman, Samuel. *Upon This Rock: The Miracles of a Black Church.* New York: Harper Collins, 1993.

Gitlin, Todd. *The Sixties: Years of Hope, Days of Rage.* New York: Bantom Books, 1988.

Glazer, Nathan, and Daniel P. Moynihan. *Beyond the Melting Pot: The Negroes, Puerto Ricans, Jews, Italians, and Irish of New York City.* Cambridge, MA: The M.I.T. Press, Second Edition, 1970.

Goodman, Robert. *After the Planners.* New York: Simon and Schuster, 1971.

Gratz, Roberta Brandes. *The Living City.* New York: Simon and Schuster, 1989.

Grebler, Leo. *Housing Market Behavior in a Declining Area.* New York: Columbia University Press, 1952.

Hermalyn, Gary. *The Creation of New York City's First Public High School: Morris High School in the Bronx.* New York: Bronx Historical Society, in press.

Hoffman, Abbie. *Soon To Be a Major Motion Picture.* New York: Perigee Books, 1980.

Horwitt, Sanford D. *Let Them Call Me Rebel: Saul Alinsky—His Life and Legacy.* New York: Alfred A. Knopf, 1989.

IAF 50 Years of Organizing For Change: Industrial Areas Foundation. New York: Franklin Square, 1990.

Jackson, Kenneth. *Crabgrass Frontier: The Suburbanization of the United States.* New York: Oxford University Press, 1985.

Jacobs, Jane. *The Death and Life of Great American Cities.* New York: Random House, 1961.

Jenkins, Stephen. *The Story of the Bronx from the Purchase Made by the Dutch from the Indians in 1639 to the Present Day.* New York: G.P. Putnam's Sons, 1912.

Jenson, Robert. "Introduction." *Devastation/Resurrection: The South Bronx.* New York: The Bronx Museum of the Arts, 1979.

Jonnes, Jill. *We're Still Here: The Rise, Fall, and Resurrection of the South Bronx.* Boston: The Atlantic Monthly Press, 1986.

Kahn, Si. *How People Get Power: Organizing Oppressed Communities for Action.* New York: McGraw-Hill Book Co., 1970.

————. *Organizing: A Guide for Grassroots Leaders.* New York: McGraw-Hill Book Co., 1982.

Katz, Michael. *The Undeserving Poor: From the War on Poverty to the War on Welfare.* New York: Pantheon Books, 1989.

Koch, Edward I. *Mayor: An Autobiography.* New York: Simon and Schuster, 1984.

Kramer, R. *Participation of the Poor.* New York: Prentice Hall, 1969.

Lemann, Nicholas. *The Promised Land: The Great Black Migration and How It Changed America.* New York: Alfred A. Knopf, 1991.

Miller, James. *Democracy in the Streets: From Port Huron to the Siege of Chicago.* New York: Simon & Schuster, 1986.

McNamara, John. *History in Asphalt: The Origin of Bronx Street and Place Names.* Bronx, NY: The Bronx Historical Society, 1984.

Newfield, Jack and Wayne Barrett. *City for Sale: Ed Koch and the Betrayal of New York.* New York: Harper & Row, 1988.

Newfield, Jack, and Paul DuBrul. *The Permanent Government.* New York: Pilgrim Press, 1981.

Oberschall, Anthony. *Social Conflict and Social Movements.* Englewood Cliffs, NJ: Prentice Hall, 1973.

O'Connor, John Cardinal and Edward I. Koch. *His Eminence and Hizzoner: A Candid Exchange.* New York: William Morrow and Company, 1989.

Oliver, Donald. *Education, Modernity and Fractured Meaning: Toward a Process Theory of Teaching and Learning.* New York: State University of New York Press, 1989.

Patton, Michael Quinn. *Qualitative Evaluation Methods.* Beverly Hills, CA: SAGE Publications, 1980.

Peirce, Neal, and Carol Steinbach. *Corrective Capitalism: The Rise of America's Community Development Corporations, A Report to the Ford Foundation,* New York: 1987.

Piven, F. F., and P. Cloward. *Poor People's Movements: How They Succeed, Why They Fail.* New York: Pantheon Books, 1977.

Ravitch, Diane. *The Great School Wars: A History of New York City Public Schools.* New York: Basic Books, Inc., 1974.

Sallins, Peter D. *The Ecology of Housing Destruction: Economic Effects of Public Intervention in the Housing Market.* New York: New York University Press, 1980.

Sennett, Richard. *The Fall of the Public Man.* New York: Alfred A. Knopf, 1977.

Smith, Dennis. *Report from Engine Co. 82.* New York: Saturday Review Press, 1972.

Sleeper, Jim. *The Closest of Strangers: Liberalism and the Politics of Race in New York.* New York: W. W. Norton & Company, 1990.

Staples, L. *Roots to Power.* New York: Praeger Publishers, 1984.

Starr, Roger. *The Rise and Fall of New York City.* New York: Basic Books, 1985.

Stegman, Michael A. *The Dynamics of Rental Housing in New York City.* Piscatawany, NJ: Center for Urban Policy Research, Rutgers University, 1982.

Sternlieb, George, and David Listokin. "Housing." Raymond Horton and Charles Brecher, *Setting Municipal Priorities.* New York: New York University Press, 1986.

Sullivan, Donald G. "1940–1965: Population Mobility in the South Bronx." *Devastation/Resurrection: The South Bronx,* The Bronx Museum of the Arts, 1979.

Sullivan, Mercer. *"Getting Paid:" Youth Crime and Work in the Inner City.* New York: Cornell University Press, 1990.

Sullivan, William. *Reconstructing Public Philosophy.* Berkeley: University of California Press, 1986.

Swiggett, Howard. *The Extraordinary Mr. Morris.* Garden City, NY: Doubleday, 1952.

Tabb, William K. *The Long Default: New York City and the Urban Fiscal Crisis.* New York: Monthly Review Press, 1982.

Traub, James. *Too Good To Be True: The Outlandish Story of Wedtech.* New York, Doubleday, 1990.

Ultan, Lloyd. "The Story of the South Bronx 1776–1940," *Devastation/Resurrection: The South Bronx,* The Bronx Museum of the Arts, 1979.

———. *The Bronx in the Innocent Years 1890–1925.* New York: Harper and Row, 1985.

———. *The Beautiful Bronx 1920–1950.* New York: Arlington House Publishers, 1979.

Ward, Lillian. *The House on Henry Street.* New York: Henry Holt and Co., 1915.

West, Cornel. *Race Matters.* Boston: Beacon Press, 1993.

Willensky, Elliot, and Norval White. *The AIA Guide to New York City.* New York: Harcourt Brace Jovanovich, Third Edition, 1988.

Williams, Terry. *The Cocaine Kids: The Inside Story of a Teenage Drug Ring.* New York: Addison-Wesley, 1990.

Wilson, William Julius. *The Truly Disadvantaged: The Inner City, the Underclass, and Public Policy.* Chicago: The University of Chicago Press, 1987.

Wolf, Peter. *The Future of the City: New Directions in Urban Planning.* New York: Watson-Guptil Publications, 1974.

Wolfe, Thomas. *The Bonfire of the Vanities.* New York: Farrer, Strauss, & Giroux, 1987.

Articles and Government Reports

Note: Not listed here but included in the research are dozens of New York Times articles about various aspects of the South Bronx.

Bondarin, Arley. "The Jewish Population and Social Service Needs in the West Bronx," New York, Federation of Jewish Philanthropies of New York, 1972.

Bradshaw, Jon. "Savage Skull," *Esquire* (June 1977): 77.

Bronx Board of Trade, "The Nation's Ninth City: The Bronx, New York City's Fastest Growing Borough," Bronx, NY: Bronx Board of Trade, 1927.

Burghardt, Steve. "Community-Based Social Action," *Encyclopedia of Social Work.* 18th Edition, 1987.

"South Bronx Churches Asks Investigation of Lincoln Medical Center," *Catholic New York* 2 June 1988.

Derienzo, Harold. "Planned Shrinkage: The Final Phase," *City Limits* (April 1989).

Dreier, Peter, and David Hulchannski. "Affordable Housing: Lessons from Canada," *American Prospect*, 1, no. 1 (Spring, 1990).

Gittings, Jim. "Churches in Communities: A Place to Stand," *Christianity In Crisis*, 2 January 1987: 5–11.

Glazer, Nathan. "The South-Bronx Story: An Extreme Case of Neighborhood Decline," *Policy Studies Journal*, 16, no. 2 (Winter 1987).

Golden, Martha. "The Grand Concourse: Tides of Change," New York: NYC Landmarks Preservation Commission, 1976.

Hermalyn, Gary. "The Bronx at the Turn of the Century," *The Bronx County Historical Society Journal*, XXVI, no. 2 (Fall 1989).

Levy, Stephen. "Why Should I talk to You," *Whole Earth Review*. Sausalito, CA (Sept. 1987).

Kasarda, J. D. "The Regional and Urban Redistribution of People and Jobs in the U.S.," (paper prepared for the National Research Council Committee on National Urban Policy), National Academy of Sciences, 1986.

Kuhta, Candace. "The Bronx in Print: An Annotated Catalogue of Books and Pamphlets about The Bronx," Bronx, NY: Bronx Historical Society, 1981.

Jones, Arthur. "Brooklyn People-Power Spreads to the South Bronx," *National Catholic Reporter*, 13 February 1987.

Manoussoff Associates. "Bronx Borough Improvement Study," New Rochelle, NY: Manoussoff Associates, 1972.

Massaro, Dominic. "Gouverneur Morris: The Constitutional Penman Revisited," *The Bronx County Historical Society Journal*, XXIV, no. 2 (Fall 1987).

Moynihan, Daniel Patrick. "The Negro Family: The Case for National Action," Washington, DC: Office of Policy & Research, U.S. Dept. of Labor (n.d.).

New Directions for the Bronx. "Task Force on Housing and Neighborhoods," Regional Plan Association and the Bronx Borough President's Office, March 1990.

New Directions for the Bronx. "Task Force on Cultural and Environmental Quality," Regional Plan Association and the Bronx Borough President's Office, October 1989.

New Directions for the Bronx. "Task on Economic Development," Regional Plan Association and the Bronx Borough President's Office, March 1990.

New York City Department of City Planning. "Alexander Avenue: Revitalization," New York: Department of City Planning, 1976.

New York City Department of City Planning. "Partnership For Change: Interim Proposals for Bronx Community Planning District 3," New York: New York City Department of City Planning, n.d.

New York City Landmarks Preservation Commission. "Bronx Survey Report," New York: Landmarks Preservation Commission, n.d.

New York City Model Cities Administration. "Bronx Plan 1968–72: A Report on the Bronx Model Cities Neighborhood," New York: Bronx Model Cities, 1972.

New York City Planning Commission. "St. Mary's Park Area," New York, NYC Planning Commission, 1974.

New York City Planning Commission. "Strengthening Hunts Point," New York: NYC Planning Commission, 1974.

Talk of the Town. "Groundbreaking," *The New Yorker*, 25 March 1991.

O'Brien, William. "Faces of Faith: Hope Blooming in the Urban Desert," *The Other Side* (May 1988).

Olmsted, Robert. "A History of Transportation in The Bronx," *The Bronx County Historical Society Journal*, XXVI, no. 2 (Fall 1989).

Paget, Karen. "Citizen Organizing: Many Movements, No Majority," *The American Prospect* 1, no. 2 (Summer 1990).

Raywid, Mary Anne "The Evolving Effort to Improve Schools: Pseudo-Reform, Incremental Reform, and Restructuring," *Phi Delta Kappan*, October 1990.

Reitzes, Donald. *The Alinsky Legacy: Alive and Kicking.* Greenwich, CT: JAI Press, Inc., 1987.

Robbins, I. D. "How To Save Money Building the City's Housing," *Crain's New York Business* (17 April 1989).

Sleeper, Jim. "Days of the Developers: Boom and Bust with Ed Koch," *Dissent*, (Fall 1987).

———. "Looking at Our City," *Dissent* (Fall 1987).

South Bronx Development Office. "Areas of Strength/Areas of Opportunity: South Bronx Revitalization Program and Development Guide," 2 vols. Bronx: South Bronx Development Office, 1980.

Ultan, Lloyd. "Jonas Bronck and the First Settlement of the Bronx," *The Bronx County Historical Society Journal*, XVII, no. 2 (Fall 1989).

Veregara, Camilo Jose. "Ruins and Revivals: A South Bronx Landscape," *The Nation* 6 Marc 89: 302–306.

Woods, Peter. (1985) "New Songs Played Skillfully: Creativity in Writing Up Qualitative Research." In *Issues in Educational Research*. Burgess, Robert G., ed. Philadelphia: Falmer Press, 1985, pp. 86–106.

Unpublished Sources

City Planning Map, Bronx Community District 1, Department of Housing Preservation and Development—Planning Coordination, July 1988.

Chambers, Ed. *Organizing for Family and Congregation,* published by Industrial Areas Foundation, 36 New Hyde Park Road, Franklyn Square, NY 11010, 1978.

DeRienzo, Harold, Eugenia Flatow, and Garnold M. King II. *Partnership for the Future: A 197a Plan for the Revitalization of Bronx Community District #3,* prepared by The Consumer-Farmer Foundation, 101 East 15th Street, NY, NY 10003, 1989.

Leaflets: From Task Force on Housing Court: *Rights of Tenants in Buildings with Fewer than 6 Apartments;* List of twenty-eight different housing, tenant rights and community organizations; *What to do if you receive a 72-hour Notice of Eviction; What to do if you receive a Dispossess.*

Letter from Jose Serrano to James Robinson III, dated 16 May 89.

Letter from Jose Serrano to Fernando Ferrer, dated 20 Mar 89.

Letter from Abraham Biderman, HPD Commissioner, to Rev. John Heinemeier, dated 28 Mar 89.

Letter from Abraham Biderman, HPD Commissioner, to Rev. John Heinemeier, dated 25 Aug 89.

Letter from SBC pastors to James Robinson II, dated 11 Jun 89.

Memorandum of Understanding Between HPD (Commissioner Abraham Biderman) and SBC 25 Aug 89 unsigned, 5 pages.

Pamphlet: *50th Anniversary Celebration of IAF,* 31 May 90.

Price, Mark. *A History of the Bronx Schools 1898–1944: From Consolidation to the Present* ("compiled at the suggestion of Hon. Anthony Campagna, Bronx Member of the Board of Education," unpublished report, 1945).

Press Release from Office of the Mayor Edward Koch and Bronx Borough President Fernando Ferrer, no. 134–89, 9 April 1989.

Press Release from office of State Assemblyman Jose Serrano, n.d.

Press Release from Office of Mayor David Dinkins, no. 68–91, 7 February 1991.

Press Release from Office of Mayor David Dinkins, no. 57–91, 7 February 1991.

SBC Handbill: "A Call to Action! On 404!" English and Spanish handout, printed in March 1989.

South Bronx Business and Community Journal: People Together with Hope,
  published by South Bronx People for Change, Spring 1988.

Telegram to James Robinson from E. Thomas Williams Jr. on subject of Site
  404, dated 3 April 1989.

Tidings: Newsletter of St. John Luthern Church. "This Land Is Our Land—
  April 2 Rally" 100, no. 4 (April 1989).

Taped Interviews

*I have talked with dozens of people about the work of South Bronx
Churches. Among the formal, taped interviews excerpted in the preceding
text are the following.*

Aguilar, Tony	5 Jan 89	SBC staff organizer
Chambers, Ed	1 May 89	IAF Director
Chambers, Ed	9 Jun 89	IAF Director
Drake, Jim	26 Jan 89	Lead Organizer, SBC
Drake, Jim	30 Jan 89	Lead Organizer, SBC
Drake, Jim	10 Mar 89	Lead Organizer, SBC
Drake, Jim	22 Mar 91	at SBC headquarters
Dunn, Kathy	4 Jan 90	Housing Commissioner of Planning and Policy
Flynn, Father John	Oct 88	South Bronx People for Change founder
Flynn, Father John	Dec 88	South Bronx People for Change founder
Ferrer Rally	10 Apr 89	at Court House in Bronx
Grange, Father John	18 Sep 89	pastor of St. Jerome's, and early SBC member
Heinemeier, John	27 Jan 89	SBC founder: first interview
Heinemeier, John	10 Mar 89	personal history (2 reels)
Heinemeier, John	7 Feb 89	second interview, material on Morris HS
Heinemeier, John	24 Apr 89	SBC finances, origins of SBC (2 reels)
Heinemeier, John	2 Apr 89	church service at St. John's
Heinemeier, John	5 Apr 89	public remarks at first Nehemiah Wednesday
Heinemeier, John	2 Jun 89	aftermath of failed demo, events in May 89

Heinemeier, John	30 Aug 89	at Long Beach
Heinemeier, John	2 Jun 90	at Long Beach
Heinemeier, John	25 Mar 91	at his home
Hermalyn, Gary	10 Mar 89	Director of Bronx Historical Society
Kramer, Sam	4 Jan 90	HPD Director of Bronx Planning
Nehemiah Wednesday	5 Apr 89	excerpts from the rally
Nehemiah Demonstration	2 Apr 89	public remarks (2 reels)
Press Conference	14 Jun 89	at American Express to pressure The Partnership
Press Conference	26 Apr 89	at St. Bart's to press for land
Ramirez, Blanca	5 Jan 89	Director of South Bronx People for Change (2 reels)
Robbins, I. D.	7 Jun 89	Gigante, 404, etc. (2 reels)
	26 Mar 91	at SBC construction office
Rodriguez, Father Juan	18 Sep 89	South Bronx resident who became a Catholic priest
Taylor, Gerald	Jul 89	IAF organizer at training in LA
Verona, Maria	7 Mar 89	personal history of SBC staffer
Wylde, Kathy	26 Jun 89	Director of Housing for NYC Partnership

Interviews

Marshall Berman	14 Jun 89	Author of many Bronx articles and book, *All That Is Solid Melts in Air*
Gil Blum	MI	Former teacher in school along the route of the Cross Bronx Expressway
Manny Colon	5 Jul 89	SBC staffer
Ernesto Cortez	12 Jun 89	IAF Cabinet Member

Peter Freiberg	MI	Journalist, columnist with speciality in Bronx issues
Mike Gecan	18 Jul 89	East Brooklyn Churches Lead Organizer
Arnie Graff	16 Jul 89	IAF Cabinet Member
John Devaux	MI	Director of Bronx Educational Services
Tom Edwards	MI	Chairman of Bronx Educational Services
Larry Mc Neil	13 Jul 89	Founding Organizer of Queens Community Organization
Robert Moses	n.d.	Builder of the Cross Bronx Expressway
Marinella Pacheo	7 Jan 89	Housing Advocate with NEED
Carmen Olemeda	7 Feb 89	Lawyer for East-West Eviction Prevention Center
Rachel Rayoff	6 Jun 89	Press officer in Bronx Borough President's office
Rev. Shelly Sampson	14 Jun 89	SBC pastor at American Express Rally
Jim Sleeper	MI	*New York Daily News* political columnist and author of *The Closest of Strangers: Liberalism and the Politics of Race in NY*

MI *stands for multiple interviews*
n.d. *stands for no date*

Index